FREE SEATS
FOR ALL

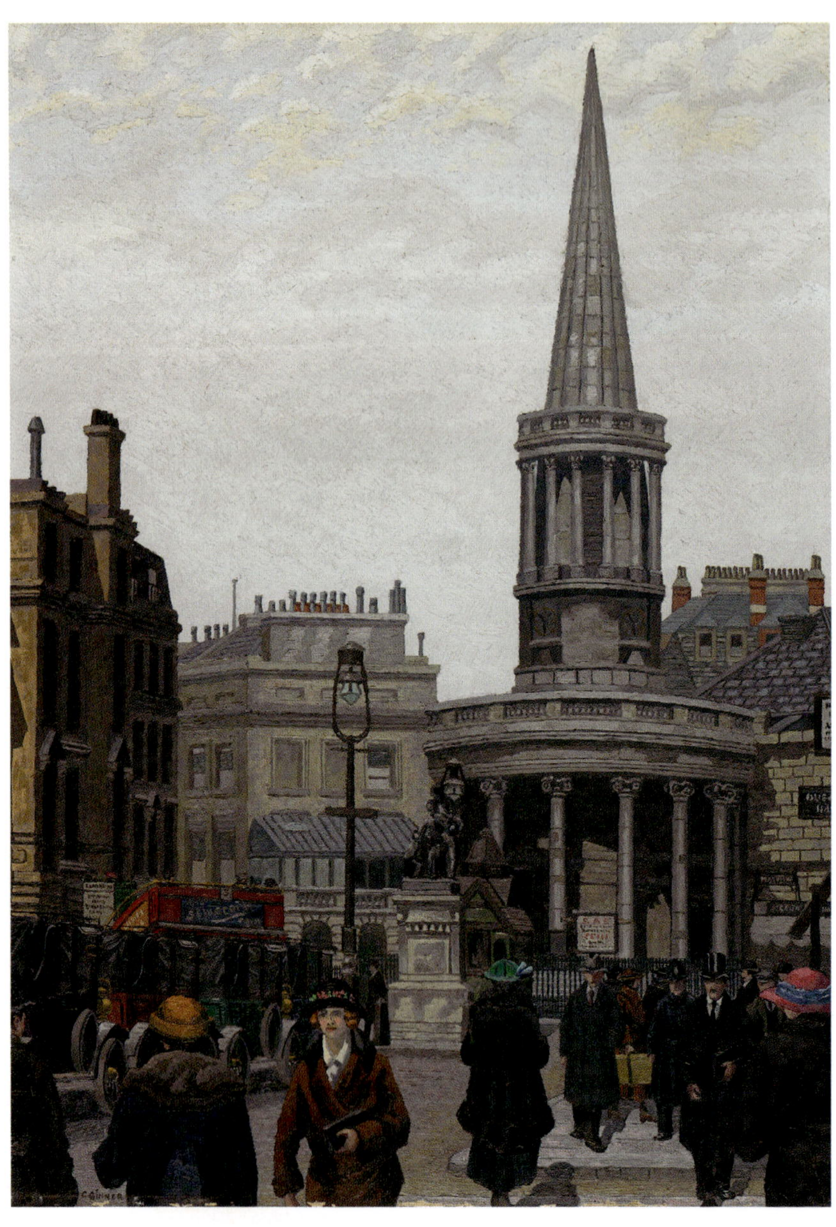

CHARLES GINNER **The Church of All Souls, Langham Place, London, 1924**
Oil on canvas

Ginner shows All Souls in relation to the odd angle at which the upper part of Regent Street meets Portland Place but before its famous backdrop, the BBC's Broadcasting House, was built in 1932.

FREE SEATS FOR ALL

The boom in church building after Waterloo

GILL HEDLEY

Published on the bicentenary of the
Incorporated Church Building Society, 2018,
by Umbria Press for the National Churches Trust

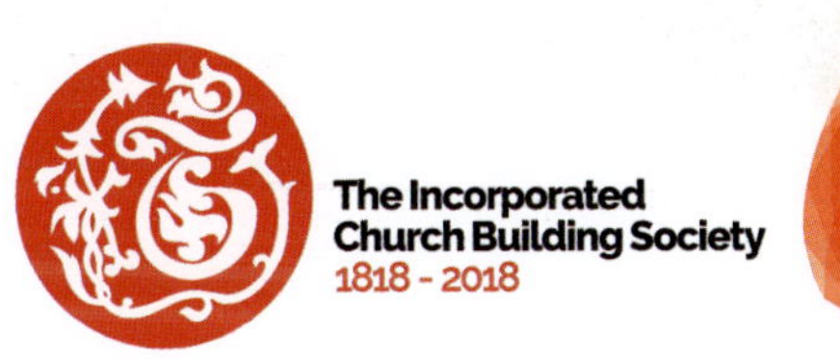

UMBRIA PRESS

ISBN 978-1-910074-16-6

Umbria Press
2 Umbria Street
London SW15 5DP
www.umbriapress.co.uk

The National Churches Trust
7 Tufton Street
London SW1P 3QB
www.nationalchurchtrust.org

C. Hoare & Co.
37 Fleet Street
London EC4P 4DQ
www.hoaresbank.co.uk

Designed and typeset in Berling
and English Engravers by Louise Millar

Printed by Ashford Colour Press Ltd
Gosport PO13 0FW
www.ashfordps.co.uk

CONTENTS

From:
HRH The Duke of Gloucester KG GCVO

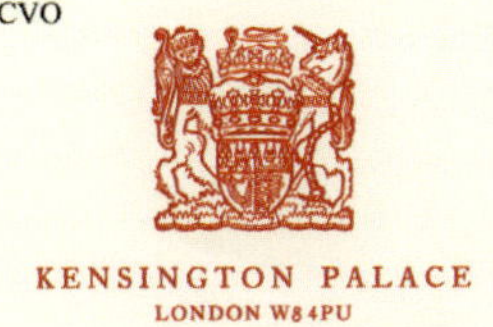

KENSINGTON PALACE
LONDON W8 4PU

Of all the arts, architecture is the noblest. At its summit lies religious architecture, where the finite nature of human existence reaches out to the infinity of the universe.

The Incorporated Church Building Society was a remarkable organisation. Founded through voluntary endeavour, it met the challenges posed by the economic and social revolutions of the 19th Century by seeking to ensure that everyone who wanted to could worship in the buildings of the Anglican church.

Today, the place of religion in both public and private life has adapted to reflect our times. Yet, whether it is small and humble or large and magnificent, through their built form churches continue to inspire and to provide a space for reflection and transcendence.

It is right that we celebrate the work of the ICBS in this, the two hundredth year of its foundation. I hope that those responsible for the care of churches today will be inspired by its work and pass on its legacy of ecclesiastical heritage safely to future generations.

ST. THOMAS'
(FINSBURY PARK)

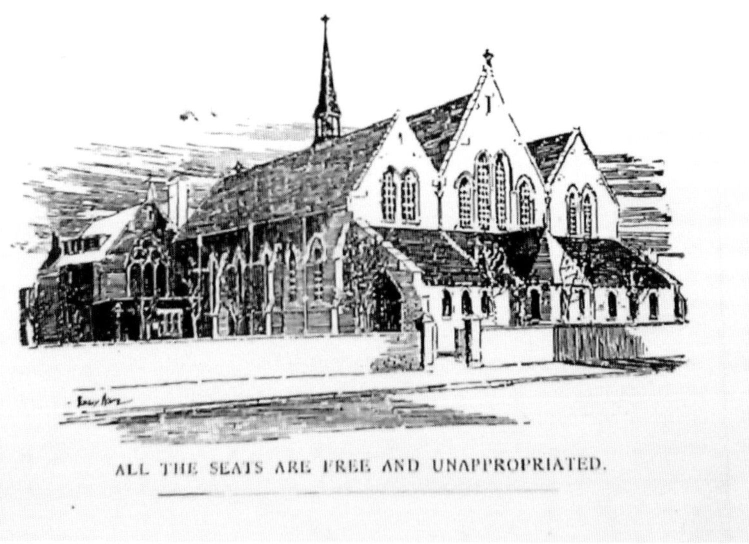

ARTIST UNKNOWN **Cover of** *St Thomas the Apostle*, **the St Thomas' Church,**
Finsbury Park, Parish Magazine circa 189Os

*St. Thomas was designed by Ewan Christian, 1888, and did not receive a grant from ICBS
but the text below this image certainly supports the cause.*

PREFACE
by Bettany Hughes

Gill Hedley is to be congratulated on writing *Free Seats for All*, a book which vividly brings to life the remarkable work of the Incorporated Church Building Society.

Following the turmoil of the Napoleonic wars and faced with the rapid expansion of industrial towns and cities the Incorporated Church Building Society (ICBS) was set up in 1818 to help keep England holy.

With a rapidly growing population, in the early decades of the nineteenth century there was a severe shortage of churches. In some parts of London there were barely enough places in parish churches for one in nine of the population. And back then, many people in the Church of England feared the rise of Nonconformity and competition from Methodism and other denominations.

In the nineteenth century, the ICBS was responsible for the building and enlargement of many thousands of Anglican churches and chapels. They include my local parish church, St Matthew's Church in Ealing, west London, and many, many churches in cities, towns and villages throughout the land.

The ICBS also provided many new pews for parish churches, the majority of them free for anyone to occupy, in contrast to the then customary provision of private pews. In just the period from 1818 to 1856, 900,000 new seats were provided, of which 700,000 were available free of charge.

The ICBS story is one of a small number of people who thought that everyone in England, and not just the prosperous, had a right to worship in the buildings of the established church. One of the leaders of this group of evangelicals was Joshua Watson, a remarkable individual. In 1811 he had helped set up the National Society for Promoting the Education of the Poor in the Principles of the Established Church in England and Wales, commonly referred to as the National Society, and which became the Church of England's network of schools.

Gill Hedley's book explains how in setting up the ICBS Watson brought together the great and the good, including the Archbishop of Canterbury, Robert Peel MP, the Chancellor of the Exchequer and William Wilberforce. They were ably assisted as treasurer by the banker Charles Hoare, and the Hoare family remained closely linked to the ICBS throughout its history.

Churches represent the lives, customs and ambitions, the hopes and fears of men and women. They are time capsules which tell us so much about local and national history. Religous buildings really are, when truth be told, the most important part of our national heritage.

I hope that *Free Seats for All* will allow people to find out more about the history of our nation's fabulous church buildings and will encourage you to visit some of the buildings helped by the ICBS, many of which are detailed in the book. ICBS-supported churches were asked to display a wooden board acknowledging their funds, the production of which had to paid for by the churches themselves! Many of these signs can still be found in churches today, making it easy for us to discover the ICBS's work!

The work of the ICBS, albeit on a lesser scale, continued through the twentieth century, right up until 2013. Its affairs are now handled by the National Churches Trust, the UK church buildings support charity, and in 2018, the Trust will be helping to celebrate the ICBS's bi-centenary.

Congratulations to everyone who today works to keep the nation's churches open to all and in good repair, and in this way furthers the original ambitions of the founders of the Incorporated Church Building Society and honours its work over the past 200 years.

Bettany Hughes
Vice-President, National Churches Trust

FOREWORD
by Michael Hoare

Church building in England started in earnest with the arrival of the Normans. It slowed at the time of the Black Death, then, following England's political independence from the continent, flowered in the glorious native Perpendicular Style of vertical lines, delicate tracery and vast expanses of glass.

Building all but stopped in 1534 and relatively few Anglican churches were built in the following 280 years, a period in which Nonconformism took root and thrived. Quakers, Unitarians, Baptists, Presbyterians, Congregationalists and later Methodists evangelised, converted and built chapels. Roman Catholics remained a small introverted minority and were forbidden to build. By 1815, only around half the population belonged to the established Anglican Church and belief within all churches was challenged by the new intellectual ideas imported from France.

On the conclusion of peace after Waterloo, the country was exhausted by over half century of war. If recent events in France were not sufficiently convincing, the Peterloo massacre and Cato Street Conspiracy brought the threat of civil disobedience closer to home and the need for institutional reform became a matter of urgency. For the Church this included the repeal of the Test Acts, which removed the civil disabilities for Nonconformists, and the Catholic Emancipation Act, which finally, after much wrangling, did the same for Roman Catholics.

If it were to maintain its place as the established church, the Church of England had to counteract Nonconformism, to adapt its churches to the fourfold increase in population since 1534 and the growth in new industrial towns, and to suppress 'pew rents', which reduced the availability of worship to the poor. Moves to reform the Church had their roots in the end of the previous century – the evangelical Church Missionary Society dates from 1799 – but the process was given real impetus by the perceived need to reinforce the structure of local government that was still the prerogative of the established church.

Against this background the Church Building Society (the future ICBS) and the Church Building Commission (CBC) were set up. Together they were to usher in an era of unprecedented Anglican church building. The CBC, with its 600 'million pound churches', is relatively well known, but the ICBS has remained largely in the shadows. Nonetheless, thanks to the efforts of a small number of committed promoters, it raised some £1.6 million (say £160 million in today's money) from rich individuals, through a well-orchestrated campaign of local societies and appeals in churches.

The ICBS also contributed actively to new thinking in church design. Under the Reformation previously rich churches had seen their plate melted down, furnishings, statues and vestments sold, magnificent rood screens ripped out and vibrant decoration whitewashed over. This austerity was, however, progressively softened in later centuries by the addition of fine monuments offered by local families.

Those churches which were built between 1534 and 1815 were largely in the Palladian style imported by Inigo Jones and exemplified by St Paul's, Covent Garden, the 'finest barn in Europe' but one with no door giving onto his new piazza due to the Church's last-minute insistence that the building be orientated to the east. Baroque passed Britain by, with the odd exception such as St John's, Shobdon, Herefordshire, described by Simon Jenkins as a 'complete masterpiece of English Rococo', but even this was largely an exercise in monochrome. In deference to Protestant teaching, altars, after a brief foray into the centre of the church, retreated to the east end and gave precedence to the pulpit. Orchestra and choir provided music from a gallery over the west door. The priest, educated at Oxford or Cambridge, was clothed in a black cassock topped by two white preaching bands and bearing thirty-nine buttons to remind him of the Church's Articles.

The early churches financed by the ICBS continued these forms. They were modest affairs designed to provide accommodation at low cost, built in Classical style with clear glass, little decoration and galleries. As the century progressed, the Church, together with the country overall, became richer and more ambitious. Under the influence of Pugin and the Oxford and other Anglo-Catholic movements, it rediscovered Gothic and the beauties of traditional Anglican medieval design. In a period as short as ten years, coinciding with the coronation of the new queen, it abandoned austerity in favour of richness, preeminent altars, large apses and glorious Neo-Gothic technicolour.

The ICBS contributed to the building of 3,508 new churches, to rebuilding and enlarging a further 10,314. In so doing it created 2.4 million new pew spaces of which 86 per cent were free.

INTRODUCTION

In May 1817 a meeting was held in London to consider a lasting memorial to the allied victory over Napoleon at Waterloo. There was a deeply held concern behind and above this topic that no single memorial was appropriate when 'not a *tenth* part of the Church of England population can be accommodated in our churches & Chapels, to worship God after the manner of their forefathers', as an open letter to the Bishop of London had warned three years previously. There was anxiety about the success with which Methodism and other dissenting groups could quickly and cheaply erect simple places of worship in urban centres newly flooded with workers who had left the countryside seeking jobs in the developing industrial heartlands. The war had changed the country and local churches could no longer house everyone. Poorer inhabitants, deprived in very many other ways, suffered most; worse, many often no longer cared whether they went to church or not. Maybe William Blake's 'dark Satanic mills' surrounding their new homes indicated to some that they could not escape hell whatever they did.

Within a year of the debate, the Archbishop of Canterbury chaired another public meeting at which the Duke of Northumberland proposed a motion leading to a first parliamentary grant of £1 million for the building of new churches. In parallel, a church-building society was created by private individuals that, over its long existence, raised even more funds for the improvement of churches, with a particular emphasis on extending existing churches and providing free seating. Working at arm's length from government, it long outlasted the state's intervention yet the same key lay figures stood behind both achievements.

The style of approved architecture for the resulting church boom was influenced by cost, fashion, prejudice and a gradual but determined change from a traditional style of theology and worship towards the ideas of the Oxford and Cambridge movements; Gothic won over classicism. Eighteenth-century classicism was viewed as suspiciously close to the revolutionary ideas of France and America, and there was also a city-versus-country tendency, with an emphasis on a notion of churches that *looked* like English churches predominating outside the capital.

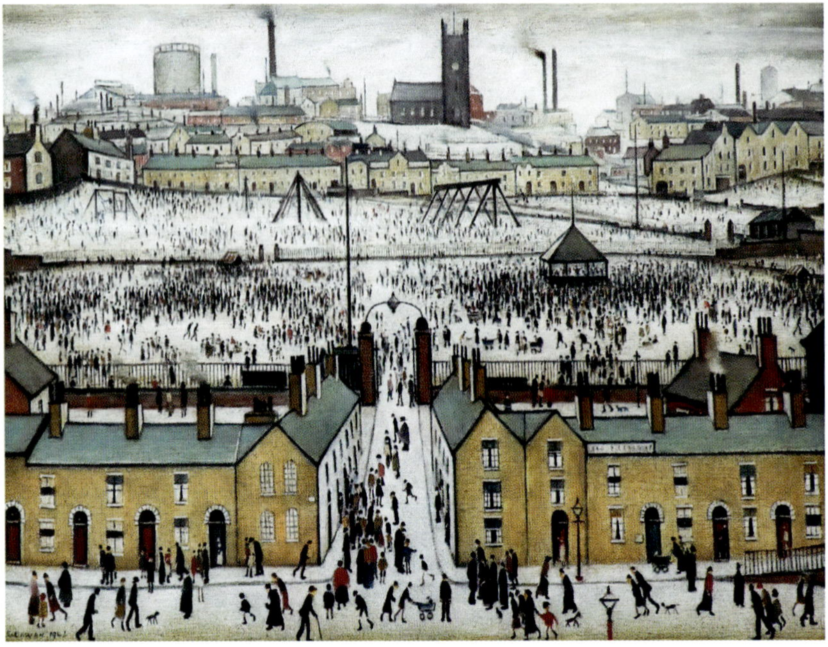

L. S. LOWRY **Britain at Play**, 1943, Oil on canvas

St Michael's and All Angels Church had been built in 1789, the year in which the French Revolution began, for a congregation of 1,000 just north east of the centre of Manchester. Lowry painted this scene of Angel Meadow Park with the church and neighbouring factories dominating the skyline during World War II. The church had been demolished in 1935 after slum clearance but the artist recalled it in this archetypal scene of a northern industrial city and its people.

Our familiar Anglican churches are largely medieval or late Victorian in origin and often a much-loved mongrel mixture of both. Changes in society and its wealth in the agrarian and wool-rich Middle Ages created a landscape of important churches; the period of industrial development after 1770 gave eventual rise to a second, very different, concentrated period of church building. In between, the City of London's skyline had been transformed by Sir Christopher Wren's building boom following the Great Fire: fifty-one churches, as well as the new St Paul's Cathedral, were built within the City to replace the eighty-eight that were burnt in 1666. In 1710 the New Churches in London and Westminster Act was passed with the intention of building fifty new churches for the rapidly growing conurbation beyond the square mile of the City. Known as Queen Anne's churches, in the end only twelve were built and eight others altered. They were paid for from the duty on coal imports that had been levied originally for the Wren churches; this duty was also used to defray costs for Westminster Abbey and Greenwich Hospital and arrears to Wren's salary. Six of the churches were by Wren's pupil Nicholas Hawksmoor. Like the post-Waterloo churches, those of the Queen Anne fund arose from a period of political upheaval when the Tories took over after twenty-two years of uninterrupted Whig power.

Britain benefited in many ways from being the first modern industrialised nation but the astonishing church-building boom that arose from this is not a simple case of a country marking its imperialism through solid, God-fearing celebrations in stone. The origin of the thousands of new church-building projects lies in philanthropic, educational and problem-solving ideas formed in the late eighteenth century, before Britain resumed war with France in 1803. Despite this, many of the new churches have become associated with the years immediately after the victory at Waterloo in 1815 which saw a small group of people concentrate their energies on creating new spaces in churches for the greatest number. There was also an overarching political response to the rise in disaffection towards the established Church, which was perceived to be especially prevalent among those members of the working class who were forced by economic circumstance to change their entire way of life and move their homes from the rural to the urban.

The strategies to achieve more room for church seating within an Anglican framework were various including two Acts of Parliament and the formation by a remarkable group of philanthropists of what they called a 'building society' to raise funds privately to build and extend churches. The instigators of these strategies were more or less the same men; the role of the building society is often overlooked because the government scheme was for a shorter duration and can be described in more detail; its churches are also more distinctive. However, both movements deserve to be compared, clarified and set in the context of contemporary politics and social reform.

Between 1818 and 1856, when the government scheme came to an end, a group of over 600 new churches was built throughout England and

Wales with £1.5 million of public money. They have various nicknames: the '600 churches', the 'commissioners' churches', the 'million-pound churches' and the 'Waterloo churches'. In parallel, the Church Building Society, formed in 1818 and becoming the Incorporated Church Building Society (ICBS) ten years later, raised £1.6 million (although over a much longer period) for the building and improvement of churches with an emphasis on church extension and 'free seats for all'. Between the same dates as the '600 churches' appeared the Society enabled elsewhere nearly a million new seats in churches, of which 700,000 were available free of charge. The ICBS itself contributed to the building of nearly 500 completely new churches in those early years and the rebuilding or enlarging of more than 1,500 others. Altogether more than 1,000 new churches, of varying quality, style and longevity, emerged in Wales and England during the decades immediately after Waterloo.

The work of the ICBS continued through the nineteenth century and well into the twentieth. Between 1818 and 1982, the period covered by the ICBS archive, it gave 14,356 grants to churches and refused only 3,804 appeals. Some 19,500 churches made enquiries and, of these, 4,397 were about new churches; 3,508 new churches were built and only 703 turned down. 4,000 grants were given to extend, reseat or build galleries while 13,822 grants enabled rebuilding or repair work, sometimes to the same churches.

While none of the new churches was conceived as a precise memorial to the Battle of Waterloo, the day that news of victory arrived in London – 21 June 1815 – is a good place to begin the story, as the church-building movement was set in train in the immediate aftermath and the link has remained. Many of the same *dramatis personae* were involved in considering a state response to victory, finally deciding upon the wider concern to create a thousand new churches and enlarge thousands more.

ONE

'Now or never is the time':
the first discussions, 1815–1817

The news that there had been a decisive battle at Waterloo was very slow to arrive in England. Rumour and counter-rumour got there first but, eventually, a messenger sent by the Duke of Wellington reached central London on 21 June 1815, three long days after the decisive battle at which the British and the Germans were finally victorious. The news was first delivered to the Secretary of State for War, Lord Bathurst, and the Tory Prime Minister, Lord Liverpool, then to the Prince Regent, all of whom were attending anticipatory victory dinner parties. The future George IV had now been his father's regent for four years.

The Duke of Wellington wrote carefully and precisely in his message of a 'desperate action' that had 'succeeded in every point', but never used the word 'victory' and stressed that the losses had been immense. Wellington's chosen messenger was Major the Hon. Henry Percy of the 14th Light Dragoons, the only one of his eight aides-de-camp to have survived the battle unscathed.

While war was still raging, four friends of the influential layman Joshua Watson had written to the Bishop of London. Bishop Beilby Porteus was a reformer and active slavery abolitionist, and was therefore receptive to such a letter, which pointed out that 'not a *tenth* part of the Church of England population can be accommodated in our churches & Chapels, to worship God after the manner of their forefathers'. The writers suggested that new churches might be offered as a national thanksgiving for victory over Napoleon, 'the most dreadful scourge that ever affected the human race'. They accepted that the Church itself could or would not confront the crisis and, whether or not it was up to Parliament or private individuals to solve it, certainly '*now or never* is the time'. At the end of 1815, six months or so after the Battle of Waterloo, Watson himself and his friend the lawyer and pamphleteer John Bowdler sent a memorandum to Liverpool, signed by 120 others, emphasising the urgent need for more churches. Their detailed planning began.

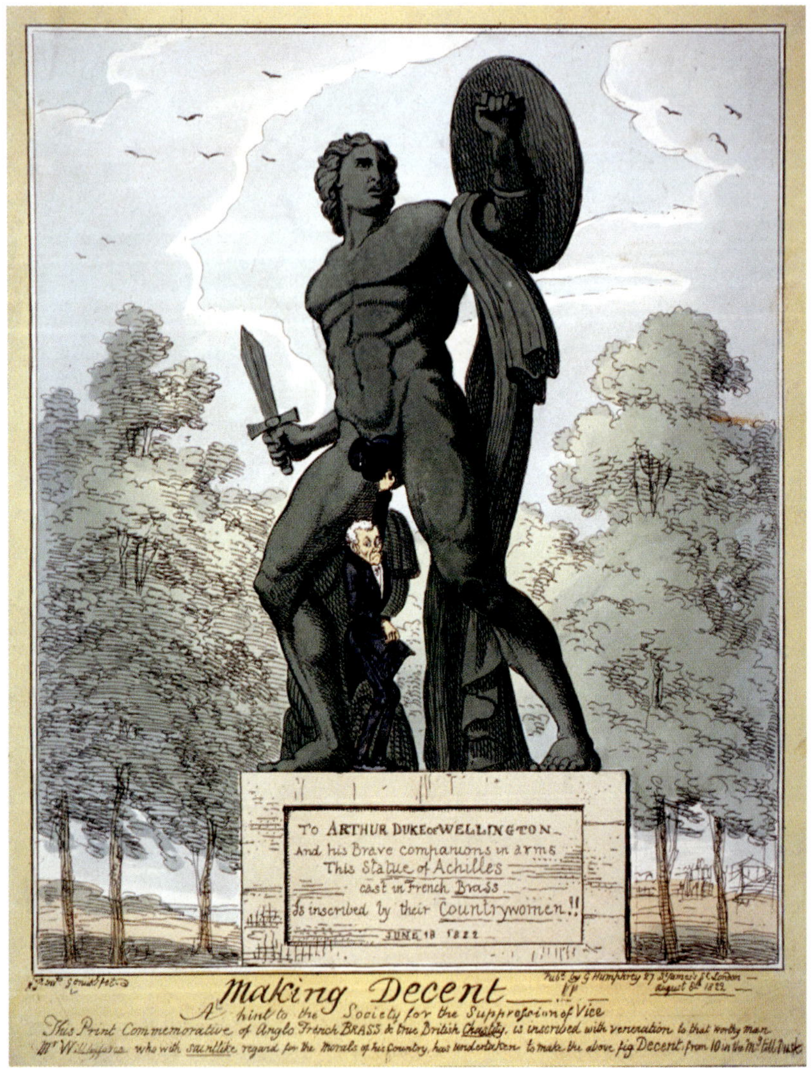

GEORGE CRUIKSHANK **Making decent – !! – ,** 1822,
Hand-coloured etching

The Achilles statue dedicated to the Duke of Wellington was funded by the women of Britain and, as the first nude public sculpture in modern Britain, caused an outcry. Cruikshank's image shows William Wilberforce, ('Mr Will-by-force') very small and weedy in comparison, reaching up to hold his top-hat over the fig-leaf which the sculptor, Richard Westamacott, had already been obliged to add. The print also carries the lines: **This Print Commemorative of Anglo French BRASS & true British Chastity, is inscribed with veneration to that Worthy Man Mr Willbyforce who with saintlike regard for the Morals of his Country, has undertaken to make the above fig. Decent, from 10 in the Mg. till Dusk.**

Eighteen months later, in the City of London Tavern on 23 May 1817, a meeting was held which recounted the discussions that had taken place since 1815 to consider a memorial to Waterloo. Such memorials were by now numerous. Waterloo Bridge, originally designed a few years earlier as Strand Bridge, was about to be opened by the Prince Regent and Wellington on the second anniversary of the battle. A Waterloo Fund gave £192,000 to the wounded and their families. A grateful nation had purchased the country estate of Stratfield Saye in Hampshire for Wellington, and the 'women of Britain' were raising funds to erect an 18-foot statue of Achilles, the first modern nude public sculpture in the country, as a monument to the duke. Later, the nearby Green Park, or Constitution, Arch was renamed in his honour. The duke had also been voted £700,000 by Parliament to build a new 'Waterloo Place', but, instead of embarking on a new building, he submitted an anonymous bid to buy Apsley House at Hyde Park Corner ('No. 1, London'), built by Robert Adam, and asked Benjamin Dean Wyatt to extend it. No other monument than Achilles – a very personal tribute to Wellington himself – was raised in London to mark Waterloo in its immediate aftermath, although a competition was started but then abandoned. Other memorials were created in the parts of Britain furthest from the capital, perhaps to emphasise, or try to persuade people, that the war had united the nation.

The Tavern meeting also revealed a deeply held concern about the success with which Methodism and other dissenting sects could erect simple places of worship in urban centres newly populated with workers who had left their homes in the countryside. Solving this problem carried more weight than celebrating or commemorating a victory that had left the country more or less bankrupt (the national debt was £679 million, more than double GDP), a country possibly no longer faithful, in the majority, to the Church of England. While parliamentary attention had been focused on the war against Napoleon many changes at home had entirely transformed the cities and villages of Britain. Allegiance to church and crown could not be taken for granted. Might dissidence, even revolution as in America and France in the 1780s, follow? The City of London Tavern, in Bishopsgate, was a notable public meeting place in the eighteenth and nineteenth centuries, a place of business as much as for alcohol and food.

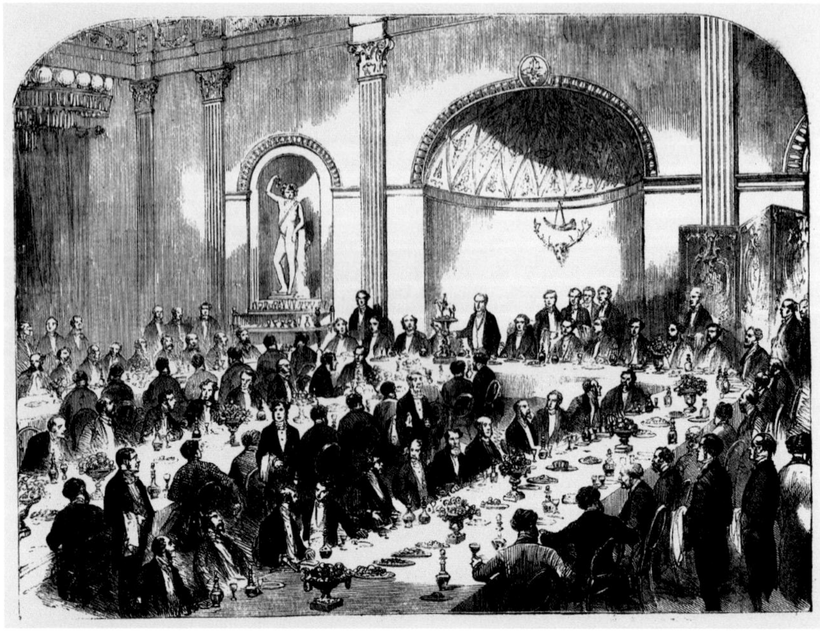

After GEORGE SHEPHERD **The City of London Tavern, Bishopsgate Street 1809**
Engraving, published in *The European Magazine* British Museum
The City of London Tavern was a notable public meeting place and, on 23 May 1817,
a meeting was held which recounted the discussions that had taken place since 1815 to
consider a memorial to Waterloo. The underlying reason for the meeting, however, was the
concern about insufficient places of worship and the risk that the country was possibly no
longer faithful, in the majority, to the Church of England.

In Dickens's *Nicholas Nickleby*, the Tavern is also the location for a public meeting 'to take into consideration the propriety of petitioning Parliament in favour of the United Metropolitan Improved Hot Muffin and Crumpet Baking and Punctual Delivery Company'.

Three days after the Tavern church-building meeting, a committee met in Lincoln's Inn Fields to form a society *'promoting public worship by obtaining additional church-room for the middle and lower classes'*. Watson and his friends William Cotton, George Bramwell and Thomas Bowdler, often now joined by the Reverend Richard Yates (author of *The Church in Danger*) met frequently, eight times in July alone. At this stage, their proposed name was 'The Church Room Society', although 'The Free Church Society' also had some support as a title.

Then, on 3 October 1817, a rebuke was received from the Lord Chancellor, the Earl of Eldon. He queried the legality of the Society and its strict conformity with the views and principles of the Church of England. He was also anxious that it might infringe on the rights of patrons and incumbents. The committee replied that the Society had not yet been formed but that it had the approval of the Prime Minister, the archbishops, and several other bishops, and that the Duke of York had agreed to be its patron. It stated that 'it had never intended planting churches or chapels through the country by any authority assumed by itself' (or, in fact, independently building any church or chapel), but would always work with the approval of the 'ordinary' – that is, the bishop or archbishop – the patron and the incumbent. The committee concluded that the legality of the Society could not be doubted and that 'the strictest conformity to the doctrines and discipline and also to the patronage by law established of the Church of England' would be ensured. Eight months after the Tavern meeting (and many more long meetings later) the proposed Society's aim was gratifyingly echoed in the Prince Regent's speech at the opening of Parliament on 27 January 1818, read by the Lord Chancellor:

> The Prince Regent has commanded us to direct your particular attention to the deficiency which has so long existed in the number of places of public worship belonging to the established church, when compared with the increased and increasing population of the country.
>
> His Royal Highness most earnestly recommends this important subject to your early consideration, deeply impressed, as he has no doubt you are, with a just sense of the many blessings which this country by the favour of divine Providence has enjoyed; and with the conviction, that the religious and moral habits of the people are the most sure and firm foundation of national prosperity.

The mood in the Palace of Westminster will have been solemn, for the speech was given in the Prince Regent's absence as he had been in mourning since November: 'The Prince Regent is persuaded that you will deeply participate in the affliction with which his Royal Highness has been visited, by the calamitous and untimely death of his beloved and only child the Princess Charlotte.' Nonetheless, the tone of the speech itself is upbeat. A year previously, on the way to Parliament, the royal coach had been mobbed and a window broken. The liberty of habeas corpus was immediately revoked and only repealed in the January 1818 session, which sought to be positive, possibly building on the temporary sympathy for the Regent's bereavement. His speech makes the economy sound buoyant and the country tranquil and at ease with itself:

> His Royal Highness recommends to your continued attention the state of the public income and expenditure; and he is most happy in being able to acquaint you, that since you were last assembled in Parliament, the revenue has been in a state of progressive improvement in its most important branches.

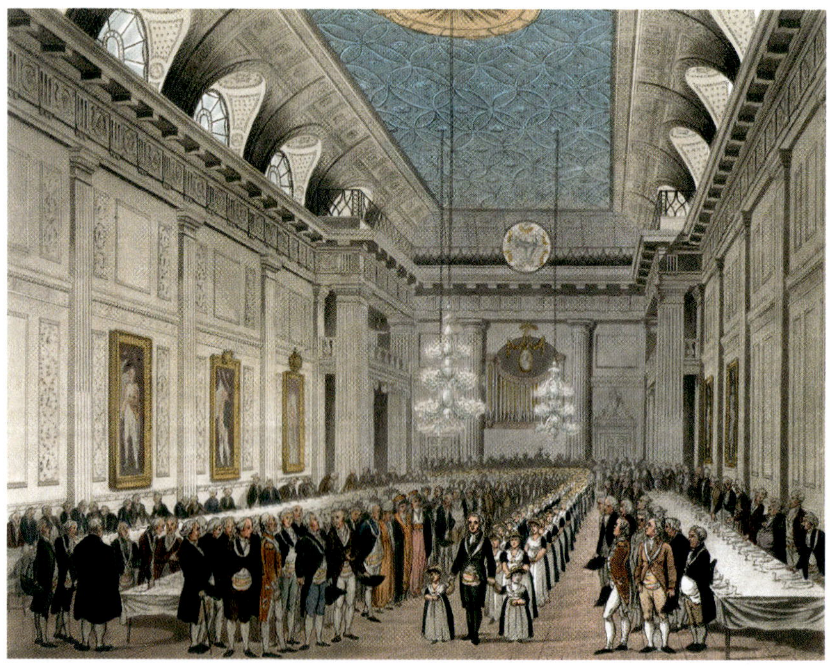

After THOMAS ROWLANDSON and AUGUSTUS CHARLES PUGIN
Freemasons' Hall, Great Queen Street, London, 1808, Aquatint
From *The Microcosm of London*, published by Rudolph Ackermann, 1808-10
The Church Building Society was first proposed at a meeting in the Freemasons' Hall on 6 February 1818.

A major church-building programme could show his concern for the nation and help imply a new financial and social stability. There was also a sense of modernity and urban change in the air. Lord Liverpool had become Prime Minister after the assassination of Spencer Perceval in 1812: a moderniser, Liverpool was the first British Prime Minister regularly to wear long trousers instead of knee breeches and to sport a short haircut instead of long hair tied in a tail. He became Prime Minister at the point when the English capital was newly lit up with gaslights and, very soon, other British cities would follow. The role that public buildings played began to change as the population became more mobile, happier and safer to be in city centres or suburbs after dark.

Ten days after Parliament opened, on 6 February 1818, the Archbishop of Canterbury, Charles Manners-Sutton, chaired a meeting in the Freemasons' Hall near Drury Lane, another centre for important public discussions. At this meeting the new 3rd Duke of Northumberland (cousin to Wellington's young messenger) proposed a motion to form the Society for the Promotion and Enlargement of Churches and Chapels, better and later known as the Incorporated Church Building Society (ICBS). Lord Kenyon seconded the motion. Its purpose was to 'remedy the deficiencies of places set aside for Public Worship in our towns and cities', and the meeting noted with satisfaction the proposed new Act 'and the probability that each will be very beneficial to the other'.

On 16 March, the nascent Society was attacked in a pamphlet addressed to William Howley, Bishop of London. 'A Clergyman of the Church of England' acknowledged the formation of the Society: 'whether within the walls of St. Stephen's, or of the Freemason's Tavern, it is pleasant, and to my feelings heart-warming, to find the important and truly national subject of enlargement and building of PLACES OF WORSHIP brought fairly and fully before the public view', but he objected to the 'apparent incongruity of two simultaneous operations, not exactly moving in union with each other'. He stated that 'either Parliament is, or is not, competent to provide for the increase and enlargement of Churches. If it be, the Meeting at the Freemason's Tavern was unnecessary; if it be not, there should be similar meetings in every Town-hall throughout the kingdom.' This was a fair point.

An account was opened at Hoares Bank on 4 March 1818 with a deposit of £4,982 3*s*. 4*d*. made by Thomas Bowdler and George Bramwell, transferred from one opened there the previous year in their joint names. Early donors included the Archbishop of Canterbury (200 guineas), the Archbishop of York (200 guineas), the Earl of Normanton (200 guineas), Hoares Bank (350 guineas), 'a friend to the Church' (£10), Eton College (£100), the University of Cambridge (£1,000) and the Worshipful Company of Goldsmiths (200 guineas). The Society announced £19,000 in subscriptions. By 25 May 1818 the account at Hoares Bank was already in credit to the sum of £39,123 7*s*. 9*d*., which is roughly the equivalent of £4,000,000 at today's values.

The apparent incongruity of two movements, private and state, clearly appeared to many as a necessary check and balance; not exactly in union but complementary and leaving the Society with nominal independence. Prominent and diplomatic laymen, with the support of many members of the nobility and the Church, made it plain that they were willing to undertake what the government did not appear ready to do.

The next public examination of the subject was in the Houses of Parliament on 16 March, the same day that the critical pamphlet appeared. George Tierney, leader of the Whig party, announced 'that soon after the holydays he intended to move, that the sum granted by parliament for the erection of a monument to commemorate our victories by sea and land, be laid out in the erection of a parish church or churches'. The Chancellor of the Exchequer, Nicholas Vansittart, replied that, instead, he himself was proposing 'an economical arrangement for the building and enlarging of churches throughout the kingdom … very different from the erection of a monumental church upon a great scale of ornamental architecture'. Tierney agreed (but voted in 1824 against funds for more churches).

Vansittart then continued, having quoted the Prince Regent's speech of January, that

> he believed no communication from the throne had ever been expected with greater anxiety, or received with more satisfaction by the public, than that which the Lords Commissioners had made, by the command of the Prince Regent, at the opening of the present session. For more than a century, the want of accommodation for

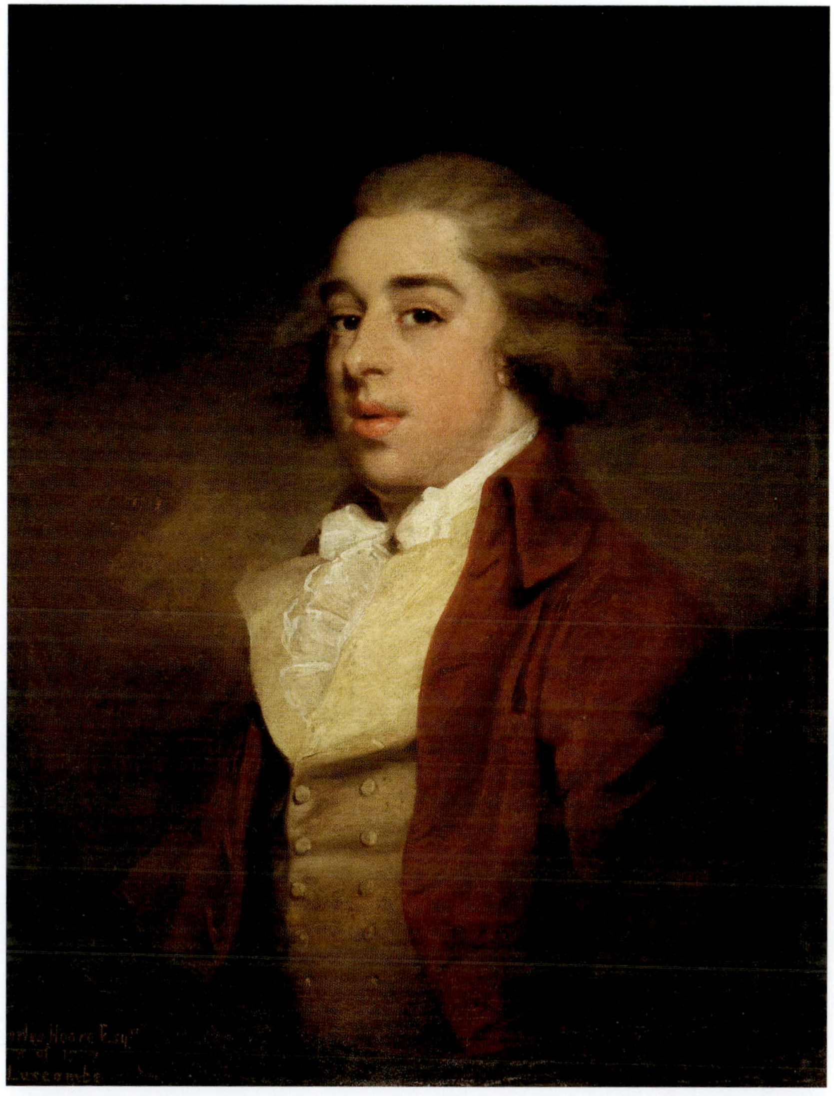

Attributed to PRINCE HOARE
Portrait of Charles Hoare of Luscombe (1767–1851)
circa 1790, Oil on canvas

*In 1799, Charles Hoare commissioned John Nash to design him a country house at
Luscombe in Devon. Charles also oversaw the new building for his family's bank in Fleet
Street in 1829. He became the Church Building Society's first treasurer and a generous
benefactor; he remained treasurer for eleven years and a trustee for thirty-three years until
his death. In all, nine members of the Hoare family have been ICBS treasurers.*

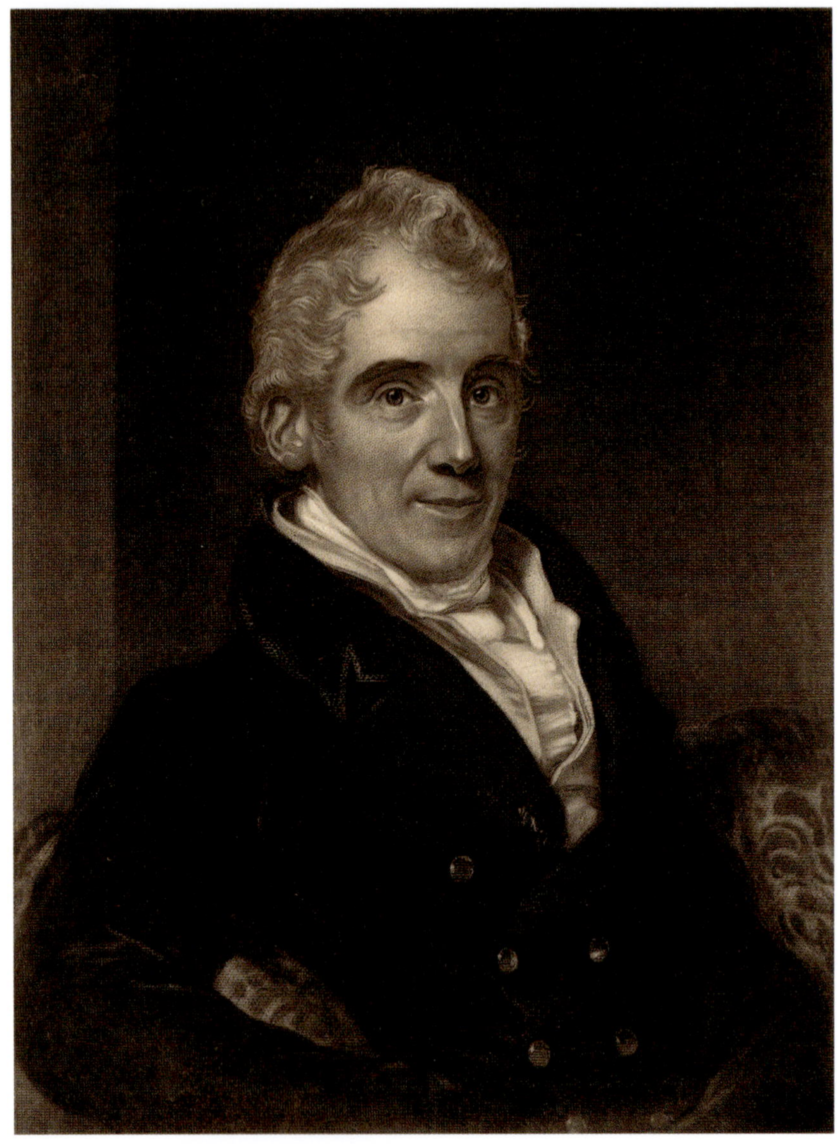

WILLIAM OVEREND GELLER, after SIR WILLIAM CHARLES ROSS
Portrait of Joshua Watson 1771–1855, circa 1825, Engraving circa 1825
By 1825, the Church Building Society had begun to run out of resources for the first, but not the last, time. The original oil painting has not been traced but clearly showed the gently humorous and informal character of the much-loved Joshua Watson.

public worship had been felt by the members of the established Church as a most serious evil; and an attempt had been made so long ago by Parliament to remedy it, so far as respected the metropolis, and its immediate vicinity. This attempt, however, though attended with considerable expense, had been very imperfect in its execution, only eleven churches having been built, out of fifty which it was proposed to erect. Since that time no farther steps had been taken by public authority, though the evil had been perpetually increasing with the growing population of the country.

Kenneth Clark, vague about the sequence of dates but accurate about the impact, later wrote in his history of the Gothic Revival: 'In 1818 there appeared the Church Building Society, and the extraordinary success of this pious enterprise shamed the government into action.'

The Church Building Act 1818 was passed that summer; the Church Building Commission (CBC) was appointed and a parliamentary grant of £1 million made 'for building, and promoting the building, of Additional Churches in populous Parishes'. The Commission first met on 28 July 1818, to form a committee which in turn sat at Lambeth Palace three days later, oddly without Joshua Watson, who was the most diligent member of both the Commission and the ICBS. The CBC opened an office at 12 (later 13) Great George Street in Westminster. A sub-committee of three was asked to draw up an abstract of rules: Watson; Francis Wollaston, Archdeacon of Essex and until recently a Cambridge professor of natural philosophy; and Richard Mant, who later became a bishop in Ireland. They reported by 7 September and it was agreed to print 500 copies of the rules and send them out to bishops, of whom Geoffrey Best has said they were 'like tenants whose landlord was responsible for repairs[:] they could hope for little beyond being consulted about the colours'.

By February 1821 it was already clear that the appetite for new churches was huge and even more money would be needed from Parliament, leading to the Church Building Act of 1824, which provided a second parliamentary grant of £500,000. This new money was distributed more widely and grants were less generous. The first parliamentary grant was shared between fewer than 100 churches; the second, half the size, was given to five times as many.

Apart from the amounts of money available to both groups, and the many regulations that governed them, the main difference between the CBC and the ICBS was their respective approaches to entitlement to the increased numbers of seats in churches for Anglican worshippers. Parliament's argument was simply towards a greater quantity of church space using pew rental as part of the means of payment, against the ICBS's goal of free seats for all. Both bodies sought to influence the appearance and form of their funded churches but worked at different speeds. Ultimately, the patient but determined guidance of the ICBS helped Gothic Revival architecture gain dominance in the building of the 'typical' English and Welsh parish church.

At the head of the ICBS was a royal patron, first Prince Edward, Duke of York (father to Queen Victoria) until 1820, followed by George IV and then Victoria herself. The Archbishop of Canterbury (Charles Manners-Sutton until 1828) was president *ex officio* of the Society. The Archbishop of York, two bishops and twenty-five lay peers and commoners were to be vice presidents; among these were three dukes, eight earls and two viscounts, Charles Manners-Sutton (Speaker of the House of Commons and son of the archbishop), Sir Robert Peel, William Wilberforce and Vansittart. A further thirty-six 'laymen and ecclesiastics' were to compose the executive committee of the Society. Prominent among the 'ecclesiastics' were the deans of Westminster, Lichfield, Chester and Canterbury; the Reverends John James Watson, Christopher Wordsworth, Richard Yates and Henry Handley Norris; and Archdeacon Charles Daubeny. Charles Hoare was appointed treasurer and George Bramwell was honorary secretary.

A donation of 100 guineas conferred the right to become a governor and to have a double vote at general meetings. Those contributing twenty guineas as a lump sum, or two guineas per annum, were to be considered members of the Society with a right to vote at general meetings and be eligible for election to the committee. A general meeting was to be held annually on the third Thursday in May, at which a report of the Society's proceedings during the previous year was to be presented by the committee together with a statement of receipts and payments. Vacancies on the committee, three auditors and a treasurer were also to be elected then.

Four trustees were to be appointed by the committee to administer 'donations, subscriptions, bequests or otherwise'. The four founding trustees were Peel, a self-made mill owner and Tory MP whose son would become Prime Minister; Charles Hoare, a senior partner in his family bank, a major donor, the treasurer for eleven years and a trustee until his death in 1851; Beeston Long, a West Indies merchant and a former governor of the Bank of England; and Lord Kenyon, an actively anti-Catholic son of a previous Tory Lord Chief Justice. Long was replaced in 1820 by Joshua Watson, who had always been the quiet force behind the movement towards church-building reform. Watson was, with Kenyon, also a member of the CBC. William Cotton (whose father Joseph chaired the first committee meeting) succeeded Peel in 1830.

In 1818, a public address was issued by the Society that described its creation and the Church Building Act as an 'extraordinary concurrence'. To a modern mind, this has a faint irony. Extraordinary it might have been but it was also very carefully planned. The address continues: 'A Society has been formed; and while the arrangements connected with its establishment and first proceedings have been going on, the nation has had the satisfaction of beholding the attention of Parliament called to this great object … a wide field is open for the exertions of the present Society.'

The ideas and subsequent planning that led both to the Act and the Society had begun even before the French wars. As far back as 1797, John Bowdler, a lawyer until he inherited a fortune, had published a forcefully worded pamphlet entitled *Reform or Ruin*, in which he decried the immorality and irreligion of the nation. His sister and brother have become eponymous moralists as 'Bowdlerisers' after they published an expurgated edition of Shakespeare's plays.

Another early reformer in religious politics was Richard Watson, Bishop of Llandaff, a professor of chemistry and a Cumbrian. In 1800 he wrote to William Wilberforce, the independent and evangelical MP for Kingston-upon-Hull, to enlist his help in proposing 'free churches'. Wilberforce was a passionate campaigner and reformer, especially against slavery, who also created the Society of the Suppression of Vice in 1802. In this capacity he was later to organise a fig leaf to preserve the modesty of the Achilles–Wellington statue in Hyde Park. In 1803, Britain declared war on France, initiating a conflict that would culminate at Waterloo. In the same year there was an ineffectual parliamentary Act to promote church building and repair. The next year, Watson preached a sermon to Wilberforce's Society on the theme of free churches.

The potentially powerful combination of Watson and Wilberforce did not develop. Instead, two other men took up the reins and skilfully guided matters towards the meeting at the City of London Tavern in 1817. Both were merchants and laymen whose influence on the nineteenth-century church would be extensive.

TWO

'The Saints' versus 'the High and Dry':
protagonists within the Clapham Sect
and the Hackney Phalanx

In the twenty years between 1801 and 1821, the population of England increased by 35 per cent, from 7.7 million to 10.4 million. At the same time, there was a great shift of population from the country to the towns. A reviewer in the *Quarterly Review* of 1820 reflected upon the habits of the people of England prior to the Reformation of the church in the 1530s: 'A peasant, perhaps, scarcely ever went thirty miles from the place where he was born, unless he were called away on military service. There were then no overgrown cities, and the few manufactories which existed were carried on upon a small scale.' In 1700 it was believed that the five most populated English counties were Middlesex, Somerset, Gloucestershire, Wiltshire and Northamptonshire. A century later only Middlesex was still in that league table, joined now by Lancashire, the West Riding of Yorkshire, Staffordshire and Warwickshire. The change was not, however, mirrored in the building and enlargement of churches and the Industrial Revolution began to demolish the traditional parochial system. An increase in the number of factories suggested to some that there was now a directly linked increase in the prison population, too, and that only more room in churches could break the cycle.

In 1815, the English Corn Laws were introduced to set tariffs on imported grain and keep prices high to favour farmers at home. This was a cause of anger in urban centres where political power was weakest. The Corn Laws were supported by Tory landowners and opposed by Whigs, many of whose voters were industrialists. The next year there were widespread food shortages following a volcanic eruption in Indonesia, although this was not understood at the time; it became known as the 'year without a summer'. At the same time income tax was abolished. By the beginning of 1819, when the church-building legislation was newly established, failing economic conditions and disproportionately low political representation

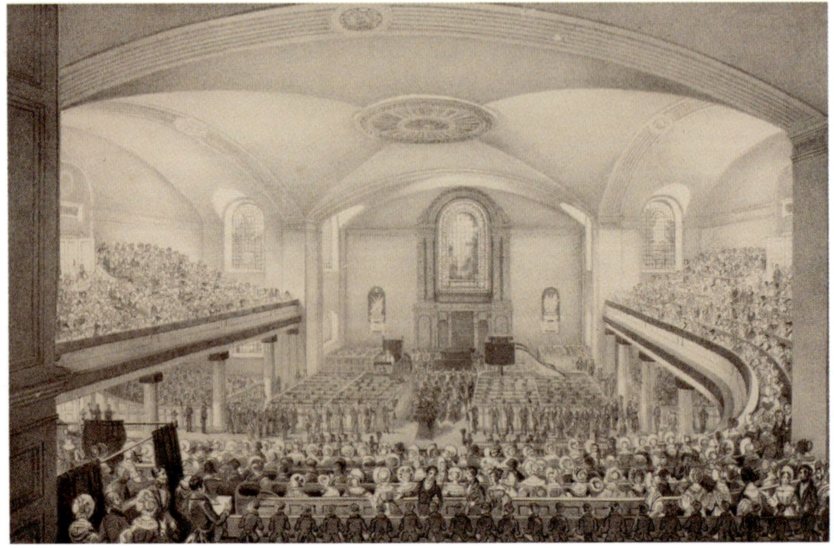

BRITISH SCHOOL **Interior view of St John at Hackney, London, during the funeral service of Rev. John James Watson, Archdeacon of St Albans, and Rector of Hackney**
Engraving 1839

Joshua Watson's younger brother John died in 1839 and was buried at St John's, near the Town Hall in Hackney, where he had been rector for forty years. The scale of the funeral shows the regard in which he was held.

in northern England encouraged and enflamed radicalism. A brief boom in textile manufacture, concentrated in Lancashire, was followed by periods of chronic economic depression particularly among weavers and spinners, whose wages were cut by about a third. The Manchester Patriotic Union, a group agitating for parliamentary reform, organised a demonstration to be addressed by a radical orator on St Peter's Field, Manchester. Local magistrates summoned the militia to disperse the crowds, who carried banners calling for 'No Corn Laws', 'Annual Parliaments', 'Universal Suffrage' and 'Vote by Ballot'. Cavalry charged into the crowd with sabres drawn, 15 people were killed and between 400 and 700 more were injured. The massacre was called Peterloo in ironic comparison to the Battle of Waterloo four years before. Two years previously, a smaller but devastating revolt of handloom workers took place on the Chatsworth estate at Penritch in Derbyshire which resulted in three men hanged, fourteen deported and six gaoled. As a direct result All Saints' Church was built in nearby Ripley, one of the very first to be funded by the ICBS.

Percy Bysshe Shelley wrote an eyewitness poem in 1819 in memory of Peterloo which did not appear in print until 1832. It ends:

> *Rise like Lions after slumber*
> *In unvanquishable number,*
> *Shake your chains to earth like dew*
> *Which in sleep had fallen on you –*
> *Ye are many – they are few!*

Unrest was also a very present danger in the capital. By 1818, when the two bodies behind the church-building impetus were being constructed, social and political unrest was at a flashpoint. George III was mentally unfit to rule and Britain found itself under a regency headed by an unpopular figure. Neither the Regency nor the Prince Regent's subsequent reign as George IV was a period of best moral example: shortly after he acceded to the throne in 1820 the House of Lords passed a bill to grant him a divorce from Queen Caroline but, because of public pressure in the queen's favour, the bill was dropped. The same year witnessed the Cato Street Conspiracy, an attempt to assassinate the Prime Minister and the entire British cabinet as part of a furious backlash against Peterloo and the repressive, anti-radical Six Acts that followed.

By the time the discussion about church room reached Parliament in 1818, in Manchester only 10,950 people out of a population of 79,459 could be accommodated in Anglican churches. Liverpool had a population of 94,376, for whom only 21,000 could be found seats in church, and in Marylebone, London, the figures were 8,700 out of 75,624. In Birmingham it was calculated that there were 40,000 people to be provided for, 'which cannot be done, but by building twenty churches'. Twenty churches each were also said to be required in Manchester, Sheffield and Stockport, and 'it was but too certain, that in every manufacturing or mining district in the kingdom, the same deficiency will be found, in a greater or lesser degree, to prevail'.

Meanwhile, technological advancement was offering some very significant advantages, notably steam printing. In 1814, *The Times* adopted this technology, which multiplied printing capacity fivefold. Pamphlets proliferated. An explosion in popular novels followed in which stories revealed or imagined the lives of the rich and aristocratic, making even more explicit the hierarchy of village and suburban life; exactly where each person sat and what they wore in church on Sunday became local news. Church alterations and new buildings were news and the stuff of literature, too.

In 1819 Mary Ann Evans, better known as George Eliot, was baptised at All Saints, Chilvers Coton, Warwickshire, which in 1837 raised its own funds to build a north aisle. Twenty years later, Eliot wrote in 'The Sad Fortunes of the Reverend Amos Barton', one of the stories that goes to make up *Scenes from Clerical Life*, that its fictional (but accurately described) counterpart

> was a very different-looking building five-and-twenty years ago … now there is a wide span of slate roof flanking the old steeple, the windows are tall and symmetrical, the outer doors are resplendent with oak-graining … pass through the baize doors and you will see the nave filled with well-shaped benches, understood to be free seats; while in certain eligible corners, less directly under the fire of the clergyman's eye, there are pews reserved for the … gentility.

William Stevens and Joshua Watson were of different generations, respectively born in 1732 and 1771, but shared a number of attributes. Both came from trade but retired as soon as they could to devote themselves to church matters. Each had close family who were church officials while they themselves strove to support the church as wealthy laymen using published tracts and private letters as their instruments.

William Stevens was brought up with his cousin George Horne, who became Bishop of Norwich. Stevens's father had been in trade and died when the boy was a baby so Stevens, unlike his wealthier friend and cousin, was apprenticed to a hosier. He rose to become a partner in the firm and retired in 1801 to concentrate on writing on religious topics from a High Church, Tory and Royalist, perspective. He was the biographer and editor of the works of William Jones of Nayland, with whom he formed the Society for the Reformation of Principles to counteract the influence of the French Revolution. The Society published a collection of tracts for younger clergy – such as *The Scholar Armed against*

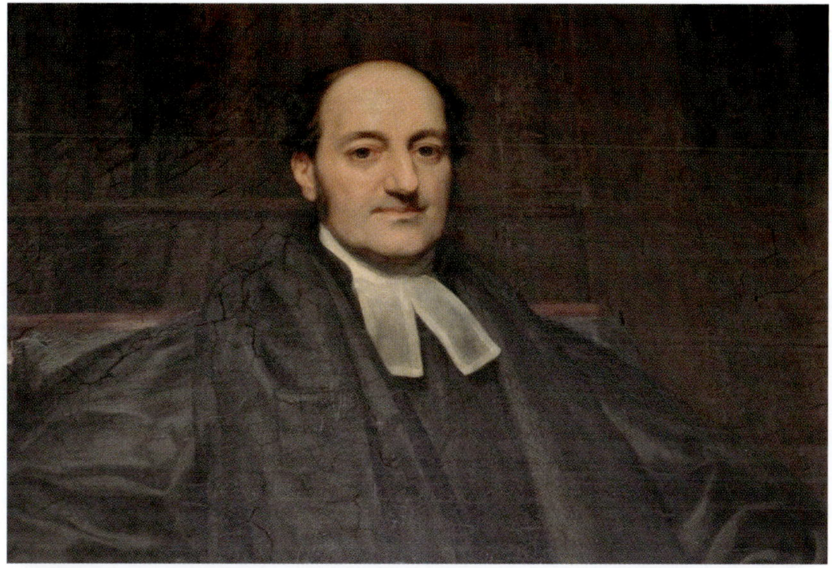

THOMAS PHILLIPS, RA **Portrait of Henry Handley Norris 1771–1850** (detail)
circa 1830 Oil on canvas

Henry Handley Norris – 'the Bishop-maker' – was the son of a wealthy merchant, like his
close friends the Watsons. His sister married John James Watson; Norris married the sister
of Baden Powell. He was rector of St John of Jerusalem and a key figure in the Hackney
Phalanx. This grand portrait was commissioned by his parishioners from a distinguished
portrait painter who also sketched the Emperor Napoleon.

the Errors of the Times, 1795 – and the British Critic, a quarterly journal.
Stevens acted for many years as treasurer of Queen Anne's Bounty (see
page 55), supported the work of various church societies, and, unusually,
interested himself in the position of the Episcopal Church in Scotland.
He was also the founder – the very Nobody himself – of the dining club
Nobody's Friends in 1800 (which still exists today) and an inspiration to
the generation that pushed for the church-building movement.

Joshua Watson, from an early stage one of Nobody's Friends but in
fact a friend to very many indeed, was forty years younger and worked
in the family wine-importing business in the City of London. He was
not directly related to Bishop Richard Watson but both were Cumbrians.
Joshua Watson became a partner in his father's business in 1792 and by his
early forties was able to retire, having spread his business interests widely

and successfully as a government supplier during the Napoleonic Wars. He could now devote himself to good works and intensive activity in church affairs: he was referred to as the best layman in England even though, or probably because, he was rarely in the public eye. Like Stevens's cousin, George, Joshua Watson's elder brother John was the member of the family that joined the church while the younger brother followed their father into commerce. John James Watson was rector of Hackney for forty years and Archdeacon of St Albans.

Joshua Watson married Mary Sikes, whose uncle, Charles Daubeny, later Archdeacon of Salisbury, and brother Thomas, vicar of Guilsborough in Northamptonshire, had been at Oxford with Joshua's elder brother John. These relations and friends were among the leading churchmen of the day. Joshua Watson, with both money and time available, became the virtual leader of the 'High Church party' and his early friends and advisers included Stevens and, among churchmen, two particular individuals. One was Henry Handley Norris, who was both curate and brother-in-law to John Watson in Hackney, then rector himself, as well as prebendary of Llandaff Cathedral (1816) and of St Paul's (1825). He was known as 'The Bishop-maker'.

The other influential friend was William Van Mildert, rector of St Mary-le-Bow in the City of London and subsequently Bishop of Llandaff (after Richard Watson), then Dean of St Paul's, and finally the last Palatine Bishop of Durham. He narrowly missed out on becoming Archbishop of Canterbury. Van Mildert's father, like Watson's, had been a wine merchant and the bishop was known as 'The Stormy Petrel' for his trenchant views.

Watson bought a house in Clapton, to the east of London, to be near his brother and Handley Norris. He worked closely with other friends and relations who formed the branches of several family trees in Hackney, entwined to a formidable degree. His only daughter, Mary Sikes Watson, married Henry Michell Wagner, vicar of Brighton (see page 174).

Clapton and Hackney became centres for various influential High Church religious and philanthropic projects under the nickname the Hackney Phalanx. This east London group was diametrically opposed to its counterpart south of the Thames, the Clapham Sect, both of them nicknamed by the witty Reverend Sydney Smith in his *Edinburgh Review*.

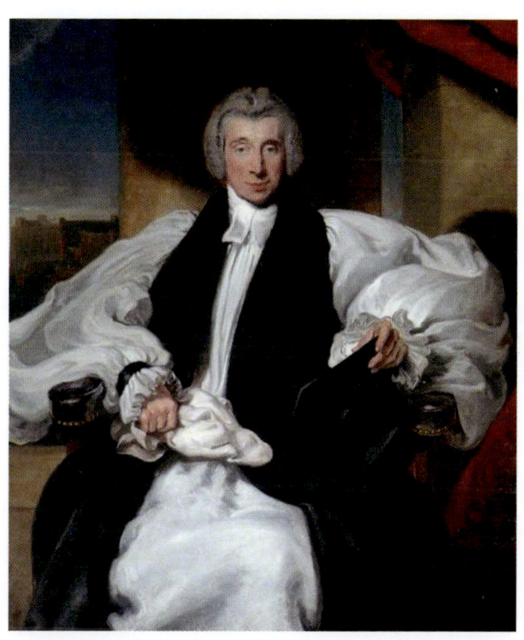

After SIR THOMAS LAWRENCE
Portrait of William van Mildert 1765–1836 circa 1826 Oil on canvas

Son of a gin distiller, van Mildert became Regius Professor of Divinity at Oxford then Bishop of Llandaff. From 1826, he was Bishop of Durham, the last Bishop Palatine, and the driving force behind the creation of the city's university, a college of which bears his name.

The Clapham and Hackney groups, also known respectively as 'the Saints' and 'the High and Dry', in newly prosperous London suburbs to the south and east, were both passionate Anglican social reformers, but the Clapham Sect was strongly evangelical and had at its centre the reformer and abolitionist William Wilberforce. A sister organisation – the Eclectic Society – had posed the question 'What methods can we use more effectually to promote the knowledge of the Gospel among the Heathen?' and provided the answer by forming the Church Missionary Society (CMS) in 1799 (still active today as the Church Mission Society). Like the ICBS, its bankers were Messrs Hoare, the first treasurer was William Henry Hoare and the first secretary was the Reverend Thomas Scott, (grandfather of the renowned church architect George Gilbert Scott; see page 102), who, in response to Thomas Paine's *Rights of Man*, published *The Rights of God*. The CMS was much concerned with the plight of the Jews but after some wrangling, it was decided in 1809 that a separate society should be set up, to be known as the London Society for Promoting Christianity Amongst the Jews (LJS).

In the early nineteenth century, the lot of the Jew, wherever he or she lived, was not an enviable one. Particularly unfortunate were those living in Jerusalem, where their numbers were steadily swollen by refugees fleeing Russian pogroms. In the words of Karl Marx, 'None equals the misery and suffering of the Jews at Jerusalem, inhabiting the most filthy quarter, constant object of Musulman oppression and intolerance, insulted by the Greeks, persecuted by the Latins.'

The LJS's work began first among the poor Jewish immigrants in the East End of London and spread to Europe, South America, Africa and Palestine. In 1823, it sent a delegation to the Holy Land with 10,000 bibles and the ambition to construct a church in Jerusalem but reactions were immediate and negative. The ruling Muslim Turks refused the construction of a new church (none having been built in Jerusalem since the time of the Crusades) and they also issued a decree forbidding the distribution of Christian reading material throughout the Levant. The Pope issued a bull forbidding Catholics from receiving or reading the bibles and the other Christian churches in Jerusalem were equally hostile. Most important of all, the Jews did not wish to be converted. The LJS was undeterred.

Under pressure from Lord Palmerston (cousin to the LJS chairman of the day, Lord Shaftesbury), the Turks finally agreed to the British opening a consulate in Jerusalem and, in 1838, the LJS was able to purchase a prominent site opposite the Citadel. From this base, the LJS, despite persistent opposition particularly from the rabbis, did much excellent work for local Jews. It built hospitals, founded schools, started training centres, educated women and set up agricultural colleges.

In 1841, the new King of Prussia, Frederick William IV, persuaded the Anglican Church and the UK government to set up, via the Bishops in Foreign Countries Act, a joint Anglo-German bishopric in Jerusalem with a converted rabbi, Michael Alexander of the LJS, as its first bishop (see page 142). This association of the Church of England with the Prussian Lutheran Church (evangelical, non-episcopalian) was strongly opposed by those of High Church persuasion and contributed to the departure to Rome of several eminent Anglo-Catholics including the future Cardinal Newman. When, later, Otto von Bismarck came to power in Prussia, he strongly objected to the 1841 agreement, particularly the clause that required that the Prussian and English churches took it in turns to nominate bishops; the bishop named by the Prussian church had to be a

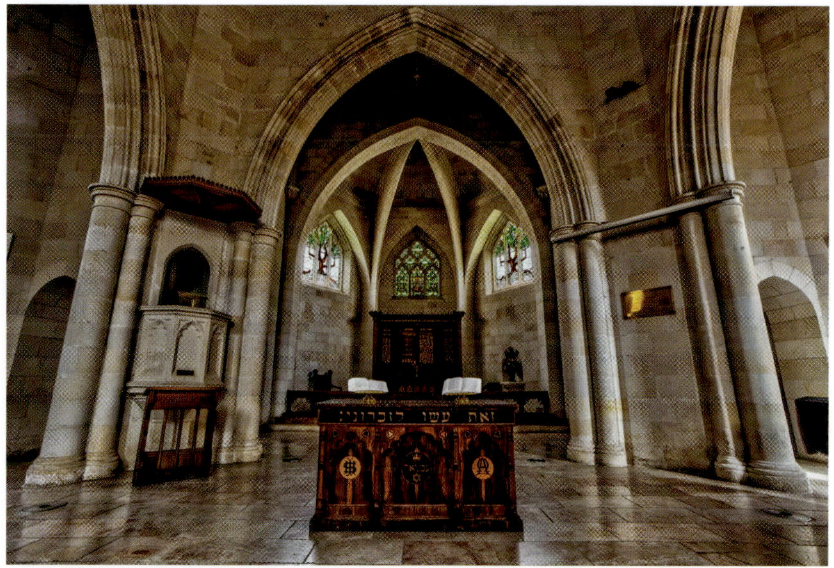

Interior of Christ Church, Jerusalem

communicant Anglican, subscribe to the 39 Articles and be approved by the Archbishop of Canterbury.

Christ Church was finally consecrated in 1849, the oldest Protestant church in the Middle East and the first to be built in Jerusalem. Kelvin Crombie, the historian of Christ Church, notes that as no silver trowel was available, the bishop lent his fish slice. The LJS continues to be an active member of the Anglican community and is still proprietor of Christ Church.

In both Clapham and Hackney groups, the evangelical focus was on the spiritual life at home, spreading the Word, active conversion, missions overseas, prison reform and the abolition of slavery and child labour. The High Church group concentrated first on education then on church building, liturgy and theology. Hackney was an area also associated with active Nonconformism in both intellectual and religious spheres, with a particular dominance by Unitarians, but the Phalanx contained remarkable organisers. By 1807, all the old guard that had influenced Watson and his friends were dead and the baton passed to the younger generation of churchmen and laymen with substantial private incomes, business experience, energy and public consciences.

The Hackney Phalanx's first major achievement came in 1811 when the National Society for Promoting Religious Education was established in a meeting at Watson's house and he became its first treasurer. Often known simply as the National Society and still active today, it was incorporated in 1817 'for the education of the poor in the principles of the Established Church in England and Wales'. The aim was to found a church school in every parish and by 1851 (twenty years before the state took responsibility for education) there were 12,000 of its schools across England and Wales. The awareness of poverty and deprivation (and of local Dissenters) led the Hackney philanthropists equally to promote information and statistics about the lack of places in church for such children and their families. Sunday schools had been founded in 1780, day schools in 1800, but much more was needed. If children were educated in the ways of the church there must be places for them to follow early learning with lifelong worship, and Watson insisted: 'It matters comparatively little how much, or even how well, we teach our children in the weekday, if we do not carry them to church on the Sunday.'

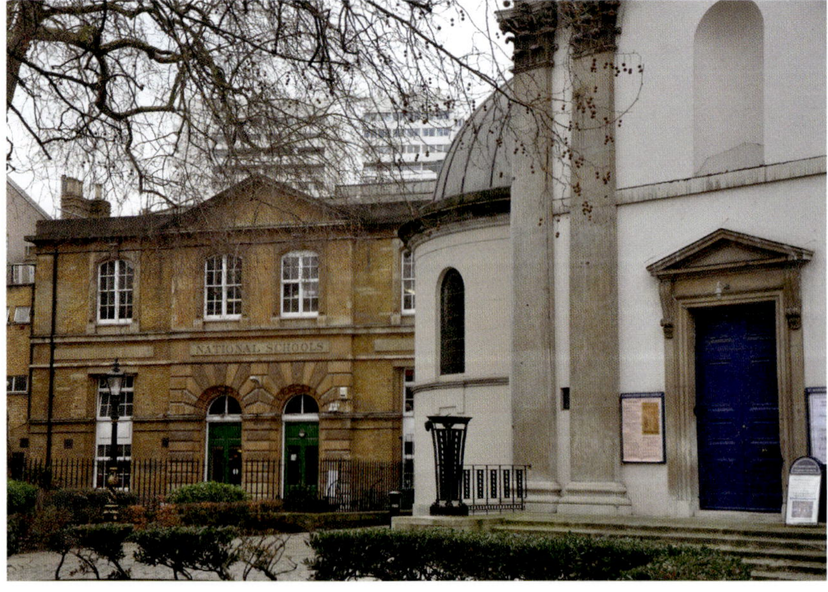

The former Central National School, Marylebone, (now St Marylebone C of E School) next to Marylebone Parish Church

Watson rarely missed a meeting of the societies with which he was involved, which included the Society for the Propagation of the Gospel, the Society for Promoting Christian Knowledge and the Clergy Orphan School as well as the National Society, the ICBS and the CBC. He remained treasurer of the Additional Curates' Society until he was eighty-two. He had been secretary of the relief fund, in 1814 for those Germans who had suffered from the Napoleonic wars. In the same year as The National Society was created Watson and Henry Handley Norris purchased the *British Critic* from William Stevens in order to restore its original function as the trenchant mouthpiece of the High Church party on the subject of society's faults: 'Ungodliness, profligacy, intemperance, improvidence, turbulence, desperation, disease: the unmitigated and intolerable penury which is ever at the heels of vice and low debauchery: the destruction of physical, mental, moral and spiritual health: the murder of soul and body: the atmosphere of pollution spreading and propagating itself without a check.'

The Hackney Phalanx's triumph was to extend its influence from education to churches. It provoked and enabled the Church Building Act 1818 with its first parliamentary grant of £1 million and directed the early years of the ICBS with its much longer life and greater reach.

It became clear to some after Waterloo that they could no longer assume that the majority in England and Wales was loyal to the established Anglican Church, but as the British Empire expanded so did the potential for new Anglican congregations and charities were set up to spread the message worldwide. Long before the new church-building projects, the Society for Promoting Christian Knowledge (SPCK) had been founded in 1698, followed in 1701 by the Society for the Propagation of the Gospel in Foreign Parts (SPG). The first Bible Society was created in 1779 'for purchasing Bibles to be distributed among British Soldiers and Seamen of the Navy, to spread abroad (by the blessing of God) Christian knowledge and reformation of manners'. The (London) Missionary Society was formed in 1795 by evangelical Anglicans and Nonconformists and in 1799 the Religious Tract Society was founded by the same group. The Sunday school movement began in 1780 so that the Word was, in theory, being delivered near and far. In 1800, a fifteen-year-old Welsh Methodist, Mary Jones, walked 26 miles through north Wales to buy a copy of the Welsh translation of the Bible. Inspired by her tale, in 1804, William Wilberforce and others formed the British and Foreign Bible Society at a meeting at the City of London Tavern.

It was not just the souls of the population that were in danger. A new Relief of the Poor Act was introduced in 1782 to organise social care on a county-by-county basis, the parishes of which could set up workhouses to help the elderly, sick and orphaned. The able-bodied but poverty-stricken were provided with poor relief in their own homes. In 1795 a meeting was held at the Pelican Inn in Speenhamland, Berkshire, where a system was devised to alleviate the poverty and distress caused by high grain prices. The Speenhamland system was a means-tested sliding scale of supplements to agricultural wages which balanced the price of bread against the number of children in each household. This system of 'outdoor relief' as opposed to help given inside the poorhouse reached its height during the Napoleonic Wars when it was used as a means of quelling potential revolt but it allowed employers to pay below-subsistence wages, knowing the parish would make up the difference.

It was little wonder that the people in the cities moved away from the Church of England. In a debate to increase church extension in 1840 Henry Knight, MP for Nottinghamshire North, commented:

> Dissent in this country has spread to its present extent chiefly on account of the difficulties which were thrown in the way of building a church, whilst none of those difficulties are in the way of building a meeting house. In this respect the Church of England should at least be placed on a level with her opponents.

In the same debate, Sir Robert Inglis, MP for Oxford University, told Parliament:

> The House will hardly believe the amount which England has paid since the commencement of the present century in building and repairing gaols. In six counties, the aggregate expense has been more than a million and a half; in all England, from 1800 to 1830, it exceeds £3,320,000. I do not suppose, or mean to insinuate, that an increase of church accommodation in the interval would have superseded the necessity of all this expenditure; but I do mean to say, that exactly in

proportion to the degree of active and pious pastoral superintendence, is, humanly speaking, the certainty of the diminution of the amount of crime, and consequently of the expense of punishment.

The first new church in or near Manchester to be considered for grant aid by ICBS was not given support until 1852: Emmanuel, Didsbury, now home of BBC Radio 4's Daily Service, was turned down because it did not follow the ICBS rules regarding a central aisle. The CBC gave early grants to two Lancashire churches dedicated to St Peter, including one in Ashton-under-Lyne. In 1795 there was only one church in the town

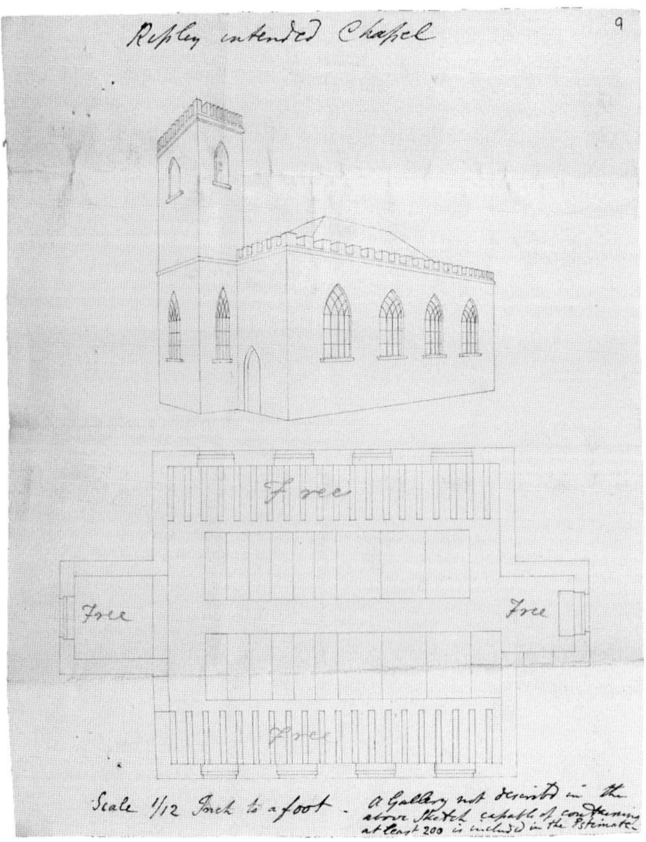

ARTIST UNKNOWN **All Saints, Ripley, Derbyshire 181?–1826**
Perspective and ground plan
All Saints was one of the first churches to be funded by the CBS as a direct result of a local workers' revolt, two years before the Peterloo Massacre.

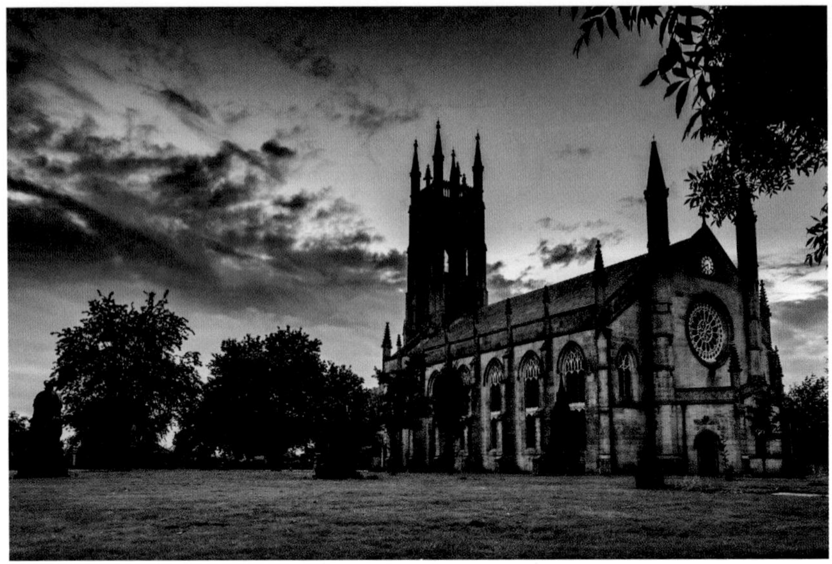

St Peter's, Ashton-under-Lyne, Lancashire
The church was built 1821-4 with a grant of £13,191: a 'particularly imposing and elaborate example of a Commissioners' Church' (Pevsner Architectural Guides).

but by the end of the nineteenth century there were no fewer than 44 Anglican churches and 138 chapels belonging to other denominations. St Peter's was the first of three churches designed by Francis Goodwin for the Commission in the Manchester area. It was built between 1821 and 1824 with a grant of £13,191 and is described in the National Heritage List for England as a 'particularly imposing and elaborate example of a Commissioners' Church'.

In *The Church in Danger* (1815), Richard Yates had estimated that in London alone 953,000 people were 'excluded from the advantages of parochial worship', although a reviewer in the British Critic specified the number of excluded, with forensic exactitude, to 627,168 people. The estimated need was for 300 new churches, at a cost of £3,000,000 'for the complete accommodation of this district only'. Besides London 'we must add the equally pressing necessities of several other large and populous places'.

Yates was unrivalled for attention to detail and Geoffrey Best has commented that 'he could not touch lightly upon any subject not even a light one'. Yates believed that not only were the existing buildings inadequate in scale, location and number, but they failed also in design. Medieval churches no longer suited a modern congregation. Catholic ritual had demanded procession as well as theatrical gesture so long aisles and soaring ceilings were appropriate. Protestant worship, on the other hand, was rooted in instruction and the sermon so the architecture could be less imposing and simply allow the words to be heard; often bleak 'preaching boxes' followed.

The church problem was many headed. The Church of England and its parochial system had been created on a rural, landowning model, relating to villages. The clergy were gentlemen and their outlook and the legal system that bound them were inflexible, each unwilling to modernise. The various sects within Nonconformism were organised on the whole more efficiently and directly through their congregations. They did not rely on the permission of an ecclesiastical hierarchy before they could build nor were they bound by ancient parish divisions. They could create a building that disobeyed traditional rules. They were not dependent on either tithes or church rates for income or on an argumentative parish in order to make any progress locally. And they did not have to seek a minister with a university degree. It was no surprise that, as a reviewer of *The Church in Danger* wrote, 'Meeting-houses have quickly sprung up, and have been thronged with persons, who turned with regret from the Church, where they could not gain admittance, and feel compelled to embrace the only remaining means of public congregational devotion within their reach.' In an attempt to weaken the appeal, Parliament had imposed a range of bans that prevented Nonconformists from holding most public offices, required them to pay local taxes to the Anglican church, be married only by Anglican ministers and forbade attendance at Oxford and Cambridge or the award of degrees. Nonconformists were defined as Protestant Christians who did not conform to the governance and practice of the established Church of England. Eventually, the term specifically included Presbyterians, Congregationalists, Calvinist sects, Quakers, Baptists and Methodists. Scotland and Wales were effectively Nonconformist countries by the mid-nineteenth century and Cornwall was also a major centre.

One of the oldest Nonconformist movements is Unitarianism. It has attracted amongst others Isaac Newton, Joseph Priestley, Neville

Chamberlain and Béla Bartók. Another staunch protagonist was Emma Wedgwood, whose husband Charles Darwin had been baptised an Anglican despite his Unitarian antecedents and sent to Cambridge to become a priest. When the family attended Anglican services, she turned their children's backs to the altar when the Creed was being recited. Whether Unitarians, who did not believe in the Trinity, could properly be considered Christian, has taxed theologians down the centuries. Parliament, however, in 1844 decided in the Unitarians' favour through the Dissenters' Chapels Act, which gave them access to funds set aside to build chapels.

The reach and effect of many Nonconformist buildings can be compared to the impact of supermarket sheds on the edges of towns today, replacing traditional high street shops in market towns and villages with their marble fish slabs or mahogany cabinets. The new buildings were plain and capacious, well placed to capture a congregation often with different working hours and less sense of commitment to the district where they now lived. The very first Methodist building was The New Room,

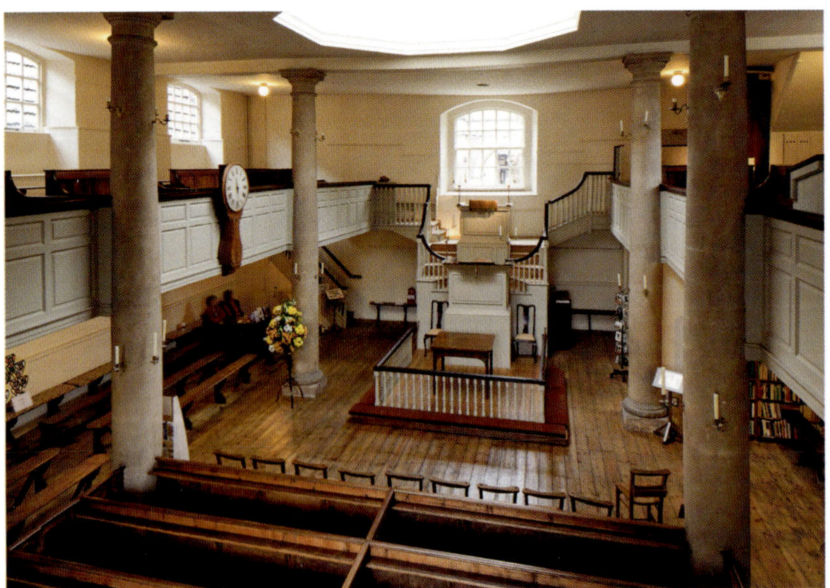

New Room, Bristol (interior)
Built in 1739, this was the first Methodist chapel in the world and is in Broadmead, Bristol. John Wesley and his fellow preachers stayed in rooms above the octagonal chapel. Meetings were held outside the normal hours of the Anglican church so as not to be in competition.

built and named with simplicity in Bristol in 1739, followed by octagonal chapels further east and north in Norwich, Rotherham, Whitby, Yarm and Heptonstall. John Wesley personally approved the design of the octagonal chapels: 'It is better for the voice and on many accounts more commodious than any other.' He is also said to have added that there were no corners for the devil to hide in. Wesley then raised a large hall on the City Road in London in 1777–8.

Mark Twain describes in his own inimitable style in *A Connecticut Yankee in King Arthur's Court* (1889) one of the many ways that Dissenters were exploited in Britain during the 18th century:

> It reminded me of something I had read in my youth about the ingenious way in which the aldermen of London raised the money that built the Mansion House. A person who had not taken the Sacrament according to the Anglican rite could not stand as a candidate for sheriff of London. Thus Dissenters were ineligible; they could not run if asked, they could not serve if elected. The aldermen, who without any question were Yankees in disguise, hit upon this neat device: they passed a by-law imposing a fine of £400 upon any one who should refuse to be a candidate for sheriff, and a fine of £600 upon any person who, after being elected sheriff, refused to serve. Then they went to work and elected a lot of Dissenters, one after another, and kept it up until they had collected £15,000 in fines; and there stands the stately Mansion House to this day, to keep the blushing citizen in mind of a long past and lamented day when a band of Yankees slipped into London and played games of the sort that has given their race a unique and shady reputation among all truly good and holy peoples that be in the earth.

During the post-Waterloo years, as church expansion was being urged, the Dissenters demanded the removal of all political and civil disabilities imposed on them but the Anglican establishment resisted until the Test Acts of 1828. Church rates, local taxes at the parish level for the support of the parish church buildings in England and Wales, were also a contentious matter for Dissenters. Buildings of the established church alone received the income from such taxes and civil disobedience was beaten back by

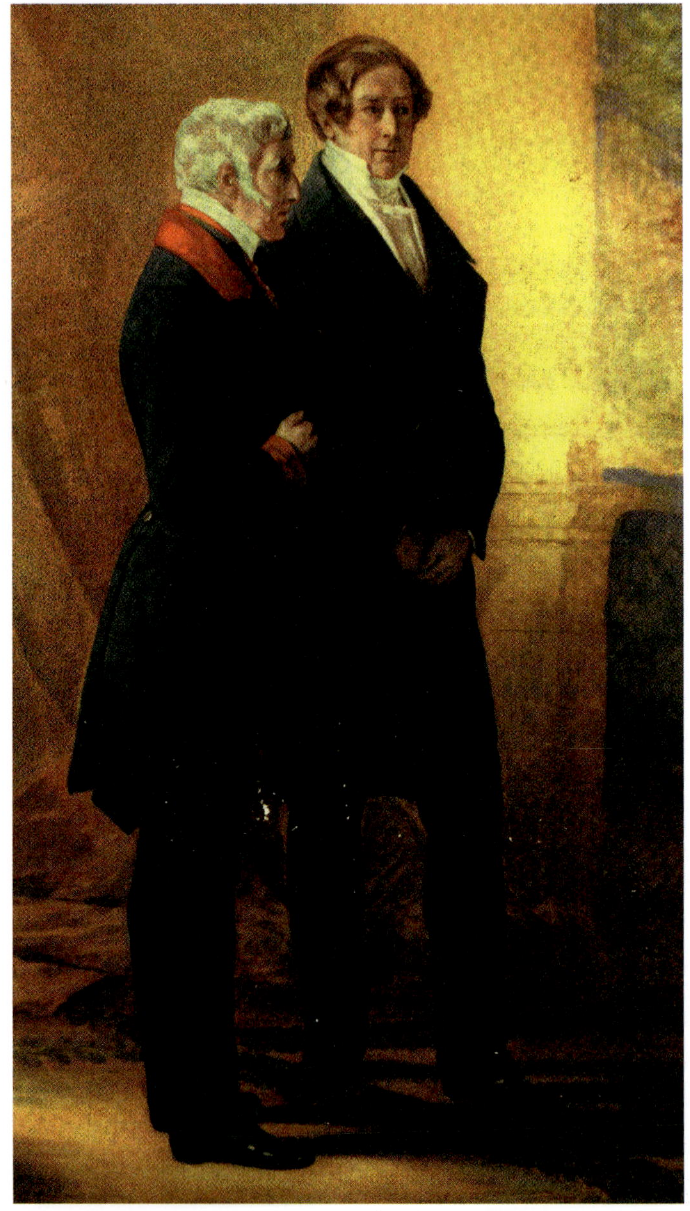

Franz Xaver Winterhalter **Wellington and Peel** 1844
Oil on canvas

*The Duke of Wellington (1769–1852), victor of Waterloo, was Prime Minster
1828–30 and is seen here with Sir Robert Peel (1788–1850), who had been
his Home Secretary. Peel was subsequently Prime Minister 1834–5, 1841–6.*

seizure of personal property and even imprisonment. Payment was finally made voluntary in 1868 by Gladstone's government, which also passed the Irish Church Act, disestablishing the minority Anglican Church in that country, expelling its bishops from the House of Lords and, effectively, preventing revolution. Three years later the University Tests Act, fought through under much opposition, opened Oxford and Cambridge to those of all beliefs or none, although with rather more modest effect as both universities remained staunchly Anglican until well after the second war. In England and Wales by the late nineteenth century the terms 'Dissenter' and 'Nonconformist' began be to replaced by 'Free Church'. However, this should not be confused with the 'free seats' movement. That phrase was the rallying cry of the ICBS and the anti-pew brigade for decades.

When Elizabeth I came to the throne in 1558 the Church of England's independence from Rome was reasserted: Parliament made the fact of being a Jesuit treasonable; priests found celebrating Mass were often hanged, drawn and quartered. The Roman Catholic Church continued in England but was subject to various forms of persecution and most recusant members (except those in some heavily Catholic areas in the north or members of the aristocracy) practised their faith in private. Roman Catholicism was entirely separate and equally disabled.

In 1766, the Pope recognised the English monarchy as lawful, which led in 1791 to the Papist Act, legalising the exercise of the Roman Catholic faith on condition that buildings carried no outward signs such as bells or steeples. During the next forty years magnificent Roman Catholic chapels were built at Wardour Castle, Wolverhampton and elsewhere, disguised from the outside as simple domestic dwellings.

The English latent mistrust of 'Popism' was finally overcome in 1829, when, following a long and acrimonious debate, the Duke of Wellington, as Prime Minister prevailed on his previously ardently anti-Catholic Home Secretary, Robert 'Orange' Peel, to support the Roman Catholic Relief Act. Until that point, Catholics suffered the same bans on public office and education as Dissenters within the Christian community.

THREE

'The mother parish ate the oysters; the districts divided the shells': funding and parallel organisations, 1818–1828

The Church Building Commission, appointed in 1818 to spend the £1 million purse, had thirty-four members, both clerical and lay, who had to decide how to apportion its funds in a manner that was to be simpler and more efficient than the 1710 commission which had built the few Queen Anne churches. The CBC set its maximum sum for each grant at £20,000 (equivalent in today's money to £2 million) but if that amount had been given every time there would have been enough to build only fifty churches, and so often the grant was less than the cost of the building, the difference being met by private donations and public subscription, like the ICBS. The recommended ceiling of £20,000 was never exceeded but in some cases the Commission provided the whole cost of the building and on occasions this also included the cost of the site and legal charges. The highest grant was of £19,948 for St Martin in the Fields, Liverpool, known affectionately as the Black Church because of the effect of the local dye works. It was destroyed in the Second World War.

Applicants for grants had to abide by a range of rules drawn up by the Commission. The CBC could grant-aid building projects, enable entirely new churches or lend money but only under certain statistical rules. The population in the area had to exceed 1,000 and there should be insufficient church room for one quarter of the population. Alternatively, more than 4,000 inhabitants had to live more than four miles from their nearest church. Statistics and data gathering were an integral part of church politics: 'visitations' every few years were originally carried out by the archdeacon or bishop and were the occasion on which churchwardens were sworn in and asked to report on the morality of the clergy and their parishioners. By the eighteenth century, visitations were required for local clergy and their assistant curates as well as churchwardens and schoolmasters. Local ministers filled in the enquiries and returned them to the bishop, either before or during the visitation, answering questions about the parish, curate, the parsonage, schools and hospitals, and Christians outside the established church such as Catholics, Methodists and other Dissenters. Locally, throughout the nineteenth century, the range of questions was extended to learn more about behaviour in the parish, the number of people attending services, how Sunday was observed by both clergy and parish, educational provision and the physical fabric of church buildings. The parliamentary Church Building Act had depended on the first detailed national census of 1811; after 30 March 1851 – 'Census Sunday' – a nationwide analysis of religious allegiance and habit was available, too.

In addition to providing grants of money, the Commission had powers to divide and sub-divide parishes; the existing parochial system had already been chopped and changed by the Industrial Revolution. Not only were there insufficient churches but many existing ones were in need of basic repair and the priests in charge were often desperately poor themselves. The two bodies behind church building and extension should be seen in the context of the many other charities labouring in the same field to gain donations from exactly the same patrons, such as the Corporation of the Sons of the Clergy, the Clothing Society for the Benefit of Poor Pious Clergymen, the Church Pastoral Aid Society and the Additional Curates Society.

The Corporation of the Sons of the Clergy had been established in 1655 in response to the distress of the large number of clergymen who were deprived of their livings under Oliver Cromwell, as long as they remained loyal to the Crown and adhered to the traditional form of service. The founders of the charity, much like the Hackney Phalanx, included merchants of the City of London as well as priests of the Church of England, all of whom were themselves sons of clergymen.

In 1820, a charity was created first in Leicestershire then nationally for the relief of poor clergymen and their families. Founded by Phyllis Peyton and Mary Lamb as the Clothing Society for the Benefit of Poor Pious Clergymen, it was one of very many charities looking after clothing and other provisions for clergy, their widows and orphans, often set up by women and enabling other women to be active in philanthropy but outside church politics. After several changes of name and amalgamation with smaller charities, Peyton and Lamb's charity exists today as the Friends of the Clergy Corporation.

The Church Pastoral Aid Society (CPAS) was founded in 1836 by evangelical social reformers including Lord Shaftesbury partly as an umbrella body under which to raise money to help church building but primarily to give grants to increase lay staff as well as help those who were ordained. One of the first recipients of a grant was the Reverend Patrick Brontë, rector of Haworth in Yorkshire and father of Charlotte, Emily, Anne and Branwell Brontë. He was able to employ as his curate the Reverend Arthur Nicholls, later to marry Charlotte,. Charlotte opens her novel *Shirley* (1849) with these words: 'Of late years an abundant shower of *curates* has fallen upon the North of England: they lie very thick on the hills; every parish has one or more of them.'

In 1837, in the final year of his reign, William IV made a subscription of £500 for a charity to take care of those lower down the pecking order and a new Society for Promoting the Employment of Additional Curates in Populous Places (more concisely, the Additional Curates Society, ACS) was created, of which Joshua Watson was treasurer and Henry Hoare a committee member. The ACS was established to complement the ICBS, providing individuals to cater for the spiritual needs of those moving into the new industrial areas. In its early days the ACS grants were used to pay a curate's stipend, often in full. Later, as the Church gradually assumed responsibility for the payment the Society helped to pay for housing and still flourishes today, as does the CPAS. Anthony Trollope pointed out in his essay 'The Curate in a Populous Parish' that the increase of curates often meant that many now stayed in that lowly role all their lives: 'The clerical babe must become a clerical old man.' Curates' Acts were put before Parliament in 1805, 1806, 1808 and 1812 until, finally, one was passed in 1813, an early attempt at church reform starting at the lowest rung even before Waterloo.

The clergy were entitled to charge fees to conduct the services required for churching, christenings, marriages by banns or licence, funerals and burials in various parts of the church, differently priced for locals and those from other parishes. These 'surplice' fees were a substantial part of the parish priest's income so the CBC had discretionary power to decide the number of occasions and rates of fees that would be appropriate in new churches to protect the interests of an existing incumbent.

In 1703, a perpetual fund was established of 'first fruits and tenths' for additions to the income of about 3,900 of the poorer Anglican clergy, earning less than £80, from a tax on wealthier clergy. The fund was named Queen Anne's Bounty. Land was purchased from which income could be derived. First fruits (annates) and tenths (decimae) originally formed part of the revenue paid by the clergy to the Pope: the fruits consisted of the first whole year's income and the tenths were one tenth of annual profits in subsequent years. After the Reformation the first fruits and tenths income reverted from the papacy to the Crown.

The CBC actively encouraged local people to raise subscriptions for each new church and gave priority for grants to those who did but, if applicants could not offer their own funds, then applications were considered on a first-come, first-served basis. The CBC could accept buildings for conversion, had the power to compel a parish to purchase land and was also able to provide endowments. Ecclesiastical patronage had been a longstanding and important class of property rights and this

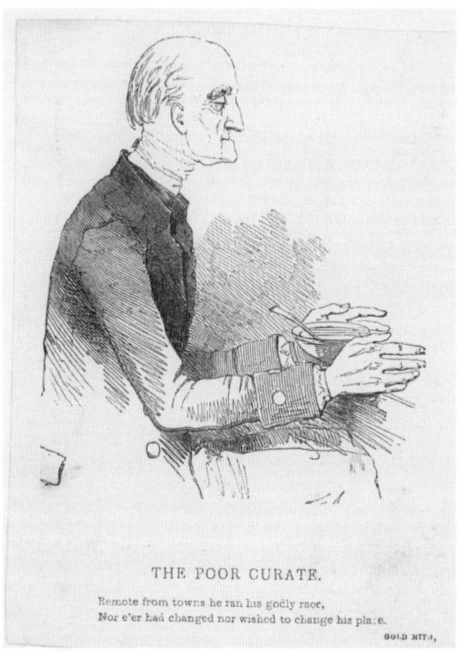

After KENNY MEADOWS
The Poor Curate from Heads of the People or Portraits of the English, 1858, Engraving
'Curates, long dust, will come and go
On lissom, printless, clerical toe;
And oft between the boughs is seen
The sly shade of a rural Dean'
(Rupert Brooke, The Old Vicarage, Granchester)

sense of entitlement had been a previous obstacle in the creation of new churches. Advowson, the right in law to nominate a parish priest (subject to a bishop's approval), was often held by the lord or lady of the principal manor within a parish, wherever their main home might be. Jane Austen has the sycophantic Mr Collins in *Pride and Prejudice* describe himself as

> so fortunate as to be distinguished by the patronage of the Right and Honourable Lady Catherine de Bourgh, widow of Sir Lewis de Bourgh, whose bounty and beneficence has preferred me to the valuable rectory of this parish, where it shall be my earnest endeavour to demean myself with grateful respect towards her Ladyship.

Mr Collins later commented, in admiration, that her Ladyship always attended church at Easter and Christmas.

In 1821, it was established that the patrons of well over half the benefices in England were laymen. There was also an added complication, in some parishes, that many lords of manors and patrons of livings had remained Roman Catholic. In broad terms, a parish is a standard unit of measure in church administration: sub-divisions might result in a chapel of ease as a more local place of worship where it was difficult for the congregation to reach the main parish church. Each chapel of ease had to pay rates to the 'mother' church, so often congregations were not keen on maintaining or expanding their underling church and incurring more taxes: as Geoffrey Best put it, 'The mother parish ate the oysters; the districts divided the shells.'

There were also proprietary chapels, like private pews writ large, sometimes associated with an institution rather than a wealthy family. According to Best:

> Proprietary chapels (open to the public but money-making) took virtue out of the parish; and if they did any good, the benefit was felt simply by those respectable persons who bought or rented the pews, and who went, perhaps because of the attractions of the minister, perhaps because it was fashionable and convenient, and perhaps because the lease of their house in a new square or terrace included a pew in the chapel provided to give the development a finished air.

Today's Church of England parishes each lie within one of forty-four dioceses, divided into thirty in the care of the Archbishop of Canterbury and fourteen administered from York. Each parish normally has a parish priest known as either the vicar or rector, rectors usually having a higher income. In the past, the priest's parochial duties were often supported by one or more assistant curates, some of whom might be deacons; some parish priests might have had more than one living, putting a curate in charge of those places while the priest lived elsewhere. Today, it is common practice for several neighbouring parishes to be placed in the charge of one priest who holds services by rotation. Every parish also has a number of churchwardens, unpaid lay officials expected to watch over the maintenance of the building. They are also *ex officio* members of the parish board, usually called a vestry or today a parochial church council, and are obliged to keep a 'terrier'(which is a record of the property rather than a dog) and an inventory of the valuables.

By February 1821, eighty-five government-funded CBC churches had been provided with seating for 144,190 and only £88,000 of the original £1 million remained. Applications for twenty-five more churches had to be postponed and it was clear that more money would be needed from Parliament. A second parliamentary grant of £500,000 was provided by the Church Building Act 1824. This was made possible because on 16 March 1824 Parliament finally ratified the payment of the longstanding Austrian war debt. Between 1795 and 1797, Britain had lent £6.2 million to its ally Austria but by 1822 the total loan, capital and unpaid interest, had reached over £23 million and the government did not expect to be repaid. The opposition, however, kept bringing the matter before Parliament and, finally, Lord Castlereagh (Foreign Secretary from 1812 until 1822) asked for a token repayment from Prince Metternich, his Austrian counterpart, who replied that any debt had been paid in full with Austrian blood, shed in defeat of Napoleon. Eventually, the Duke of Wellington as a diplomat and Solomon Rothschild as a banker succeeded in extracting £2.5 million to be paid in instalments between December 1823 and June 1827. While not beginning to address the question of interest owed (the repayment was only one third of the initial loans) it was still an unexpected windfall. From it, £60,000 was spent on acquiring paintings from the John Julius

Angerstein collection, which went on to form the basis of the new National Gallery; £300,000 was spent on repairs to Windsor Castle; an unspecified sum was given to the King's Library; and a vital £500,000 was made available for new churches.

The new funds were distributed much more widely and, on the whole, the grants were less generous. The second parliamentary grant went to more than 500 churches and payments covering the full cost of building were less frequent than from the first. The highest grant was of £10,686 to All Saints' Church, Skinner Street, in the City of London, but this was exceptional. The church was demolished in about 1869. Most grants were between £100 and £1,000, but on some occasions a mere £5. This did not mean less work for the board, which met about thirty times each year on average. During negotiation for the second grant, a select committee, including Joshua Watson, expressed regret at 'the vast disproportion' that still existed between church room and population and recommended that the focus should now be on the largest towns 'with very inadequate provision of church-room which have received nothing from the first grant'. With the population in each of these specified locales exceeding available seating by 15,000 the slant was now rather more firmly directed towards the principles of the ICBS.

In 1825 the board of the CBC gained five new members including Charles James Blomfield, recently made Bishop of Chester, and a close friend of Watson's, who remained the sole layman on the board. Like his friend, the Bishop had a passion for business and took over some of his roles when Watson became too frail.

The ICBS had different criteria to the CBC. Each applicant had to state the population, and what means and efforts to raise funds were being made or had already been made. The rules stipulated that 'no expense shall be incurred for ornamental architecture beyond what shall by the committee be deemed essential to give such building the character of churches or chapels of the established religion'. No grant of more than £500 was to be made unless approved by two thirds of the committee. Other resolutions referred to statements of accounts and the composition of the Society's committee and set the tone of the Society's operations for virtually the whole of its existence. There was no question of the Society purchasing sites for church building or building new churches in opposition to local interests. Everything depended on local initiative and the Society would only then make a proportionate grant. Although this limited the Society's scope, it also meant that with limited resources it could help a large number of cases, unlike the smaller number of large-scale building projects at relatively few places which define the Commission's approach between 1818 and 1824.

At an early meeting of the Society on 18 February 1818 in the vestry room of St George's, Hanover Square, it was decided to publish the proceedings of the general meeting in more than a dozen provincial newspapers across England to promote the scheme and emphasise that it should be locally led. Exeter established the first of the regional church-building societies in 1825. A deputation successfully petitioned the Chancellor of the Exchequer for a free postage concession for sending and receiving the Society's correspondence. Sub-committees were created, one to deal with correspondence and enquiries, another to superintend finance and a third to handle architectural plans and estimates. The editor of the New Times in Middlesex agreed to publish details of the Society's proceedings free of charge. An enquiry as to whether grants would be available for 'a new arrangement of the pews and seats in churches' was told that this would not be inconsistent with the Society's rules so long as it resulted in 'further accommodation to the poorer classes'. A decision was taken to sell previously purchased Exchequer bills and invest some of the proceeds in government securities; the treasurer retained £300 in hand. A letter was sent to 'Principal Bankers in the Cities and considerable Towns' so that subscriptions could be received locally.

While the established church may have rejected the architectural taste of the Dissenters, the Society was designed to provide some of their enviable independence and flexibility. However, the committee had to wait until someone in a destitute parish was ready to take the initiative of enlarging or building; only at that point could it respond. From Walsden in Lancashire George Dowtey, the phonetically well-named perpetual curate, wrote to the Society:

Having exhausted the resources of our own neighbourhood, I have gone far and near, from town to town, from village to village, and in

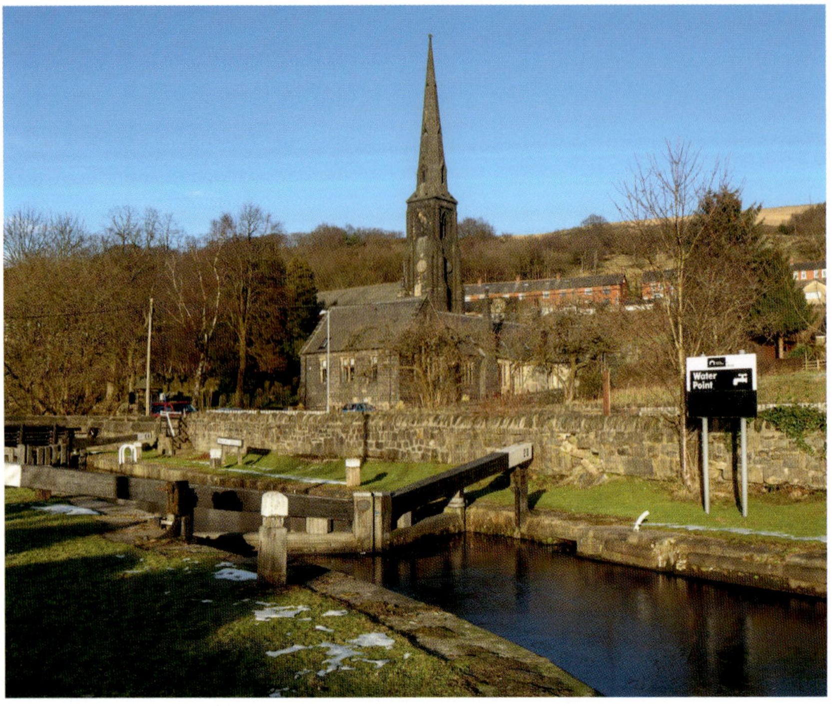

St Peter's, Walsden, Rochdale

*A doughty minister, in name and temperament, was 'obliged to walk from morning 'til night'
to raise funds for his new church, which was first built with a grant from the ICBS in 1845,
then had a history of disasters and triumphs until it was rebuilt one hundred years later.*

some instances almost from house to house, exposed to all weathers
and not unfrequently to the censure and unfeeling repulse of
individuals who have regarded me as a common beggar, or seeking
to achieve my personal interest rather than the cause of the church.

Although his income was only £150 per annum, Dowtey spent more than
£12 in travelling expenses and was now 'obliged to walk from morning
'til night'. His church, St Peter's, was finally built in 1845 with a grant
from the ICBS and consecrated on 7 August 1848 in the presence of a
congregation of 3,000; a spire was added in 1864 with a clock and peal of
bells in 1872. However, within two weeks, the weight on the clock broke
and fell through three floors, smashing through the tiles of the porch and
sinking into the earth.

On Friday 28 May 1948, amid preparations for a great centenary celebration, the church caught fire. Many treasures were lost, including the stained glass windows, church manuscripts and music. The undaunted parishioners set up a rebuilding fund and, although a grant was refused by the ICBS as the claim was not made soon enough, the rebuilt church was thankfully reconsecrated on 10 March 1956 by the Bishop of Wakefield.

The CBC was allowed to spend a maximum of £20,000 on any one church, while the ICBS was rarely able to contribute its maximum of £500. Even so, the Society assisted (sometimes with amounts as small as £20) many more parishes than the 600 or so which the Commission helped provide with new churches. The Society was also much more flexible in that it possessed no fixed rules as to the density of population or distance of residence from the parish church. It could take into account local circumstances, such as the kind of countryside, the existence of outlying hamlets in one parish lying nearer the church of another or the poverty and wealth in different places. One of the Society's main principles, which particularly distinguished it from the Commission, was that it was prepared to give money not only for the building of entirely new churches but for the enlargement and extension of old ones. In many cases it was possible to obtain as much extra accommodation by adding to the floor space of an ancient church or installing galleries as by building a new one and often at much less expense. By the close of the Society's first financial year just nine out of forty-seven grants made were for building new churches. The remainder were for rebuilding and enlarging existing churches or chapels, for an improved arrangement of pews and, in three cases, for the addition of galleries.

On incorporation, monies left over from the 1705 Act (known as 'brief money') in the care of the bankers Stevenson, Salt & Co. were transferred to the ICBS. The Society's initial success in fundraising had been with a small number of individuals, members of the various committees set up for the purpose who both took out subscriptions and later provided legacies, Anglican institutions such as the Oxbridge and Eton colleges – curiously Oxford gave twice as generously as Cambridge – livery companies, senior ecclesiastics and its royal patrons. The ICBS was to go on to raise further impressive sums through a well-orchestrated campaign with diocesan societies and in churches themselves. Of particular value was the vital granting of royal letters or letters patent, a form of public proclamation that authorised the Archbishops of Canterbury and York to exhort clergymen to raise funds for the newly incorporated Society to distribute. The royal letters were read out to congregations from the pulpit three times a year and between 1828 and 1851 raised £233,000, £41,000 in 1830 alone. The ICBS benefited in alternate years with two other privileged sister bodies, the Society for the Propagation of the Gospel (whose treasurer was Charles Hoare's partner Henry Hoare) and the National Society.

All donations, subscriptions and bequests were collected via the various subscriber banks and agents, centralised at Hoares (bankers to the Society for 200 years) and then deposited in the Bank of England in the names of four trustees. Any sums not immediately required were invested initially in annuities and in exchequer bills and later in government securities such as consols. In 1887, the Society bought and held for some fifty years 4 per cent Turkish bonds, which, despite being guaranteed by the British and French governments, provided a useful 1 per cent premium.

The address that invited contributions to the Society's funds, in June 1818, made a modest and realistic case:

> [It is] in promoting the enlargement of the building, and the increase of accommodation in existing churches – a department altogether out of the contemplation of the parliamentary vote, and in which moderate aids may be productive of the largest returns – that the peculiar usefulness of the society will be most strongly felt.

Each year between 1819 and 1825, the Society more or less gave out the same amount of grants but in 1825 funds began to be exhausted and it never again reached the success of those first seven years. The appeal that year resulted in a donation from the King of £1,000, which 'strongly marks His Majesty's sense of the value of the services which the society has performed, and His earnest wish that it may be enabled to continue its useful work'. One of the most consistently generous individual supporters of the Society was Charles Hoare, its treasurer.

After ten years, the Society had received 935 applications and helped in 577 of them; 88 churches had been given a second grant. A total of

£119,967 worth of grants had been allocated but only £108,627 had been paid out. Nonetheless funds were running low and, on its tenth anniversary in 1828, the Church Building Society was incorporated by Act of Parliament as the Society for Promoting the Enlargement, building and repairing of Churches and Chapels. SPECC never stuck as an acronym and the Society remains known as the ICBS.

In 1828 a new Act was guided through Parliament by Robert Peel in the nick of time to save the Society from financial collapse. This recognition of Parliament elevated it now to the status of a quasi-governmental agency. The new Bishop of London, Charles Blomfield, wrote to an enquirer earlier that year that the Society had not 'more than four or five hundred pounds in hand' but now it became the Incorporated Church Building Society, a legal entity rather than a private society. Peel referred to the 'admirable system of economy with which this excellent society had been conducted', and commended it on its efficiency. The King's Letter on the subject, published in the *Morning Herald*, stated that the Society 'has tended greatly to promote the good and laudable objects for which it was instituted' and gave it the additional and vital function of being able to contribute towards the repair of dilapidated churches. The letter continued:

> There was no doubt that a great improvement had in a stroke been achieved in the method of raising money by appeal from the pulpit in pursuance of church extension. First, every farthing bestowed by charitable individuals will be transmitted directly to the treasurer, without the least diminution and secondly, the money so subscribed will be applied by a committee of able and conscientious men.

Joshua Watson, Charles Hoare and others had proved their point through perseverance and integrity and handed it down to several generations. In 1831, the annual report stated with a hint of humour: 'The object of this Institution is so definite, and its operations so uniform … that the Reports cannot be expected to present much novelty or variety.'

FOUR

'Give me leave to say yet more about pews.
There can never be enough said ... I fully believe
that most of the mischief comes from pews'

In fact, there can easily be more than enough said about pews, but it is necessary to define terms. Today the word 'pew' is used to describe both a long bench seat and an enclosed box used for seating individuals within a congregation or a church choir. In the battle for church provision in the nineteenth century there were endless skirmishes about privately enclosed box pews versus open benches. The founder of the Cambridge Camden Society (see Chapter 7), J. M. Neale, who is also quoted in the title of this chapter, called it 'the battle of Catholick principle against puritan selfishness'.

The Church Building Commission needed twenty-one church-building Acts of Parliament to achieve its aims between 1818 and 1856. The designs for its churches were to be decided by competition but each one was supposed to be soundly built with an overall intention for 'proper accommodation for the largest number of persons at the least expense'. It was stipulated by the CBC that part of the seating was to be enclosed and rented out, the rest to be open sided and free for anyone's use. The income from pew rental was to produce a stipend for the minister and his clerk. The principle of free versus rented seating, more than any other aspect of the much-debated church-building boom, defined the difference between the parliamentary approach and that of the private ICBS, who finally won the day. By 1830, the ICBS had enabled 193,711 appropriated seatings and 142,222 that were free, 'cheaply purchased', it felt, at £135,990.

Before the first Church Building Act in 1818 the renting of pews had only been legal where specific Acts of Parliament authorised it, but the Church Building Act permitted, even encouraged, rents without specific parliamentary authorisation. Many new churches took advantage of this, resulting in a substantial rise in income from pew rental but also a continuous source of controversy in the 1840s and 1850s. A very significant contrary resolution made by the Church Building Society on

24 June 1818 referred to 'free sittings', stating that preference would be given to buildings with the largest number of free seats in proportion to grants given. This was a fundamental aspect of all grant aid given by the Society, ensuring not only that churches should be built, but that they should have at least part 'of their interiors allocated wholly to the lower classes, who could not afford pew rents and did not possess the local influence to be given proprietorial rights over pews'.

Before the thirteenth century, English churches were empty of seating and congregations had to stand, but then a few backless stone benches gradually began to appear, sited along the walls so that the elderly or sick might be able to attend for longer periods: 'the weak go the wall'. Eventually the benches were moved to the nave and finally became fixed to the floor. Wooden benches began to replace stone from the fourteenth century and became commonplace in the fifteenth. The medieval church buildings were simulacra of their town or village: spaces were sub-divided by those with vested interests: parish officials, trade guilds, local landowners and wealthy families.

Permanent seating began to be installed after the Reformation and as the sermon became a central, and increasingly lengthy, act in Protestant worship so pews and benches became a standard item of church furniture. Often seating was installed at the expense of individuals in the congregation and became their personal property. Pew deeds recorded each entitlement and purchase from the church: the price of seating went towards the costs of building the church and was therefore approved as a form of direct taxation by the Church Building Commission. The ICBS saw it instead as divisive in its exclusivity and subject to abuse through sub-letting and plural ownership in families with homes both in town and country.

Certain parts of the church interior were considered to be more desirable than others, offering, like the front stalls or grand circle of a theatre, a better view of or ease of listening to services. Just like the theatre, and indeed the wider world, this arrangement also gave prominence to certain families or individuals. Until 1650, attendance at church was compulsory by law and failure subject to heavy fines so the placing of seats offered a model view of social hierarchy. Seats, like other property, were handed down through families from one generation to the next. Gradually wealthier and generous inhabitants often came to expect the prestige of a 'good seat' in return for contribution to the material upkeep of the church. Income from pew rents varied enormously but a pew for a family of six might cost from a few shillings to a few pounds each year depending upon its position within the church. A church might raise £200 each year from pew rental, which was a substantial sum at a time when a clerk or a curate was unlikely to be paid more than £100 per year. Bigger churches or those in fashionable areas could generate much more income and pews were often advertised for sale in local newspapers.

The Reformation had abolished chantries, which were a type of trust fund through which prayers for the specified dead were purchased in perpetuity. Chantry chapels subsequently became private enclosures in which a manorial family could sit in state and be seen to do so. A growing middle and lower middle class began to emulate the practices of the gentry and the wealthy and, subsequently, those with more modest incomes from trade and professions, particularly small business owners, began to expect equal benefit. Disputes over ownership were inevitable.

In spite of the ICBS's best endeavours, pew letting continued in many churches well into the twentieth century, in some instances into the 1950s and 1960s, and one Anglican church in the British Isles continues to rent sittings to this day. Other abuses included informal pew renting in the form of tips paid to those who acted as pew openers to secure preferred seating for a single church service.

St Philip's, Clerkenwell, a Commissioners' church, was the first London church to dispense with pew rents, although Commissioners' churches were only required to offer 20 per cent free seating, the Commission believing that rental was a necessary taxation. There was also a belief in some quarters that family pews encouraged family attendance. Attitudes began to change from the 1840s thanks to the ICBS and others within the High Church party fighting for 'equality within the House of God'. By the 1860s and 1870s that view had become quite orthodox: 'free and open churches' began to be built. The Free and Open Church Association was founded in 1866 by Samuel Ralph Townshend Mayer, who was also one of the first important religious figures openly to support homosexuality.

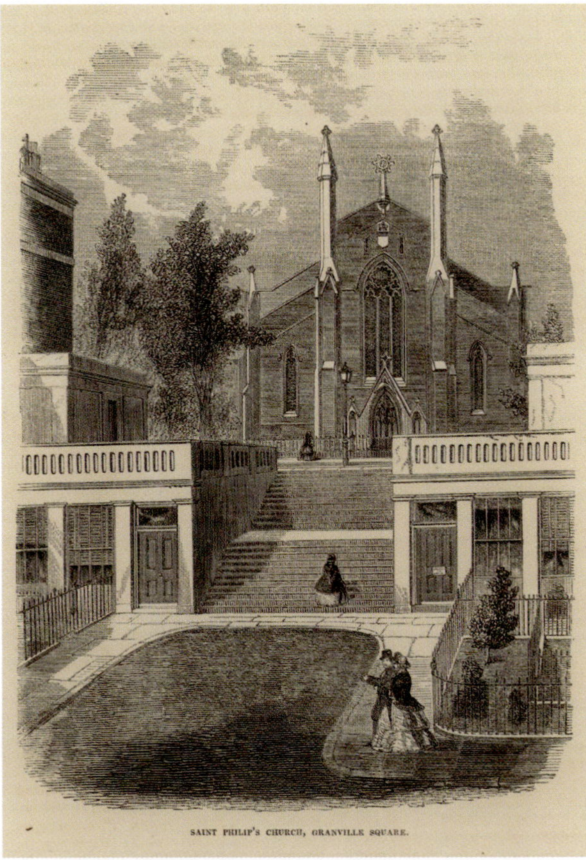

BRITISH SCHOOL
St Philip's, Granville Square, Clerkenwell, London 1831–2
Engraving
A Commissioners' church, it was the first London church to dispense with pew rents. Built by E.B. Lamb, it received a CBC grant of £4,893, cost £4,805 but was demolished in 1938. One of its vicars subsequently became secretary to the ICBS.

In 1819 the Society first published for applicants and others a set of 'Suggestions and Instructions', which were practical rather than aesthetic. The primary advice was about the site. This should be central in terms of population density rather than spacious; dry and elevated but not high or steep; away from 'steam-engines, shafts of mines, noisy trades, or offensive manufactories' and from main roads all to avoid noise, while still being easy to get to on foot or in a carriage. The Society counselled good foundations and covered drains, with all vaults and graves more than 20 feet away. It recommended at least 18 inches of paving around the church to prevent damp and that vaults should provide storage 'for coals for the use of the poor, fire-engines, or the like, and for stoves for warming the interior; others … apartments for clerk, sexton, &c.'

In building walls the Society advised 'durability to be regarded more than beauty'. The roof, gutters, chimneys ('may be concealed in pinnacles') and floor were considered in precise, pragmatic detail and, if a tower were part of the design, it was stated that 'the vestibule and staircase may be placed in the Tower, so as to leave the whole Church available for sittings'. Windows 'ought not to resemble modern sashes, but whether Grecian or Gothic, the glass should be in small panes, and not costly'. Ventilation was sensibly addressed and applicants were advised that 'fresh air may be introduced from without, and conveyed through pipes carried under the floor into the body of the Church, at convenient apertures; and the foul air may be expelled at or near the roof, either by horizontal or perpendicular channels or tubes'. Tellingly, horizontal pipes are referred to as those used in 'the best barrack infirmaries', implying that souls, like bodies, were to be healthily, if regimentally, treated. The implication was also that a big, brick box might just be enough to solve most problems.

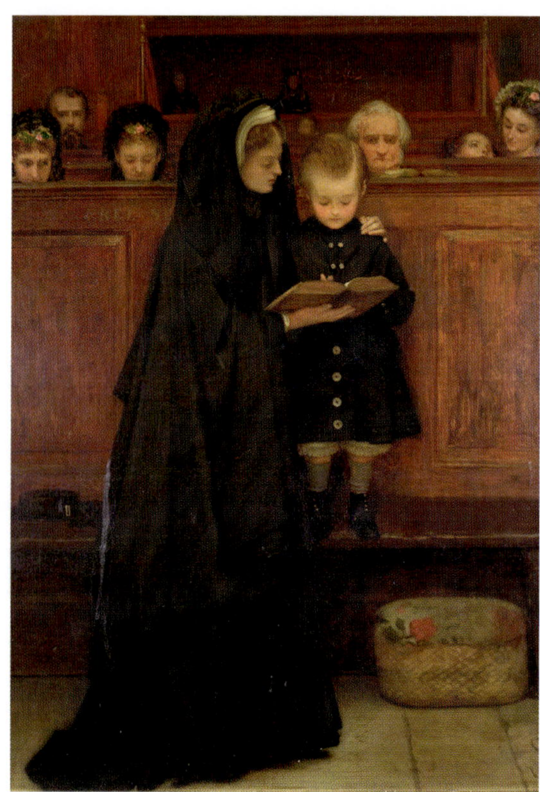

CLAUDE ANDREW CALTHROP
In Church 1869
Oil on canvas

A stage-like use of pews where the congregation is a backdrop to the widow and her child who stands on a pew to share her mother's prayerbook.

All doors were to be opened for an hour before service and one hour after, except the winter evening service. Internally, the first stricture was to prevent echo so that 'domes and coved ceilings (except of the waggon form)' and circular walls were to be avoided; 'all wood work is favourable to the voice'.

There was to be a central aisle from the west to the east and the congregation should all be able to see the minister as well as hear him, 'therefore no square, or round or double … pews should be allowed, and as few pews as may be'. The rest of the seats should be open benches with backs, although there was disapproval of sloping back-boards.

> A narrow shelf fixed behind the back-rail will serve at once to strengthen it and to support the prayer-book; under the shelf may be placed pegs, or other conveniences for great-coats and cloaks, sticks and umbrellas; about half-way under the seats may be fixed a shelf for receiving hats. Kneeling-boards should in all cases be provided.

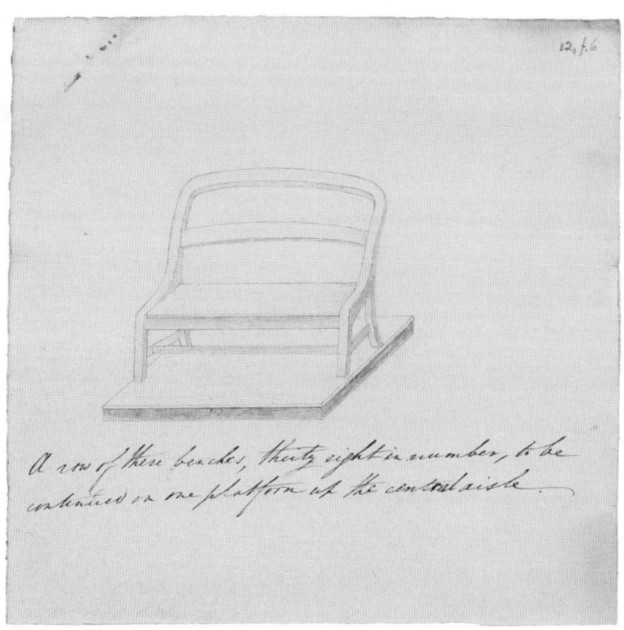

THOMAS PHILPOTTS **Design for pews at St Mary's, Malvern 1818**
Pencil on paper Lambeth Palace Library, ICBS Archive
The inscription reads: 'A row of these benches, thirty eight in number, to be continued on the platform up the central aisle.' *A grant was refused.*

Open seats with backs were to be preferred on the grounds that they accommodated considerably more seats per square foot. Three feet was the recommended pitch between the back of one seat and the next. The higher the seat, the greater the distance required between them. Seats for schoolchildren could be just twenty-four inches from back to front, and fourteen inches in width, while seats for adults were to be twenty inches wide.

All seats were to face the preacher, as far as possible, and the benches, 'whether pewed or not', should be set from east to west so that no part of the 'congregation may turn their backs upon the altar'. Laying out seats longitudinally, at a right angle to the altar in the manner of a choir or college chapel, was condemned, with St Peter's, Treborough, Somerset given as an example of bad practice. The pulpit should be placed with as little visual interruption for the congregation as possible. Galleries were expected to be fitted with benches and 'back-railings for children and others entitled to the use of free seats; and the eastern end of them, if they lie nearest to the pulpit or reading desk, may afford the best accommodation to the aged and infirm'. Very precise measurements for each type of seat were prescribed and, if pew comforts were considered, then it should be remembered that 'woollen linings and cushions are apt to harbour dust, damp, and vermin'.

The approved forms for the interior plan were the parallelogram and octagon; polygons 'would bring a large congregation nearer to the Preacher than any other [form], except a circle, which is objectionable, as confounding articulate sounds'. Finally, the most significant comments are plainly addressed. Internal ornament must be 'neat, simple, never gaudy or trifling', and externally the building should be in stone, 'pure and simple, yet venerable, and having the character of a Church or Chapel; none preferable to the simplest Gothic. The Grecian Doric is also eligible.' The overriding rule at all times was 'to deviate not a tittle from the fixed laws of church arrangement and the authority of antient examples'.

The 'Suggestions and Instructions' were reconsidered and amended in 1842, when architectural style came higher up the list:

No style seems more generally suitable for an English Church than the Gothic of our own country, as developed in its successive periods. The Norman (or Romanesque) style is also suitable, and offers peculiar advantages under certain circumstances, especially when the material is brick. The Society earnestly recommend that, in the proportions and great features, as well as in the details, good ancient examples should be closely followed.'

The ideal form was now defined as a cross with nave, transepts and chancel, or a double rectangle, composed of a nave, with or without side aisles, and chancel. A chapel could be a single rectangle, the length at least twice as great as the breadth. It is clear that much had been learned during the twenty-three years between the two sets of 'Suggestions':

If the circumstances of the neighbourhood render it probable that, at no great distance of time, the building may be enlarged, it is better to leave a part of the original design, as, for example, side aisles or transepts, to a future period, than to attempt the completion of the whole design at once in an inferior manner.

Each element of the building was considered in forensic detail: for the roof

the best external covering is lead, which should be not less than seven pounds to the foot, or copper of not less than twenty-two ounces to the foot. Blue tiles, commonly called Newcastle tiles, or stone tiles, are perhaps the next best covering. Westmoreland slates are better in colour than those commonly used, but are, in most cases, expensive. All slates to be fixed with copper nails. Flat ceilings are inconsistent with Gothic.

This time, more attention was paid to fittings directly related to the liturgy, and the suggestions were entirely in line with the Oxford Tractarians and the Cambridge Camden Society:

The Lord's Table should be raised two or more steps above the floor of the chancel, which should be raised a step or two above the floor of the nave. Where the rails do not extend across the chancel, no seats should be allowed between the rails and the north and south walls; and as much room as possible should be left about the rails for the access of communicants.

Hassocks were now to be preferred to kneeling boards. Galleries were no longer permitted in any part of the chancel and should not enclose columns against which they rest 'so as to break the sight lines'. They should as much as possible, be made to appear as adjuncts and appendages to the architectural design of the interior, rather than as essential parts or features of it. The Society will not sanction any plan involving the erection of a gallery, unless in cases where it is distinctly shown that no room is unnecessarily sacrificed, by inconvenient arrangements, on the floor.

Good book keeping was the final dictum in the ICBS 'Suggestions': 'Architects are particularly desired to take care that an accurate account be kept of the quantities of customable and exciseable articles used, where the expense of enlarging or building a Church or Chapel will amount to £500, or upwards, such as may be duly certified or verified by affidavit.'

The clarity of these new suggestions indicates that many mistakes had been made in buildings of the 1820s and 1830s. During the parliamentary stages of discussion towards the creation of the Commission, the elements that might go wrong had already been rehearsed. The Earl of Liverpool was 'wholly and completely adverse to incurring a heavy expense for mere useless splendour' and recommended 'decent decoration which would mark the character of the established church'. The Earl of Harrowby said that while he 'could never agree that it was intended by this bill merely to erect four walls like a barn, solely on the principle of affording the greatest possible accommodation to the largest number of persons', he was 'decidedly hostile to incurring unnecessary expense'.

Between the original 'Suggestions and Instructions' and the amended second edition lay debate and controversy over whether the Society's main aim should indeed be to rid churches of private pews and, if so, the best way in which this might be accomplished. The whole system of family pews and pew rents became increasingly the subject of furious battles in the pages of the leading ecclesiastical journals. The ancient parish church was out of touch, not suited to a modern world. In 1872, Charles Locke Eastlake, architect, recalled:

The white-washed walls, the damp stone floors, the ceiled roof, the high stiff pews, with mouldy green baize cushions and faded red curtains, allotted to all the principal houses and farms in the parish: the hard benches without backs, pushed into a corner or encumbering the aisle, where the poor might sit: the mean table with a moth-eaten red cloth upon it in the chancel, the dirt, the indescribable dank smell of decay, are experiences of their childhood familiar enough to many now living, and almost universal to those who lived a century ago.

Eventually, in 1837, the validity of exclusive appropriation was challenged in a legal case in the parish church of Yeovil in Somerset. A pew auction was to be held and a local solicitor, George Hancock, demanded a pew in the church of which he was a parishioner. He was entitled to this in law but all the seats were already appropriated. The case was referred to the bishop, who declared the system illegal and that everyone was entitled to a seat in their parish church without fee or payment. Nor would he agree to houses in the parish being automatically entitled to pews. As elsewhere, in Yeovil several pews were owned as an investment and owners, who often had pews in more than one church, rented them out at a profit. One hundred and one pews were owned by twenty-nine persons (one held eleven, another six). The abuse was stopped and the solicitor got his rightful place.

A more pragmatic attempt to justify the existence of pews lay in the argument that they represented much-needed protection from freezing churches so they were often constructed to achieve warmth as well as privacy, rather like four-poster beds or theatre boxes. Curtains, rugs and cushions were brought along to prevent draughts and make the pews distinctive; some were even equipped with fireplaces. A large number of churches were still unheated at the beginning of the nineteenth century although a few had primitive coke stoves. The Society, in its first set of 'Suggestions and Instructions', recommended the building of a vault or crypt in which coal could be stored or, with equal pragmatism, the parish fire engine be kept.

The topic of pews exercised all sorts of writers including Mrs Strutt in *Chances and Changes: A Domestic Story* (1835):

'What a contrast,' said Catherine to Edward Longcroft, 'is this little church upon the mountains to the fashionable churches in London, – when I saw the benches of hewn stone, without any distinction of

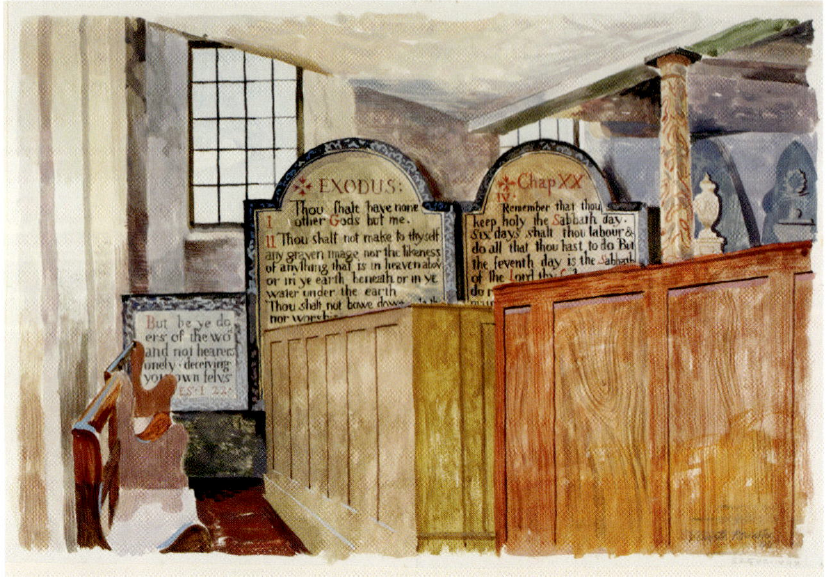

KENNETH ROWNTREE **Pews in St Mary's Church, Whitby 1940**
Watercolour and body colour on paper

*The work was commissioned as part of 'Recording the Changing Face of Britain', established
by Sir Kenneth Clark, then the director of the National Gallery. It ran alongside the official
War Artists' Scheme, which he also initiated. St Mary's is noted for its 18th-century box
pews, some inscribed 'For Strangers Only'.*

pews, the single pulpit, the unadorned altar, the rough walls, backed
by the solid rock, – I bethought me of your uncle's pew, in Mary-
le-bone, carpeted like a drawing-room, lined with crimson cloth,
padded like a carriage, for the more luxurious ease of the shoulders
that rested against it: the chandelier, the fire-place, with its polished
cut steel fender and fire-irons, and Mr Longcroft rattling them and
regularly stirring the fire, as soon as the text was given out.'

Richard Mant, the Bishop of Down, Connor and Dromore, in a lecture
published in 1843, commented that religious worship was 'not best
answered by spacious rooms, inclosed with lofty partitions, and secluded
from common observation, however convenient they may be for concealing
the apathy of the indevout, the slumbers of the indolent, the playfulness
of the young, the sallies of the witty and the whispers and smiles of the
gay and fashionable'.

The campaign to eliminate pews reached its peak in the early 1840s, spearheaded by contributors to *The Ecclesiologist*, where one writer in 1842 hoped for the day when every parish would 'have escaped from the misery of pews, by ejecting the whole of these wooden boxes together'. At St Nicholas's, Hereford, for example, the Dean of Hereford refused to grant a faculty for the appropriation of pews. One of the grounds for refusal was his 'unwillingness to perpetuate a property in seats, which gives rise to trafficking'. Nevertheless, some pews survived. St Mary's, Whitby still retains its eighteenth-century box pews, some of which are inscribed 'For Strangers Only' and, north of the chancel arch, there is even a Jacobean pew.

Church rates were another source of tension. Funds for future repairs and maintenance were to come from locally levied rates and this caused problems if churchwardens were hostile, for whatever reason, to a new church. It was not unknown for Dissenters to campaign actively for election as churchwardens. *The Family Churchman* of 4 July 1890 contained this tale:

On the 12th February last reference was made to a curious dispute at Harwich where a Church rate is still levied under Acts of Parliament passed in 1821 and 1824 for rebuilding the parish church. At the last Easter vestry two Dissenters were elected as churchwardens and they have just issued circulars to the holders of appropriated seats that they will henceforth be required to pay rents which will be applied in relief of the church rate. In the event of their declining to do so, they are requested to remove their cushions, hassocks etc., and the seats will be let to anyone who may apply for them. The churchwardens profess to be acting in conformity with the statute but the vicar urges that pew rents can only be levied by the 'vicar or curate and churchwardens' jointly, and he has issued a protest refusing his consent.

So far, the dispute does not greatly concern the Free and Open Church Association, the question being merely whether persons who have hitherto enjoyed the privilege of appropriated seats gratis shall now pay for such seats. But there is one feature of the matter upon which we have something to say. Over the west door of the south aisle of the church there is (or was) a tablet which reads: 'This church was rebuilt and enlarged in the year 1821 by subscription and rate, by which means 1000 additional sittings have been obtained, the whole of which number are hereby declared free and unappropriated for ever in consequence of a grant from the SPEBCC'. The names of the vicar, the curate and the churchwardens are appended. Section 2 of the Act of 1821 directs the churchwardens to prepare a plan of the sittings, showing the mode in which they are allocated, the thousand free seats being specially mentioned. A copy of this plan ought to be found in the parish chest. What if it should turn out that the churchwardens are offering to let some of the sittings forming a part of the thousand sittings which were 'declared free and unappropriated for ever'? It appears to us that the vicar would do well to ascertain where these free seats, and to make the announcement on the board a reality.

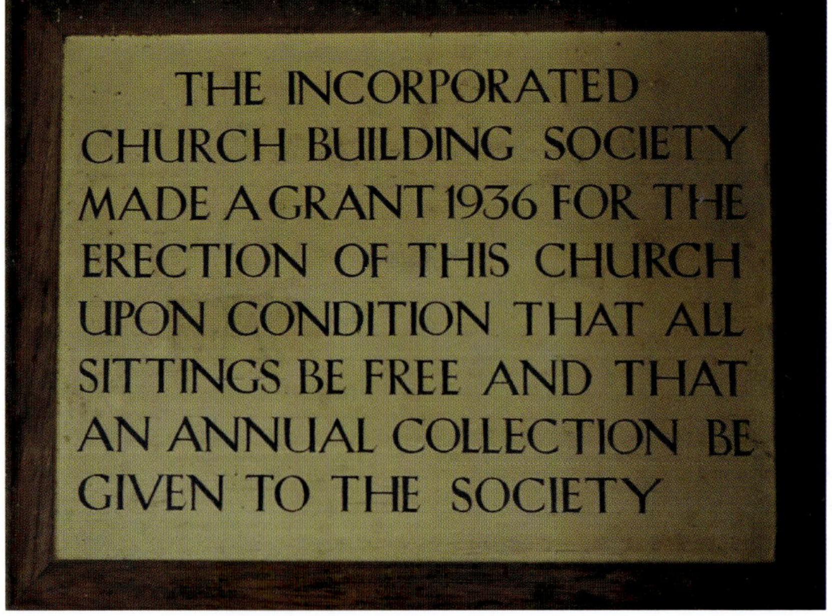

Every church was required to acknowledge grant from the ICBS. This plaque is from St Francis of Assisi, West Wickham, Kent, a church built in 1936 by J.E. Newberry and C.W. Fowler. As each board was made at the church's own expense it often caused annoyance but provides a range of splendid designs across the decades (see back cover).

The board mentioned in connection with the Harwich incident was an obligation for each church to display details of the grant from the ICBS and the number of free seats obtained. Irritation was often caused by the fact that each church had to pay for its own board, however modest the grant.

There was a popular hostility to church rates on principle and the second Act in 1819 empowered the CBC to pay all expenses if sufficient cause could be shown. The '4,000 people and church room for one quarter' rule was relaxed for the great northern parishes with their scattered but numerous hamlets and small chapelries. Experience of what worked and what caused problems was all learned on the job and an amending bill followed in 1821, then a third Church Building Act in 1822, which was the last to rely on a rates levy. After that point, the CBC rules stated that repair funds had to be secured first.

Let Charles Dickens have the last words on pews, their custodians and how extra money was solicited, in his description from *Dombey & Son* of Paul Dombey's christening in Dickens's own local St Marylebone church:

> After another cold interval, a wheezy little pew-opener afflicted with an asthma, appropriate to the churchyard, if not to the church, summoned them to the font – a rigid marble basin which seemed to have been playing a churchyard game at cup and ball with its matter of fact pedestal, and to have been just that moment caught on the top of it. Here they waited some little time while the marriage party enrolled themselves; and meanwhile the wheezy little pew-opener – partly in consequence of her infirmity, and partly that the marriage party might not forget her – went about the building coughing like a grampus.

FIVE

'To make a great show at the west end':
the Church Building Commission and its architects

One of the first Englishmen ever to call himself an architect was John Shute, who was sent to Italy in 1550 by his employer, the Duke of Northumberland. For a couple of centuries afterwards almost anyone could call themselves an architect as there was no official training, qualifications, governing bodies, guilds or legal safeguards but, by 1768, George III's favourite architect, William Chambers, 'waited upon the King and informed him that many artists of reputation together with himself are very desirous of establishing a Society that should more effectively promote the Arts of Design'. Thus the Royal Academy of Arts was formed, to promote and to teach, with eighty members among whom, still today, there must be at least fourteen sculptors, twelve architects and eight printmakers. The Architects' Club was formed in 1791 and The Royal Institute of British Architects (RIBA) was established in 1834, after which a campaign followed to protect the title 'architect' and to regulate the profession. During the early years of the Commission and the Society the profession of architecture was being consolidated and by the first years of Victoria's reign it was firmly established, based on offices of pupils and dynasties. Not only did the government build churches during this period but it also commissioned extensively within London, producing a central post office, a customs house, a treasury, law courts, a royal palace out of Buckingham House, royal parks and a national museum and art gallery.

The Royal Household had an Office of Works headed by a surveyor-general and comptroller and from 1761 employed named architects. In 1813 a non-professional surveyor-general was appointed, Colonel B. C. Stephenson, assisted by three 'attached architects': John Soane, John Nash and the much younger Robert Smirke, each paid a salary of £500 per year plus 3 per cent commission on finished works. This arrangement ended with 1832 with the formation of the Works Department, when Henry Hake Seward was appointed surveyor of works and buildings.

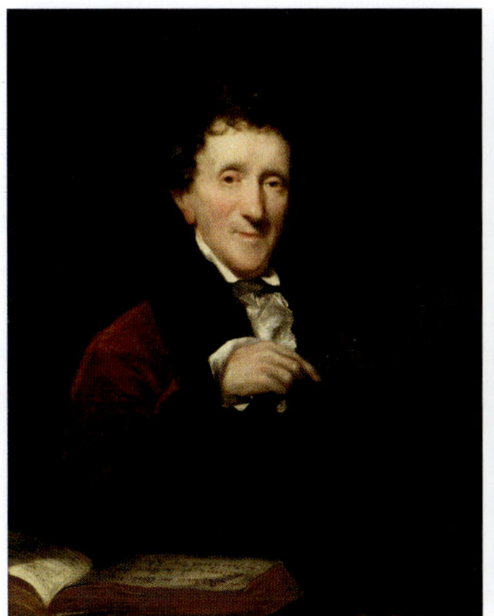

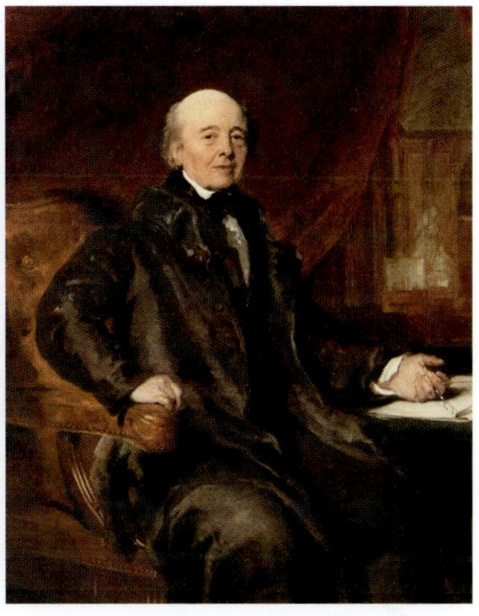

JOHN JACKSON **Portrait of Sir John Soane, RA (1757–1853)** 1828 Oil on canvas

The maverick architect Soane is portrayed three years before his knighthood and in the year he published Designs for Public and Private Buildings.

SIR THOMAS LAWRENCE PRA **Portrait of John Nash (1752–1835)** circa 1827 Oil on canvas

Nash spent many years working in Wales then became a specialist in picturesque country houses. Charles Hoare was a patron. He is best known for his work for the Prince Regent from Brighton Pavilion to Regent Street and the terraces that surround Regent's Park.

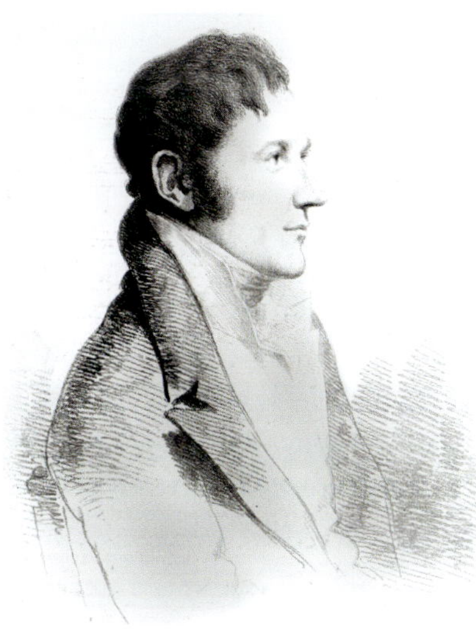

WILLIAM DANIELL after GEORGE DANCE **Portrait of Sir Robert Smirke, RA (1780–1867)** 1809 Etching

Smirke designed the first Greek Doric building in London, Covent Garden Theatre, which this early portrait commemorates. He later designed the British Museum and seven churches, six in the Classical style, for the Church Building Commission, for which he, along with Soane and Nash, was official architect to the Office of Works from 1813.

The triumvirate of Soane, Nash and Smirke were consultants to the CBC and Joseph Henry Good, son of a clergyman and a pupil of Soane's, was surveyor to the Commission from 1826 to 1857. From 1829 to 1848, Good was also the examining architect to the ICBS. Nash was George IV's favourite architect and worked in a Picturesque style, often quoting widely from various cultures as at the Royal Pavilion, Brighton. Smirke, briefly a pupil of Soane, was the foremost Greek Revival architect in Britain. The difference between them is summed up in this couplet:

> *Go to work, rival Smirke.*
> *Make a dash,* à la *Nash*

Soane was a maverick, often critical of the work of his contemporaries, and of whom it might be said in new doggerel: 'Go it alone, be like Soane.' He designed the Bank of England and the Dulwich Picture Gallery – the first purpose-built public art gallery in Britain – and created his own museum of architecture, always employing a brilliant approach to space and light. He was a committed Freemason, cynical about Christianity and had never previously built a church but, as consultants, all three were expected to produce designs for the Commissioners' churches. Nash had previously worked as a jobbing architect in Wales on church repairs; Smirke had advised on several cathedral and church restorations and had built a private chapel.

The first church built with a CBC grant (£3,500 out of the total costs of £12,600) was probably St Philip's, Stepney, in east London (1818–19), now demolished. The architect was John Walters, who had already enlarged the Old Black Lion pub in nearby Poplar and had also built St Paul's, Shadwell to replace an old parish church built in 1656, traditionally known as the Church of Sea Captains. Appropriately Walters was familiar with naval architecture, too, and invented a metal ship's brace to be placed on the bottoms of vessels. He died aged only twenty-nine from overwork.

Next between 1818 and 1820 from a range of architects came a number of churches grant-aided by the CBC throughout the country, all now demolished: St Peter's, Blackburn, Holy Trinity, Bath and St George's, Birmingham (all 1819–22); St Philip's, Regent Street, Westminster (1820); and St Paul's, Southsea (1820–22). The CBC now gathered speed and built

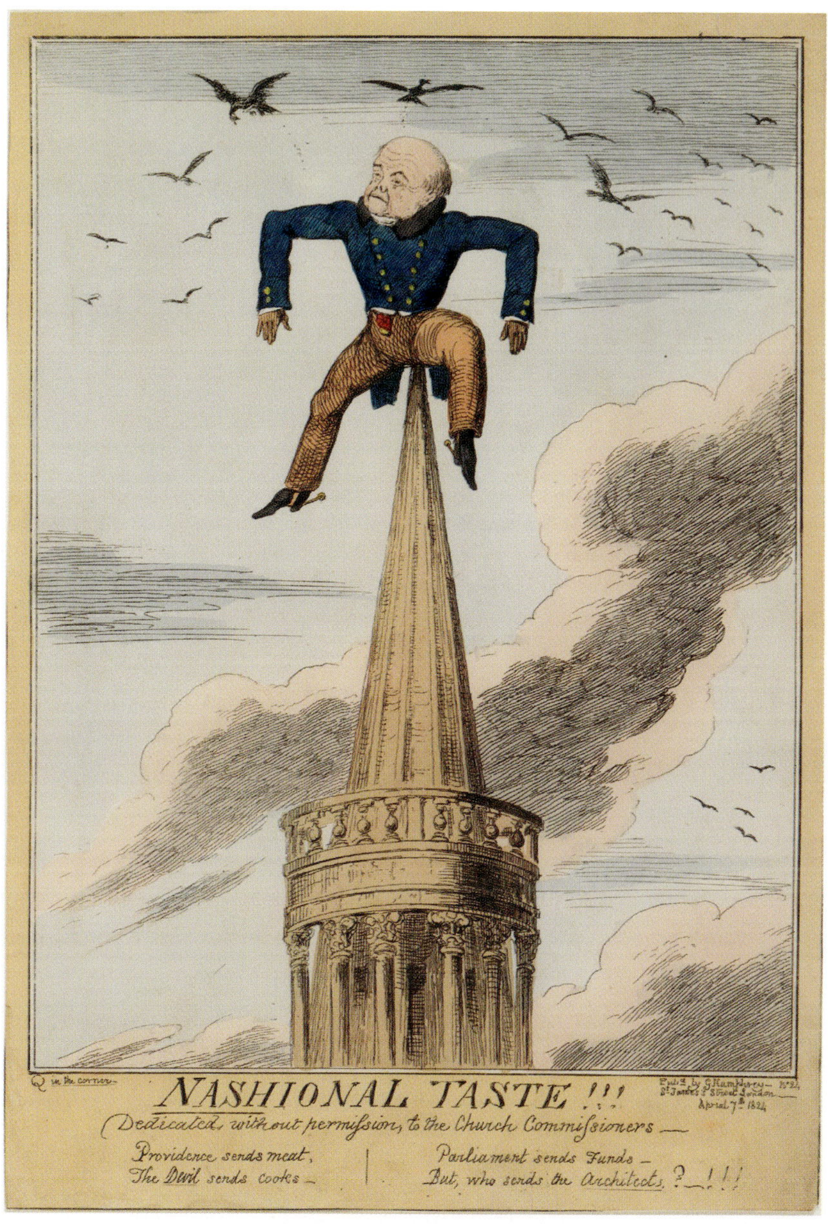

GEORGE CRUIKSHANK **The Nashional Taste!!!** 1824 Etching

The inscription reads: 'Dedicated, without permission, to the Church Commissioners — Providence sends meat, the Devil sends cooks, Parliament sends funds, But who sends the Architects?..!!!'

John Nash's All Souls, Langham Place, 1822–4, was a Commissioners' church that was not always praised at the time; one MP described it as 'a flat candlestick with an extinguisher on it'.

a range of Neo-Classical churches in London where its own architects, Smirke, Nash and Soane, built eight out of the Commission's twenty-three new churches between 1820 and 1826, at which point Charles Barry began to dominate the capital's new church building.

By 1818, the north London parishes of Marylebone and St Pancras had grown huge, 'swelling with the wealth and pride of merchants and "nabobs"', as Sir John Summerson described them. These new inhabitants sought to replace the tiny chapels that had served the areas when they were simply small hamlets.

Marylebone had already obtained four Acts of Parliament for a new church between 1770 and 1813 when a proprietary chapel was proposed on the south side of Marylebone Road (then called New Road), opposite the royal hunting grounds. Two powerful elements then came into play. Nash, under commission to convert the hunting grounds into the new Regent's Park, built York Gate on the chapel's axis, while the Duke of Portland decided that the chapel should instead become the parish church. A final Act was obtained and Thomas Hardwick (a pupil of William Chambers) was required to extend and elaborate his original design.

Meanwhile in St Pancras, a mile to the east, a committee was plotting a more ambitious scheme to build a new church to a brilliant Grecian design by William and Thomas Inwood. Both of these churches were outside both the Commission's and the Society's remit but were the best and most current examples of new church building while the institutions of 1818 were being considered and launched. The Inwoods' St Pancras was completed in 1822, at a cost of £76,679, the most expensive church to be built in London since Wren's St Paul's Cathedral. It was designed to seat 2,500 people and would have been a benchmark in terms of style and costs when the careful 'Suggestions' for applicants to the Society were being composed.

The new churches were not universally admired. 'E.I.C.' (Edward Carlos) wrote to the *Gentlemen's Magazine* on 9 August 1820:

The late Act of Parliament having revived the spirit of Church building, some edifices have been recently erected, in which are introduced every extravagant, novel, and fantastic appendage, formerly only appropriated to Theatres, but foreign to Churches, until this age of improvement: these innovations are most glaring in the New Church at Mary-le-bone, where the place of the grand window above the altar, to be seen in almost every Church, antient or modern, is supplied by a transparency, such as decorate the fronts of houses in a general illumination, fixed in the centre of the organ, which, in violation of all custom, is erected over the altar, and to complete the absurdity, accompanied by two tier of private bor[x?]es, fitted up with fire-places and fashionable chairs, giving this part of the Church the appearance of the proscenium of a Theatre. The Altar itself is placed at the South, instead of the East end of the Building, an arrangement which Sir C. Wren strictly adhered to, as his Cathedral plainly shows. The favourite model of the day is the Parthenon: the New Church building at Pancras is said to be copied from it. The incongruous additions of a steeple, and a plain body, with two series of dwelling-house windows, to the magnificent portico of Minerva's Temple, would have as much surprised its architect, if he could have witnessed the absurdity, as appropriating the same portico to the box-lobby entrance of a playhouse. It is not improbable, if the present taste

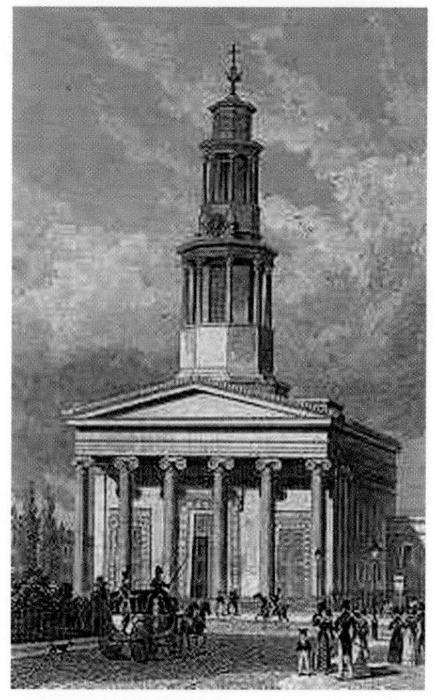

THOMAS HOSMER SHEPHERD
St Pancras New Church, Euston Road, London 1826–7
Engraving from T. H. Shepherd's
Metropolitan Improvements; or London in the Nineteenth Century

William and Thomas Inwood began their masterpiece before either the Church Building Commission or the Church Building Society were fully established. It was completed in 1822, at a cost of £76,679, the most expensive church to be built in London since Wren's St Paul's Cathedral.

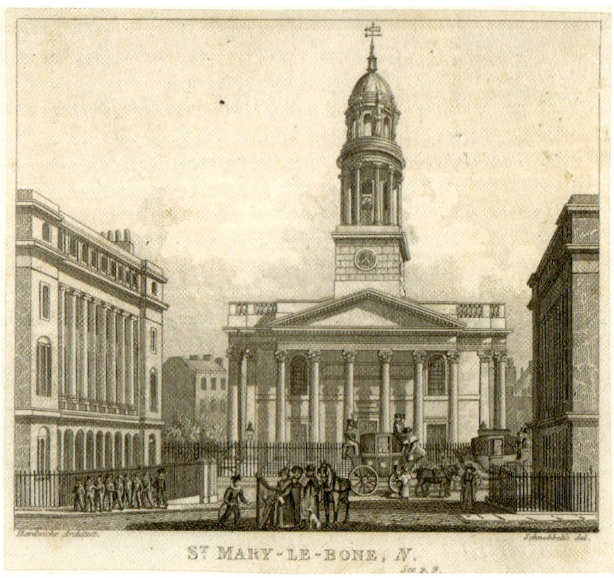

After THOMAS HARDWICK **St Marylebone, London 1817** Engraving

Cleverly placed opposite Nash's new York Gate entrance into Regent's Park, this became the new parish church of St Marylebone. Its construction continued during the early discussions about the need for funds to build churches throughout the country.

should exist for a century longer, the Church Architects will choose for a favourite design, the Coliseum; the Roman edifice will, no doubt, be as accurately copied as the Grecian, and with the same propriety be metamorphosed into a Church; and which is not unlikely to be the case, if the Methodists should have a voice in the selection.

Nash, the great Regency town planner, designed his All Souls, Langham Place (1823) for the Commission as an eye catcher to mark the oddly angled junction between his new Regent Street and the Adam brothers' older, wider Portland Place. This is a witty and clever church, but often loathed at the time. An MP called the steeple 'a flat candlestick with an extinguisher on it' and a reviewer commented:

To our eye, the church itself, apart from the tower, (for such it almost is) is perhaps, one of the most miserable structures in the metropolis, – in its starved proportions more resembling a manufactory, or warehouse, than the impressive character of a church exterior; an effect to which the Londoner is not an entire stranger.

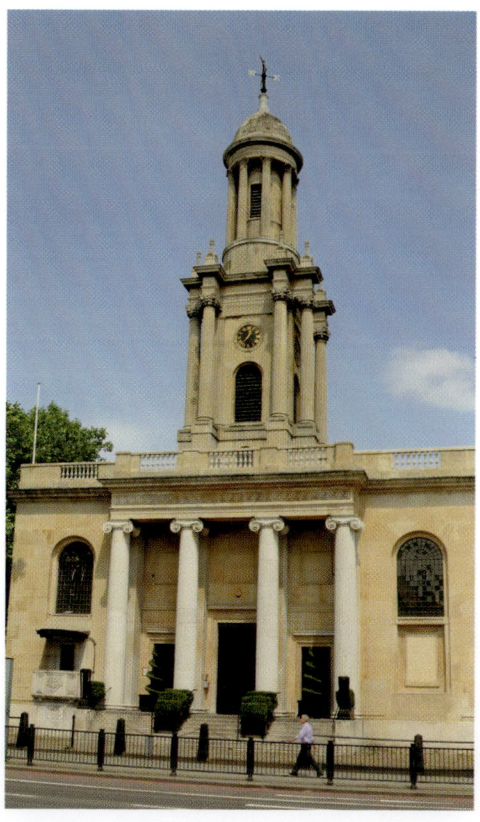

Holy Trinity, Marylebone Road, London

The Church Building Commission enabled John Soane's design for fashionable Marylebone: Holy Trinity was built on the edge of the new Regent's Park in 1826–7 for £24,708. By 1936 it had fallen into disuse and was used by Penguin Books, then the Society for Promoting Christian Knowledge (SPCK), an Anglican missionary organisation. It is now known as One Marylebone and is owned by a company of events organisers.

Soane's contribution to fashionable Marylebone was Holy Trinity, which immediately led to a demand from the Commissioners to reduce his costs, which he did, in part, by 'a quantity of enrichments lessened'. None of Soane's churches for the Commission allowed him licence nor resulted in a masterpiece. Smirke was better suited to the Commission's needs and, for the same district and within a mile of Soane's and Nash's contributions, added his St Mary's, Wyndham Place (1821) as a focal point for the new Bryanston Square in the Portman estate.

Each of the three Commissioners' architects created a Classical church for a new fashionable metropolitan district while producing in parallel much cheaper churches in the eastern and southern districts of Walworth, Bethnal Green, Wandsworth and Hackney. Outside London, the advised maximum of £20,000 per church was often halved. Smirke built in total seven Commissioners' churches, six Greek Revival and

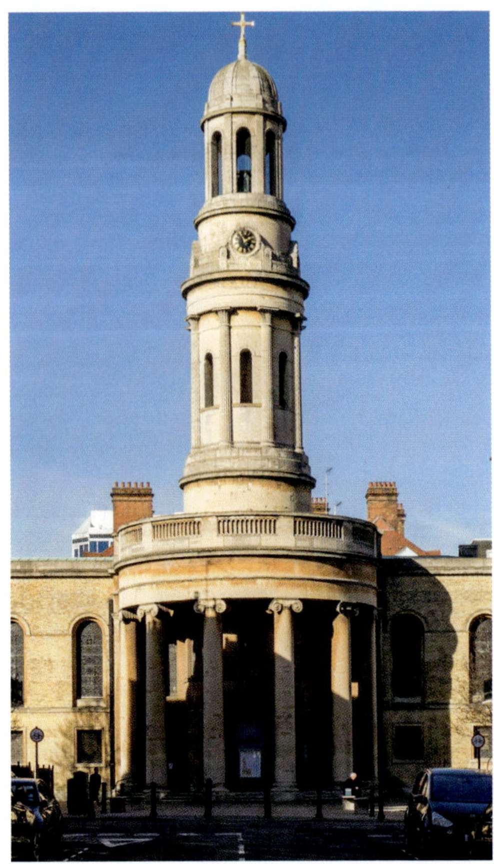

St Mary's, Wyndham Place, London

Robert Smirke's design for Marylebone was built in 1823 for £19,955. He also used the same design for another Church Building Commission church, St Philip's, Salford, but only got half the fee. He then used the design of its tower for St Anne's, Wandsworth, in south London.

one Gothic; Nash submitted ten designs, Neo-Classical and Gothic, but only built two: in complete contrast to the Classical All Souls Church, Langham Place is his Gothic St Mary's, Haggerston (1825–7), bombed during the Blitz in 1941.

The Commissioners made the requirements that each church should seat 2,000 people at a cost of £12,000 or less but Soane thought the fixed cost far too low and acted accordingly. His three churches for the Commission were all Neo-Classical in style: St Peter's, Walworth (1823–4) cost £18,348; Holy Trinity, Marylebone (1826–7) cost £24,708; and St John's, Bethnal Green (1826–8) was built for £15,999. Soane was approached in 1821 to prepare designs for the church seating in All Saints, Stand, Lancashire, but rejected the cost per seat, which was set at £12,000 for 1,800 people, or £6 13s. 4d. per seat. He passed the project to Charles

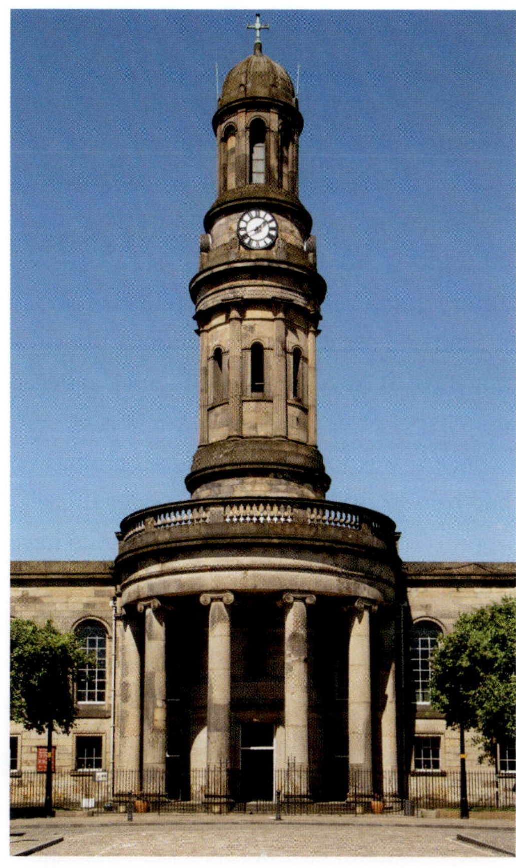

St Philip's, Salford

Robert Smirke reused a design that he had employed the previous year for St Mary's, Wyndham Place. St Philip's cost £14,670.

Barry, aged only twenty-seven, and the budget was raised to £20,000.

The only examples of the three Crown architects' own churches built outside London were all by Smirke for the Commission. St John the Divine, Chatham (1821–2) was Italianate with Doric pillars, receiving a grant of £13,797; it closed in 2004. St George's, Tyldesley, Lancashire was begun in 1821 with a grant of £9,706. As construction progressed, it was realised that the structure was too big for the site and that the plans had been inadvertently exchanged for those of St George's in Chorley, a few miles to the north-west, which seems like a very metropolitan blunder. It was built in Early English Gothic and its website describes the moment when it finally opened: 'Bells for the tower were transported on carts from Leigh on 10 August 1825 arriving to celebrations in the town when the largest bell was upturned and filled with ale supplied by all the local inns.'

Staying in Lancashire, Smirke's Neo-Classical St Philip's, Salford was built between 1822 and 1824 and received a grant of £16,804, indicating to some that Gothic was always a cheaper option. Smirke certainly practised economy here by reusing his design for St Mary's, Wyndham Place, but earned only half a fee. He also used the design of its tower for St Anne's, Wandsworth, in south London.

The most distinguished of Smirke's churches is St George's, Brandon Hill, Bristol (1821–3), and its story is an example of the conflicts that lay behind many similar projects. Smirke's design was contentious from the beginning. In 1821, the parishioners of St Augustine's and their vicar began to discuss the construction of a chapel of ease but the vicar was at odds with the vestry, whose main concern was for the large burial ground on Brandon Hill for which they had paid £2,400 of their own money the year before. The Commissioners proposed a design by Smirke, who would have been well known in certain circles outside London for his design of the new opera house at Covent Garden (London's first ever Doric building) in 1810 at the age of twenty-seven. The vestrymen insisted instead on a competition between Smirke and their own favoured candidate, Henry Hake Seward, later to be Royal Surveyor, who had already designed modest, elegant churches in Northumberland in the vestry's preferred Gothic style. Seward won the competition locally and Smirke was paid off with fifty guineas but as the Commissioners were to foot the bill so they also called the tune and overturned the decision. The vicar had applied for a grant to the Commission less to help the poor of his parish than to achieve a fashionable Neo-Classical church designed for his wealthy parishioners in the newly built terraces on Brandon Hill, a steep walk up from St Augustine's.

Brandon Hill and its 20 acres were associated with protests and meetings of Chartists and other reform groups: Bristol had been the site of the worst riots leading up to the Reform Act and was also home to the first ever Methodist building. A Great Reform Dinner in August 1832 was organised on Brandon Hill by supporters of the victorious Whigs who chose the location as it was beyond the right of the corporation to deny access to the land. Tickets were issued to 6,000 tradesmen, tables set on the grass and barricades erected around the perimeter to keep out those

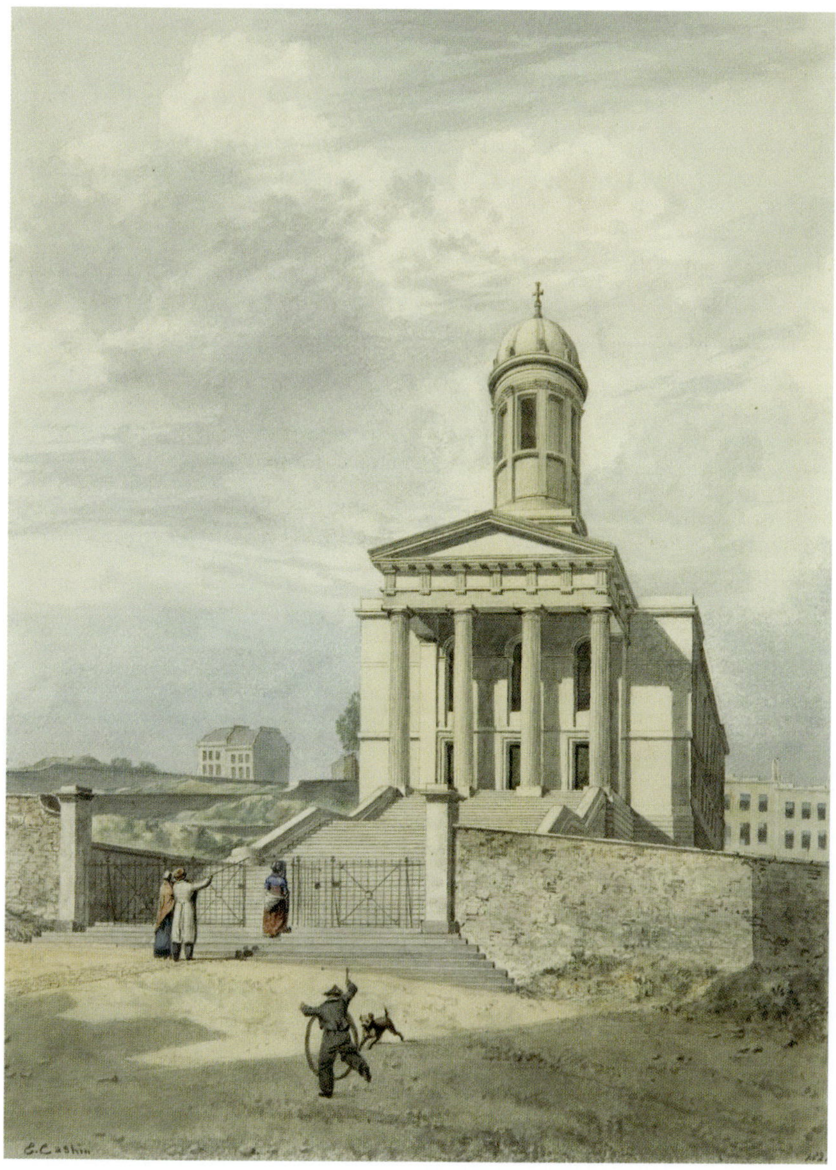

GEORGE CASHIN **St George's, Brandon Hill, Bristol 1824**
Watercolour on paper

St George's, Brandon Hill, is one of the finest of the CBC's churches, costing a modest £10,042. Its place in Bristol's radical history and its current incarnation as a concert hall give it an exemplary role in the story of British church building and it fulfilled one of the Commissioners' objectives, which was 'to make a great show at the west end'.

without tickets even though a peaceful celebration was planned. As the ticket holders waited patiently for their celebration a crowd of 14,000 gatecrashers took over, dancing on the tables and rolling barrels of beer down the hill to the docks at Hotwells, and violence broke out.

St George's fulfilled one of the Commissioners' objectives, which was 'to make a great show at the west end' and Smirke achieved this with an imposing Doric portico surmounted by a cupola, all raised above a grand flight of steps. The church received a grant from the ICBS for a rebuild in 1843. In the 1870s, G. E. Street created a 'chorus cantorum' at the east end, using marble to transform the previously plain and simple interior; a central aisle of red quarry tiles led to a marble font at the west end. In 1881 a reredos by Bloomfield was installed, as well as elaborate decoration to the gallery panelling, and the original Georgian box pews were replaced. The church was transformed into a concert hall in the late 1980s. Ian Hamilton Finlay, the classicist-poet-sculptor, was commissioned to make a series of inscribed sculptures and benches that commemorate St George's history of radical politics, transformation and music.

There are four churches in south London which from their earliest days have been known as the Waterloo churches. The reasons for singling them out with this name are not quite clear although one of them, St John's, Waterloo Road, is at the end of Waterloo Bridge and faces the railway terminus, which explains at least why its name has stuck. The others are St Matthew's, Brixton, St Mark's, Kennington and St Luke's, West Norwood, and the link between the Gospel writers certainly explains the grouping of the quartet. They were all built between 1822 and 1824 with Greek porticoes and towers, costing between £15,000 and £18,000 and each of the architects had a local connection. The Church Building Act recommended that parishioner-architects should get special privilege.

St Matthew's is by C. F. Porden, about whom little enough is known beyond his involvement with St Pancras New Church and Fonthill in Wiltshire, James Wyatt's Gothic Revival monument to hubris, built for William Beckford. In Brixton, Porden's Classical statement for St Matthew's was bold and rare as he placed his tower at the east end, leaving the elevation of the Doric portico plain and simple. It was the first of the quartet to open by a few days and the first ecclesiastical building to

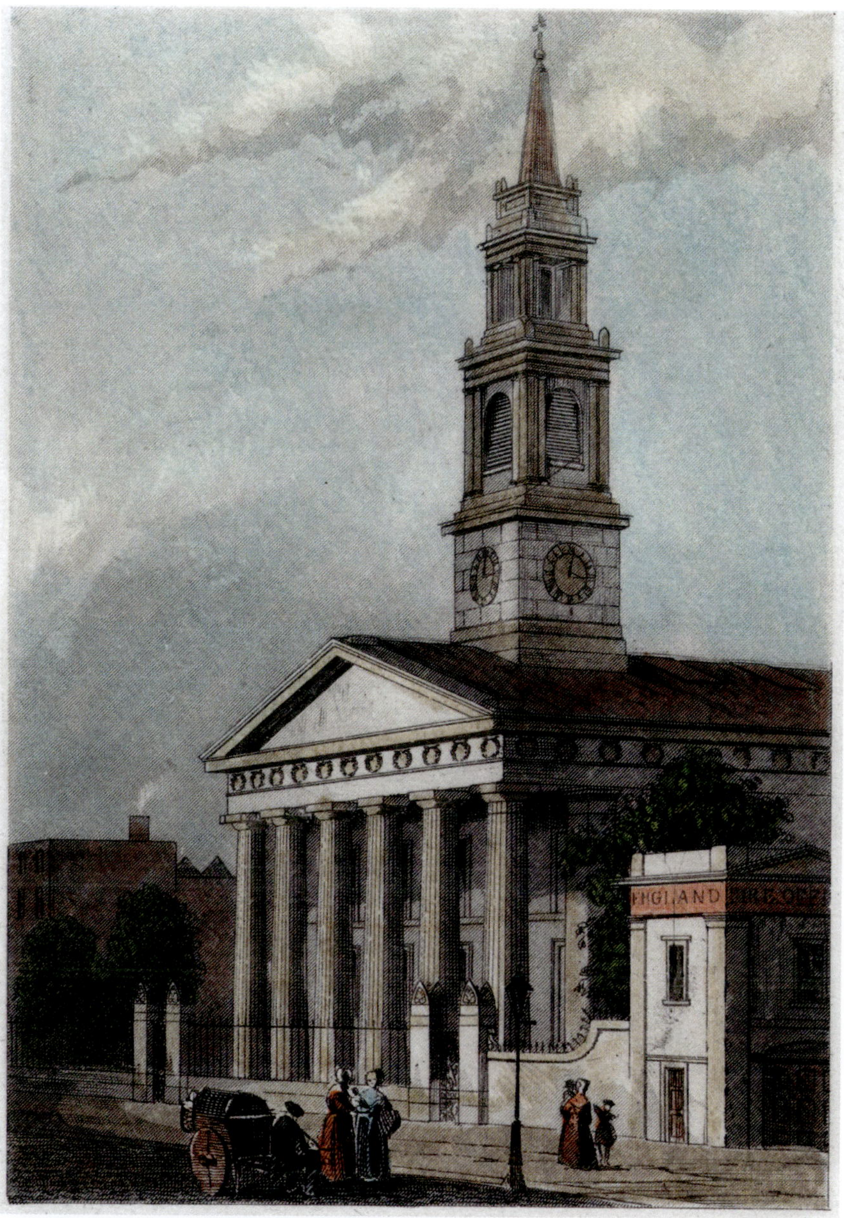

BRITISH SCHOOL **St John's, Waterloo, London 1824** Engraving

Of the four churches, each named after one of the Four Evangelists, St John's can lay claim best to the title Waterloo Church. It was built to a design by Francis Bedford at the south end of Waterloo Bridge, which had opened in 1817, one of the few memorials in London which are named after Waterloo. The railway terminus, which the church faces, opened only in 1848 and, in its present design, in 1922.

be lit by electric light in Britain. Now, sadly, it bears a little typed notice declaring that, due to alterations in the 1970s, the building no longer has anything to show of historic or architectural interest. Today the church has been divided into a tapas restaurant, a club, offices and a tiny, compromised lobby space for worship.

St Mark's was built on the corner of Kennington Common where the old gallows stood. The common was an area associated in the eighteenth century with the radical preacher George Whitefield, whose diary entry for Sunday 5 May 1739 estimated 'the crowd at no less than 50,000'. The architect of the new church was David Riddell Roper working with Alfred Bower Clayton. Roper described it as being of the 'Grecian Doric Order … with Portico, and Tower, terminated with a Cupola of the Grecian Ionic Order' and cost £16,093 4s. 3d. with half the cost raised locally and the balance paid by the Commissioners. The building accommodated more than 2,000 people with 1,082 pew seats rented out. The surplus left after paying the minister's stipend was used to build a parsonage.

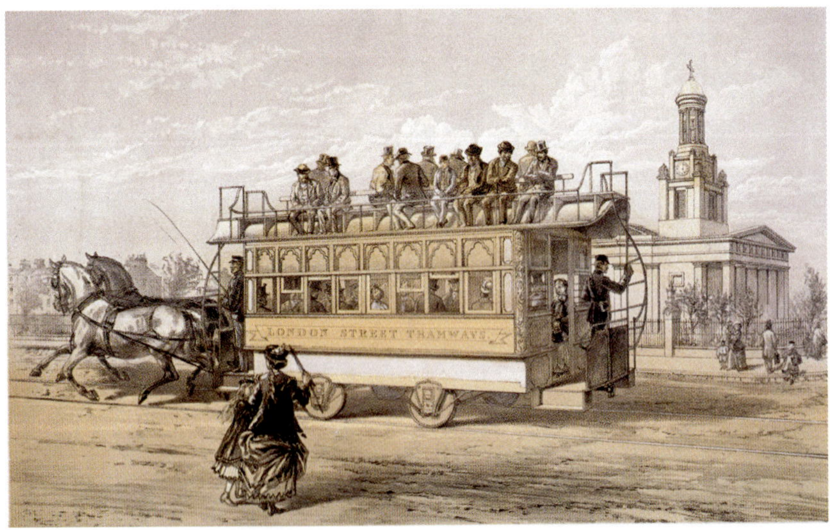

ARTIST UNKNOWN **Horse-drawn tram passing St Mark's, Kennington**
Engraving c 1870
St Mark's was built by David Riddell Roper, 1822-4, and like its three sister churches had half the costs paid for by the Church Building Commissioners. Half the pews were rented out.

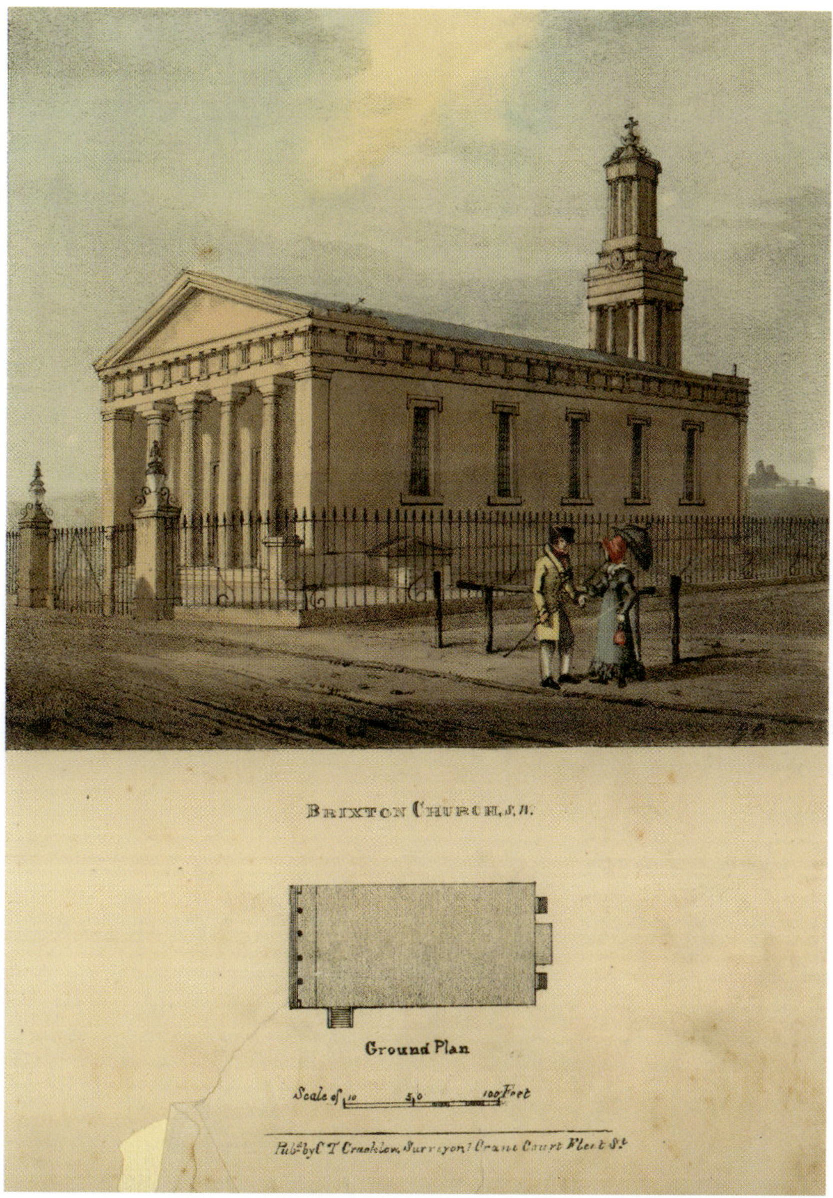

St Matthew's, Brixton, London 1824
Engraving

C. F. Porden designed St Matthew's for the Church Building Commissioners. Of the four Waterloo churches, it was the first to be built, stands in a central position in Brixton and was the first church building in Britain to be lit by electricity. Currently, it has only a very limited space available for worship and its main interior space is rented out as offices.

St Luke's and St John's were both built by Francis Octavius Bedford, who had been a runner-up in the St Pancras New Church competition. He designed two more Greek and two Gothic churches in London and four regional Gothic churches. Sir John Summerson archly describes the tower at St John's as 'the kind of tower Ictinus might have put on the Parthenon if the Athenians had had the advantage of belonging to the Church of England'. It remains the defining example of the Waterloo church in London and holds a festival each summer. It cost £18,034 with a CBC grant of £9,976 to contain 1,181 rented pews and free seats for some 851.

The first Gothic church in London under the new dispensation was built with a rather modest grant from the Commission. The soaring St Luke's, Chelsea, by James Savage, came at the request of the rector of Chelsea, the Honourable and Reverend Gerald Wellesley, nephew of the Duke of Wellington himself. Summerson commends the seriousness of the architect's approach to Gothic but acknowledges that it was learned at second hand; Charles Locke Eastlake decried it at the time as 'machine-made'.

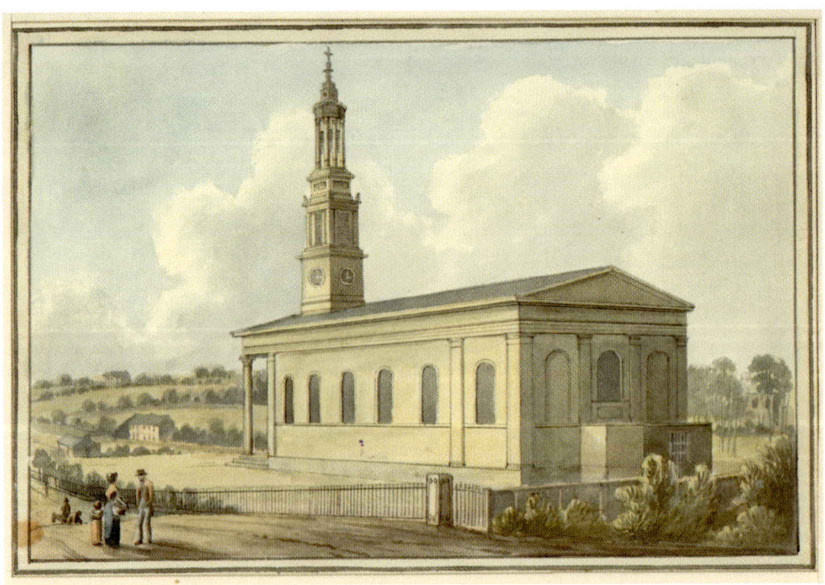

GIDEON YATES **St Luke's, West Norwood, London 1825**
Watercolour on paper
One of the four churches always known as the Waterloo churches in south London,
St Luke's, like St John's, was built by Francis Bedford.

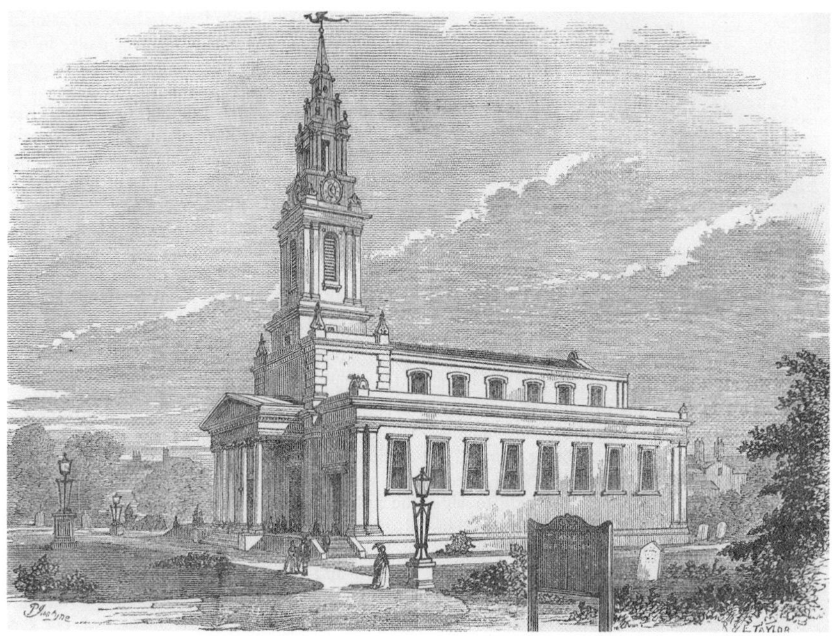

BRITISH SCHOOL **St James's, Bermondsey, London 1878** Engraving
Designed by James Savage, St James's, Bermondsey, was built 1827–9. John Betjeman subsequently wrote: 'Of all the churches built in London by the Waterloo Commission, it is the finest, the most original and the most impressive.'

In Bermondsey, Savage built his splendid St James's in 1827–9, which is widely accepted as one of the finest Classical churches of the period. It was consecrated in 1829 but the spire, copied from Wren's St Stephen's Walbrook, required a separate Act of Parliament to borrow the extra cash in 1831. John Betjeman said of it, 'Of all the churches built in London by the Waterloo Commission, it is the finest, the most original and the most impressive.'

SIX

'To correct a vicious taste': the Incorporated Church Building Society and its architects

While the CBC set its stamp on certain major churches, especially in London, the first enquiries that came into the Church Building Society in 1818 were from Durham, Lancashire, Flintshire, Yorkshire, Staffordshire, Derbyshire, Worcestershire, Monmouthshire, Dorset and Cheshire. St Paul's, Peel, Lancashire received the Society's first ever grant, which was for enlargement, followed by All Saints, Dewsbury, Yorkshire and St Gwynllyw, Newport (today Newport Cathedral) in 1819. The same year, a quintessential English village church, All Saints, Godshill, Isle of Wight, was given a grant for a gallery.

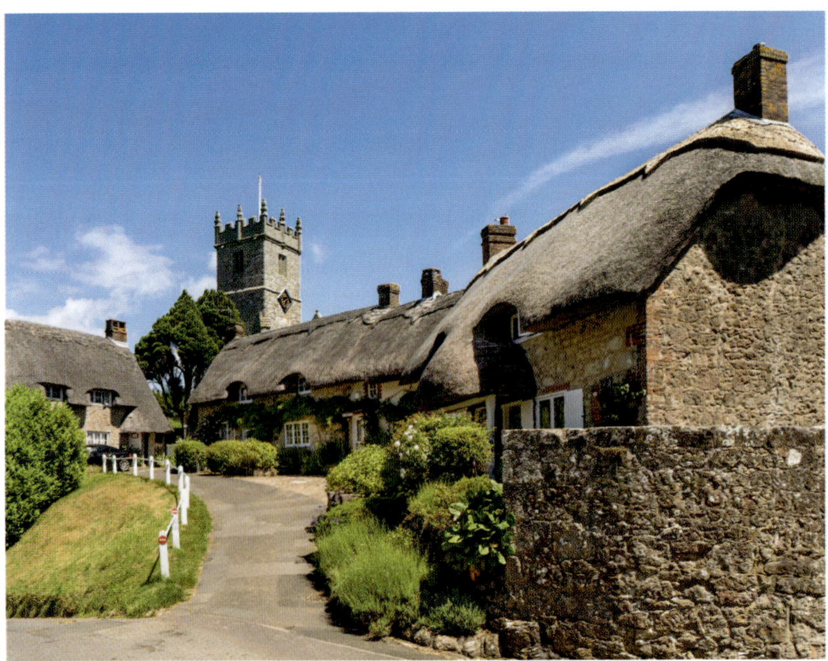

All Saints, Godshill, Isle of Wight
The church at Godshill received a very early CBS grant in 1819 but such picture postcard-perfect buildings in rural settings were rare amongst the churches that the Society supported.

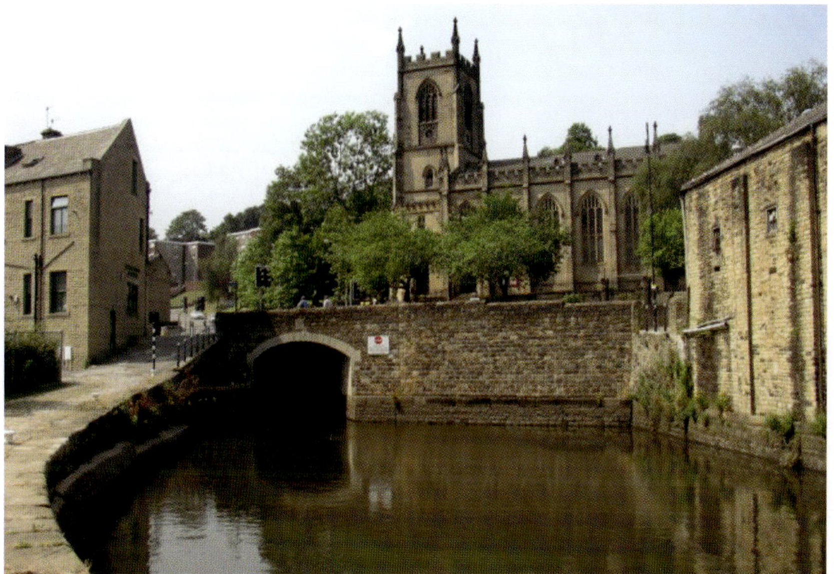

Christ Church, Sowerby Bridge, Yorkshire
Christ Church, Sowerby Bridge (1819), was an early example of a new church funded by the CBS. The Calder and Hebble Navigation meets the Rochdale Canal in Sowerby Bridge and the church was built to accommodate the rising population in this industrial area.

During these early years, the Society gave grants to many new church projects, of which some took a long time to get off the ground and others suffered from a lack of experience or foresight. Very early on, on 22 April 1819, the foundation stone was laid for Christ Church, Sowerby Bridge, Yorkshire. The church was opened two years later but only under licence as the Archbishop of York was not able to carry out the consecration until 1824, due to the large area of his diocese. The architect was John Oates of Halifax, who produced what was described in 1836 as being 'a handsome and commodious chapel of the Gothic order of architecture' and which provided 962 sittings. Nikolaus Pevsner paid it a compliment in 1959 by calling it 'a big church without the paperiness of so many churches c. 1820'.

Over on the Channel Island of Sark, church attendance had lapsed while the pub remained open for most of the Sabbath. In 1796 a Methodist chapel was built at La Ville Roussel, providing the moral leadership for the working population. A plan for a Sark parish church was conceived as a means of re-establishing the authority of Anglicanism and, by midsummer 1821, a plain rectangular building dedicated to St Peter was complete although it was not until 1829 that the Bishop of Winchester finally crossed the sea to consecrate it. At that point, the east end was dominated by the three-tiered octagonal pulpit centrally placed between the two arched windows and on a platform six feet above the pavement and was reached by a staircase rising from the minister's pew. Below the pulpit, three feet above the pavement, were square stalls with desks for the clerk and the reader, who made public proclamations. The cost came to about £1,000 and, on top of the Society's grant, forty tenants paid subscriptions for closed and perpetual family pews, which secured nearly £300 before building started. Today still, uniquely in Britain, this ensures an income (now minuscule) for maintenance. Thanks to the ICBS, at least half the 333 seats were free for all.

Blackpool's first ever church, St John the Evangelist, was consecrated on 6 July 1821. Only forty years previously Blackpool had been a hamlet but then it developed into a destination for the summer season. In 1840, the railway arrived and between 1801 and 1851 the population multiplied

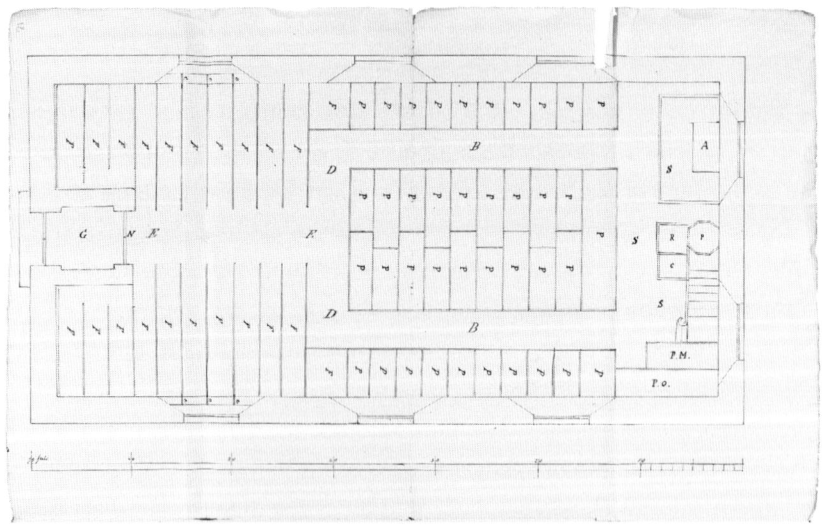

Attributed to NICHOLAS BLONDELL **Ground plan of pews at St Peter's, Sark, 1826**
Pen and ink on paper

A new parish church was grant-aided by the CBS and opened its doors in 1821 although the Bishop of Winchester did not consecrate it for eight years, due to the problems involved in travelling to the Channel Islands. It remains the only church in the British Isles where an income is still derived from pew rental.

fivefold. Within ten years of its consecration the church was already outgrown and was replaced in 1875. The ICBS helped create three other Blackpool churches in the early twentieth century.

St John's, Lacey Green, Buckinghamshire was built over the course of two years from May 1823 as a chapel of ease. The building was financed partly by a grant of £460 from the Society and partly by a public appeal which raised £2,200. The appeal was organised by the Reverend Richard Meade and subscription lists were available at six addresses in London, including Hatchard's bookshop in Piccadilly, and in Aylesbury, Buckingham, Oxford, Cambridge, Banbury and Windsor. This resulted in donations from 300 very great and good benefactors including Lord Grenville and Sir Robert Peel (past and future Prime Ministers), the dukes of Bedford, Portland and Buckingham & Chandos, and All Souls', Balliol, Magdalen and New colleges, Oxford. There were eleven trustees of whom one, John Norris of Hughenden House, an antiquary and a scholar, drew up the design but J. Chadley (who wrote a treatise on flues and chimneys) is described as its architect. It had west and south galleries and pews that faced across the church rather than towards the altar. Alterations by J. P. Seddon later removed the galleries and created a chancel.

In 1831 the ICBS grant-aided Holy Trinity in Seaton Carew, a coastal village near Hartlepool and a fashionable eighteenth-century holiday destination for Quakers from Darlington. Another shift in demographics came in the same year when they enabled St Ann's, Old Swan, Liverpool to respond to the influx of population the year after the Liverpool and Manchester Railway opened. The church was built on the site of an iron foundry and was consecrated on 13 October 1831 but was replaced in 1890.

In 1837, the ICBS grant-aided three more churches, now genuinely Victorian. St John the Baptist, Leeming, near Northallerton in Yorkshire, was declared to be 'in a ruinous condition, and dangerous for the inhabitants to assemble therein' and a new, larger church replaced it on the same site at a cost of £674 raised by subscriptions. St John the Baptist, Rowlands Castle, near Portsmouth, was built in less than a year with local subscriptions of £783 and has long links with Jane Austen's family. St John's Church, Uxbridge Moor, Middlesex was the nearest new Victorian church to London built with the help of the Society and is now a private home. There is no pattern to any of the grant aid as it was so widespread and varied: there is simply no typical ICBS church, either by style or location.

St John the Evangelist, Hildenborough, Kent was the first church built by Ewan Christian at a cost of £2,300 with a grant from the ICBS and private contributions in 1843 and won through competition. During his long career Christian produced over 2,000 works and carried out about 1,300 restorations and additions to churches, including 90 complete new churches. At Hildenborough, he retained a conservative approach to the 'preaching box', perhaps reflecting his own Evangelical beliefs: he originally intended to become a clergyman and was a Sunday School teacher and superintendent at St John's, Downshire Hill, Hampstead for more than thirty-five years. Built in an early English style, Hildenborough has a very wide nave and transepts, the seating all cruciform. Pews in the nave faced east; those in the north transept faced south and accordingly the south transept and its gallery seats faced northwards. The seats on the south side of the chancel faced west towards the pulpit, which was still three tiered. In 1847, Christian was appointed consulting architect to the Lichfield Diocesan Church Building Society and also became a consulting architect to the ICBS. Later in life he designed the National Portrait Gallery and was architect to the Ecclesiastical Commission (see page 133) from 1851 until just before his death in 1895.

Both the CBC and the ICBS were, in most regards, deeply conservative and looked back to an ideal period and *status quo* between the Restoration and the Napoleonic Wars or even to a more golden Tudor Reformation era but their approaches were deliberately, usefully, different. In his biography of his father, Thomas Bowdler recalled that John Bowdler saw the ICBS as a means to 'correct a vicious taste and encourage and compel a plainer and less expensive method'. From the outset, the Society had observed the Commission's flurry of activities with quiet interest and, from 1848, changed its approach to the design of the churches that it helped fund. At the beginning, it had simply been responsive to requests but after a decade of experience it appointed Joseph Henry Good as an examining architect alongside his work as surveyor for the Commission. In 1848 the Society set up an Architects' Committee of eleven experts, each allocated a geographical area to visit where they could monitor progress and try to prevent errors in planning.

These experts were comparatively young, the oldest being not yet fifty and the rest mostly in their thirties – much younger than the members of the committee to whom they offered guidance. By virtue of the length of service most of these architects gave to the ICBS, the average age of future consulting architects to the Society was much higher. When the first generation finally retired or died they were replaced by their elderly peers, not by men at the start of their careers.

The medievalist among the eleven was Anthony Salvin, the oldest at forty-nine, from Durham. Salvin specialised in church repair and remodelling with the intention of returning each building to some previous idealised state rather than restoration as it is understood today. He was made an honorary member of the Cambridge Camden Society in November 1841, early in his church designing career, because of his work on the Round Church in Cambridge (1841–4). In total Salvin worked on twenty old churches and three cathedrals, and built thirty-four new churches. Of the latter, his first, Holy Trinity, Ulverston, Lancashire, was built for the CBC in in 1829–32; he next built an ICBS church, St John's, Shildon, in his native county, of which only the nave survives subsequent remodelling. He worked extensively in the north east, building two churches at the expense of the dukes of Northumberland, for whom he subsequently worked on Alnwick Castle. His work will be looked at again later.

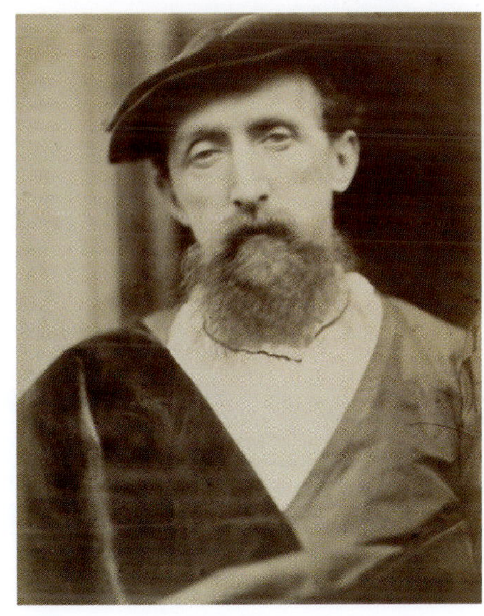

DAVID WILKIE WYNFIELD
Portrait of Anthony Salvin
(1799–1881), 1860s, Photograph
Wynfield often asked his artist sitters to wear fancy dress alluding, flatteringly, to their link to the Old Masters. In the case of Salvin it underlies his reputation as an architect who was a medievalist, often returning buildings to an idealised, rather than an historic, earlier state.

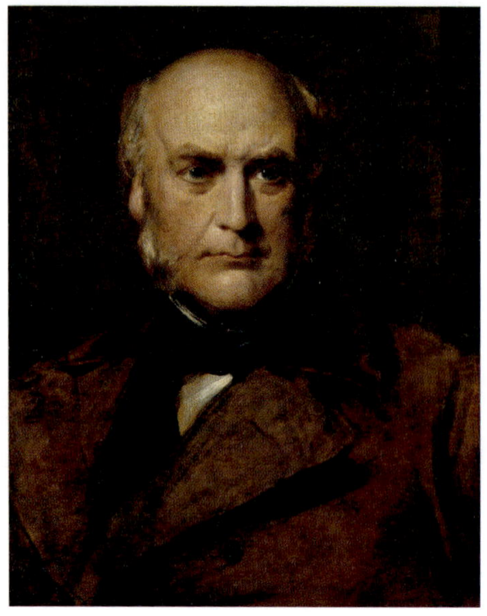

Portrait of Sir George Gilbert Scott, RA (1811–78), 1877, Oil on canvas

Although originating in a commission to mark Scott's presidency of the Royal Institute of British Architects, this version was painted by George Richmond on his own account. Architect and artist had known each other for many years; Scott wrote to Richmond to ask his advice about his work to preserve the paintings in the Chapter House of Westminster Abbey.

George Gilbert Scott was thirty-seven and had recently built the neo-Norman church of St Peter in Norbiton, Surrey. Son of a cleric and grandson of the biblical commentator Thomas Scott, he would go on to be the patriarch of a dynasty of architects, one of whom married a member of the Hoare family (see page 149). For many years before his appointment he had been a specialist in workhouses, later becoming a major figure in the Gothic Revival. His most famous buildings are among the greatest of Victorian icons. Scott's St Giles's Church, Camberwell (1844) had helped establish his reputation within the Gothic Revival: with its long chancel it was precisely the style advocated by the Ecclesiological Society (see page 121). Charles Locke Eastlake said that 'in the neighbourhood of London no church of its time was considered in purer style or more orthodox in its arrangement'. It did, however, have distinctly un-medieval wooden galleries, highly disapproved of by the Ecclesiological movement.

Scott's involvement with St Mary the Virgin in Aylesbury, Buckinghamshire (first built about 1200–1250) is an exemplary tale of argument and restoration from 1848 onwards. An earlier surveyor from London gave a very concise report, which was that the church might probably stand until he got to Watford but would likely fall down before he reached home. On 24 September 1848, during the Sunday morning service, the fastenings of the bells gave way and the noise from the tower made many believe the surveyor's prophecy had come true. In their panic the congregation scrambled over the pews and for a time there was total confusion. However, when they got outside and found nothing whatever the matter, the service was resumed. But Scott was called into make a survey, rather than a prophecy, shortly afterwards which revealed considerable problems with the foundations.

Instructions were received by the vestry from the archdeacon to repair the fabric of the building and a vestry meeting discussed borrowing £3,000 for the purpose but the idea was vehemently opposed by the Nonconformists. Nonetheless the vestry decided for the loan, which resulted in a poll of the parish over two days, ending in a majority of 281 in favour. At the next vestry Mr. Z. D. Hunt (whose initials suggest he was a Dissenter) was elected as churchwarden and asked if he might make his case for repairs only when 'necessary in furnishing the poor with religious instruction'. Not a penny should be spent on decorations or ornamental

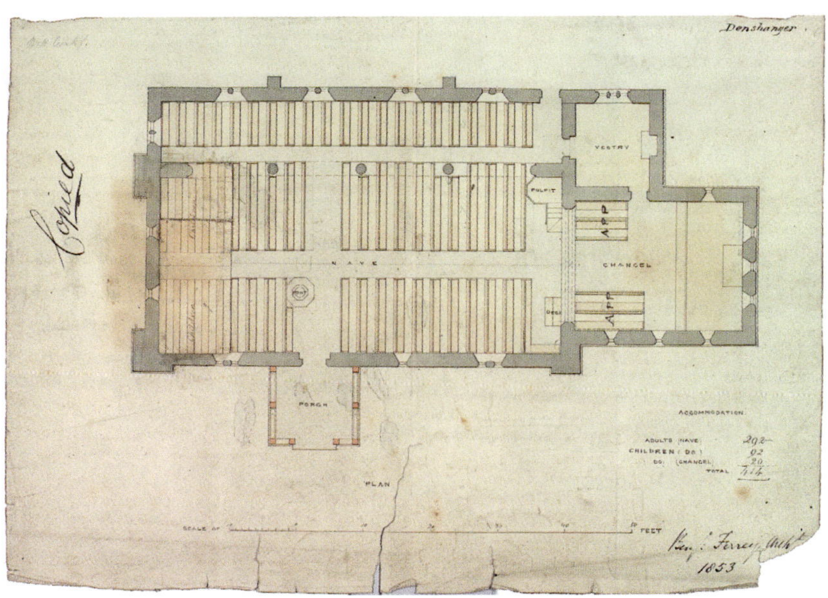

BENJAMIN FERREY **Plan of Holy Trinity, Deanhanger, Northamptonshire, 1853**
Watercolour and pen on paper,
Ferrey designed Holy Trinity as a new chapel of ease in 1853; funded by the ICBS, it cost £3,000 and is now Grade II listed.

work of any kind. Pews, galleries and partitions were swept away and sold and work began on necessary repairs and the restoration of the interior. The church was closed and public worship moved to the County Hall.

In May 1852, a vestry meeting considered the necessity of providing new seating and a plan for voluntary contributions was approved. An application to the ICBS for seating and for work on the roof, the walls of the clerestory and the south transept was also successful. Work began again, delayed only by disputes raised by some parishioners about their rights to seats, some demanding that they should occupy the places on which their old pews formerly stood. The exterior of the building was also substantially repaired and paid for on the basis of voluntary contributions as the vestry remained opposed to church rates. A Restoration Committee was appointed and the monies were raised. The entire cost of repairs and restoration was about £16,000. The church received subsequent ICBS grants in the 1920s and 1970s.

This pattern of regular grants as needs, fashions and priests change has been central to the lives of so many churches. No less frequent are the arguments, often fuelled by Nonconformists who otherwise had little voice in the way their lives were run, about whether church rates should be mandatory. Many churches failed to get sufficient local support to apply to the Society. or else plans faltered during negotiations.

Benjamin Ferrey was thirty-eight and had been both a pupil to Augustus Pugin as a very young man and then, in complete contrast, apprenticed to the Classicist William Wilkins. Ferrey was one of the original members of the Architectural Society, a fellow of the Royal Institute of British Architects from 1839, and subsequently twice its vice-president. Eastlake spoke highly of him: 'He was one of the earliest, ablest, and most zealous pioneers of the modern Gothic school. His architectural taste was for years in steady advance of his generation, and as an authority on church planning and general proportions he had scarcely a rival.'

John Henry Hakewill was another 38-year-old appointed to the committee. He was the son and pupil of Henry Hakewill, who been architect to Rugby School, and began to practise himself in 1838, going into partnership with his brother Edward by 1840. He built churches and rectories, mainly in Wiltshire, Suffolk and Essex, and was the architect of Stowlangtoft Hall, Suffolk. He also helped to set up the Architects'

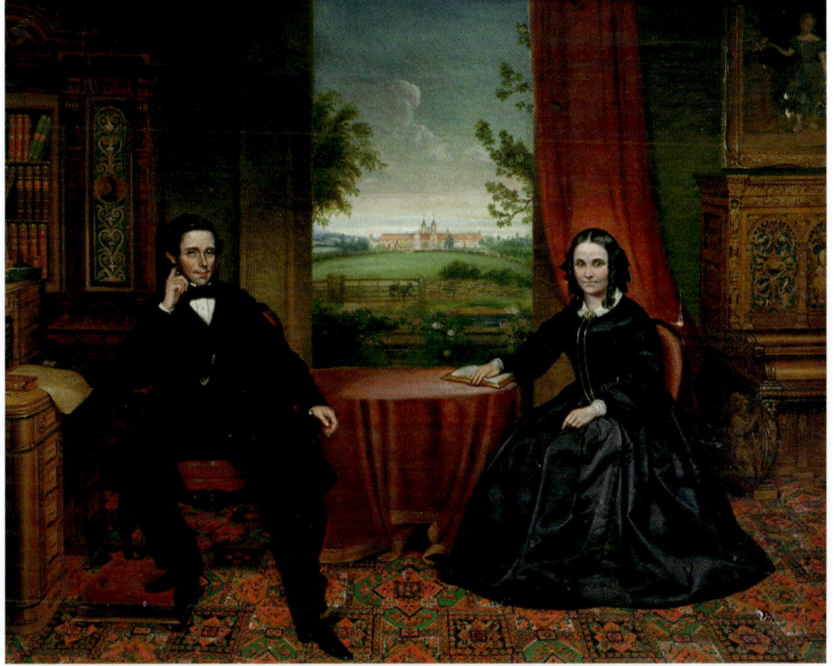

J. SIMPSON **Portrait of John Henry Hakewill (1810–80)** and his wife Lucy, Circa 1860, Oil on canvas

The couple are seated in the library of their house at Stowlangtoft Hall, Suffolk, which Hakewill built for them in 1859, probably at the moment when he also commissioned this portrait.

Benevolent Fund, while Edward was the architect of St John of Jerusalem, South Hackney, Henry Handley Norris's last great project in 1848.

Thomas Henry Wyatt was forty years old and had begun to practise on his own account in 1832 when he was appointed district surveyor for Hackney (a post he held until 1861) and was therefore well known to Joshua Watson and his circle. He was considered a safe pair of hands and was later elected president of the Royal Institute of British Architects 1870–73. The Wyatts were another significant architectural dynasty in both the eighteenth and nineteenth centuries.

John Hayward was also forty and had recently left the office of Sir Charles Barry, to whom he was related by marriage. He was the official architect for the Exeter Diocesan Architectural Society, which meant that all new designs for the churches in that district, whether ICBS applicants or not, were passed to him for approval. He later became a member of

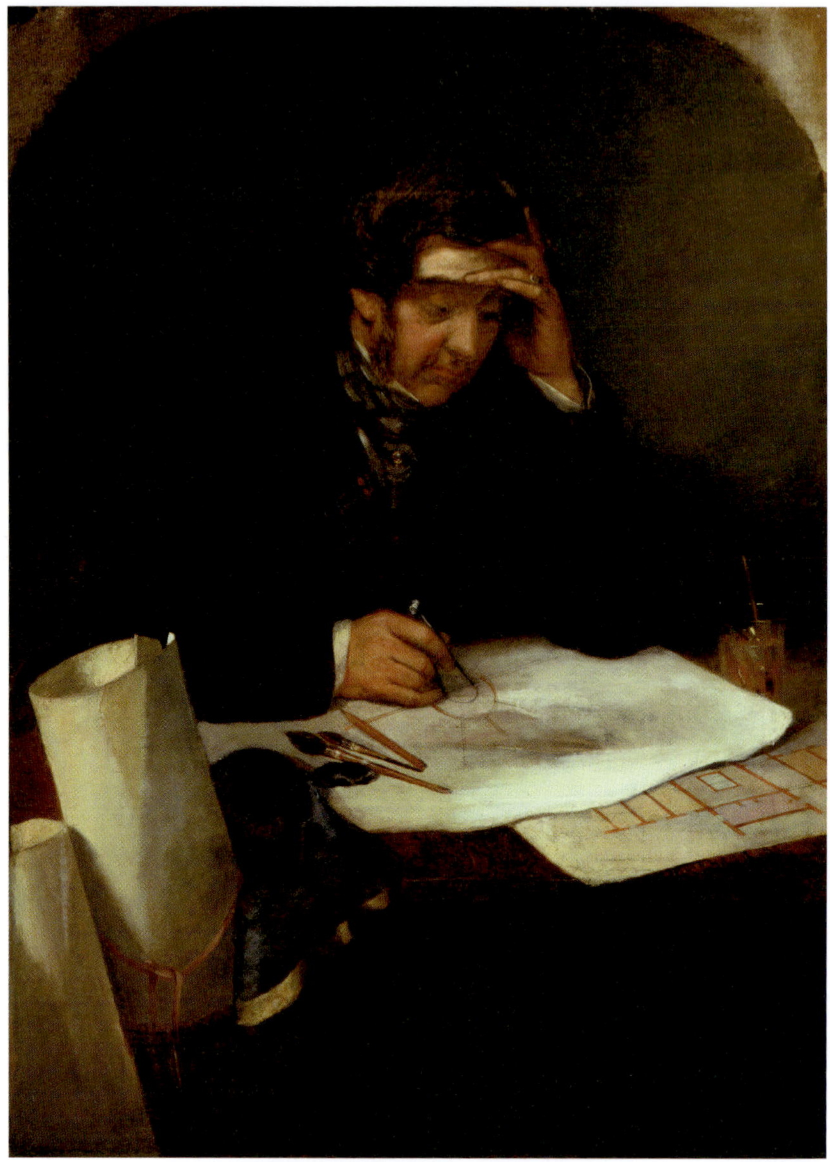

GEORGE LANDSEER **Portrait of Thomas Henry Wyatt (1807–80)**
1850, Oil on canvas

Unlike the grand portraits of Salvin and Scott or the homely view of the Hakewills, Wyatt is shown here as a working professional at a desk covered in plans, brushes and pens, two years into his period of service on the architects' committee of the ICBS.

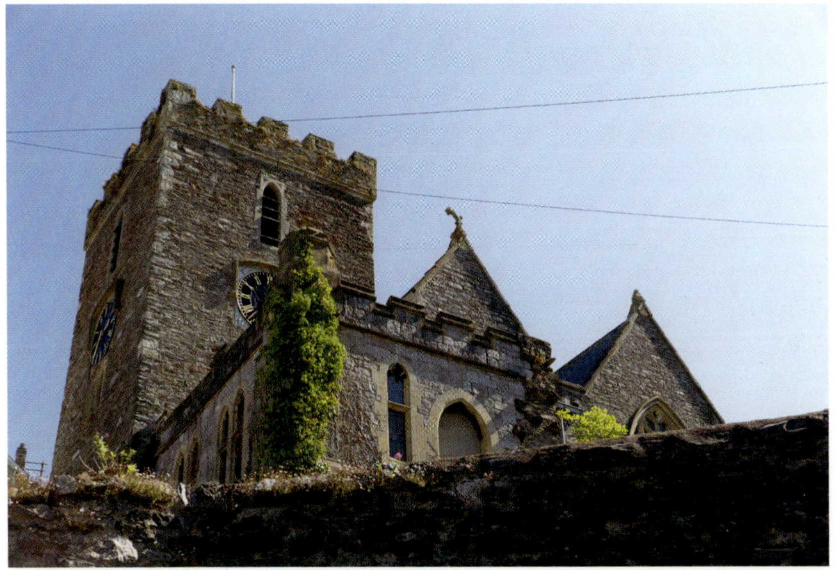

St Thomas of Canterbury, Kingswear, Devon
St Thomas was designed by John Hayward (1807-91) with an ICBS grant. Incorporating a medieval tower, it was completed in 1847. Hayward was based in Exeter and appointed to the architects' committee the following year. The church is Grade II listed.

the Cambridge Camden Society and his Gothic allegiances were clear. His St Andrew's, Exwick was described by *The Ecclesiologist* in July 1842 as the 'best specimen of a modern church we have yet seen'.

Richard Cromwell Carpenter was thirty-six in 1848. He worked in the Gothic style and was an early member of the Cambridge Camden Society, introduced by Pugin. His St Paul's, Brighton (1846–8) is looked at in Chapter Ten (see page 108).

Harvey Eginton, aged thirty-nine, was based in Worcestershire. In later years, William Butterfield would be his pupil. An encaustic tile was manufactured in 1844 by Chamberlain's of Worcester at Eginton's request, directly copied from medieval examples such as those in Great Malvern Priory Church. His Gothic Christ Church, Catshill, Worcestershire was built for the Commissioners (with a £200 grant) the year after his appointment to the ICBS. Its first vicar was the Reverend Thomas Housman, whose grandson the poet A. E. Housman was baptised by him there on Easter Day in 1859.

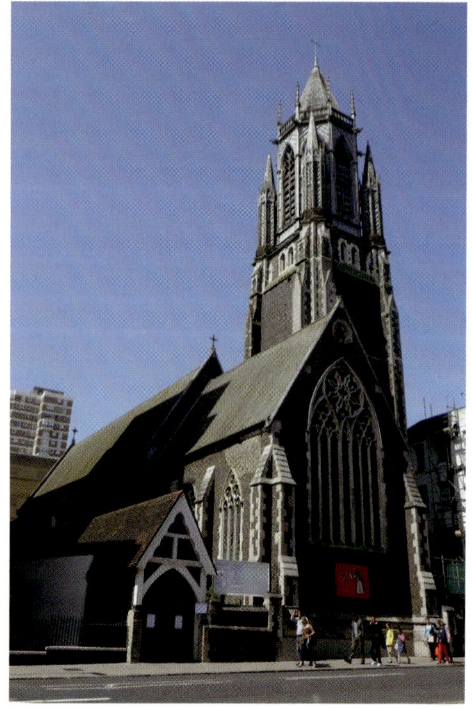

St Paul's, Brighton

St Paul's was designed by Richard Cromwell Carpenter (1812–55) for Henry Michell Wagner, vicar of Brighton since 1824, as the first ministry for his son Arthur. Arthur Wagner wanted his church to have free seating for all but his father insisted that 460 of the 1,200 seats should be reserved for rental. Henry Wagner was married to Joshua Watson's daughter Mary.

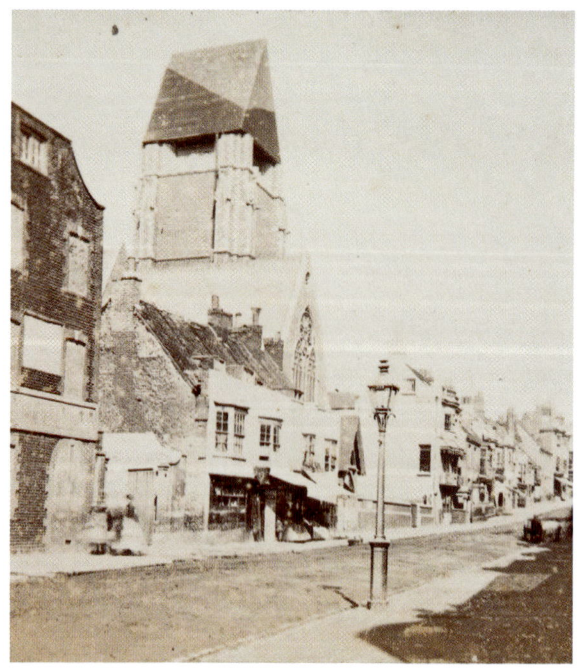

St Paul's, Brighton 1860s

Although the church was consecrated in 1848 its Gothic lantern tower remained unfinished for decades. Arthur Wagner became perpetual curate in 1850 and was criticised for his adherence to High Church practices. His morning choral service, unique in Brighton, was known as 'the morning Opera at St Paul's'.

Encaustic tile, 1844

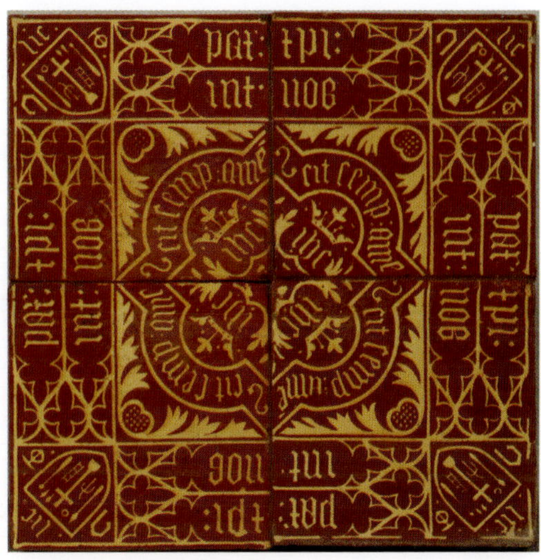

Harvey Eginton (1809–49), a Worcester-based architect, commissioned Chamberlain's of Worcester to manufacture modern tiles directly copied from medieval examples such as those in the Great Malvern Priory Church, Worcestershire. In 1833 a medieval drying oven or kiln was discovered near the church, which excited a great deal of interest in medieval tiles. Described as 'an unusually serious and competent gothic designer', Eginton died only a year after his appointment to the first architects' committee.

Eginton was involved in a major rebuilding of the church of St Lawrence in Evesham, whose story is a sad but familiar one. St Lawrence's was originally built by the monks of Evesham Abbey in the twelfth century but significantly rebuilt about 1470. From 1659 it ceased to have its own vicar and the fabric of the church deteriorated so that by the winter of 1718 it had become unusable. Repairs began in 1737, but were badly executed; the roof collapsed in 1800 and the church was abandoned. Eginton was commissioned to rebuild it in 1836 with an ICBS grant which included extending it with a north aisle in a similar style to the south aisle, and replacing the roof. In 1890, an enquiry was made to the ICBS about a grant to alter 'Eginton's abominable plan'. No grant followed and the church is now redundant, in the care of the Churches Conservation Trust.

Richard Charles Hussey, thirty-two, designed St John the Evangelist, Stoke Row, Oxfordshire in a thirteenth-century style in 1846. Stoke Row has an independent chapel built in 1815 and Dissenters have been meeting in the village since 1691 when they gathered in the drawing room of a local farmhouse. St John the Evangelist's church served to recreate an imagined Anglican history for the village.

Hussey had been in partnership with Thomas Rickman (1776–1841) from 1835 and took control of the business in 1838 as the latter's health

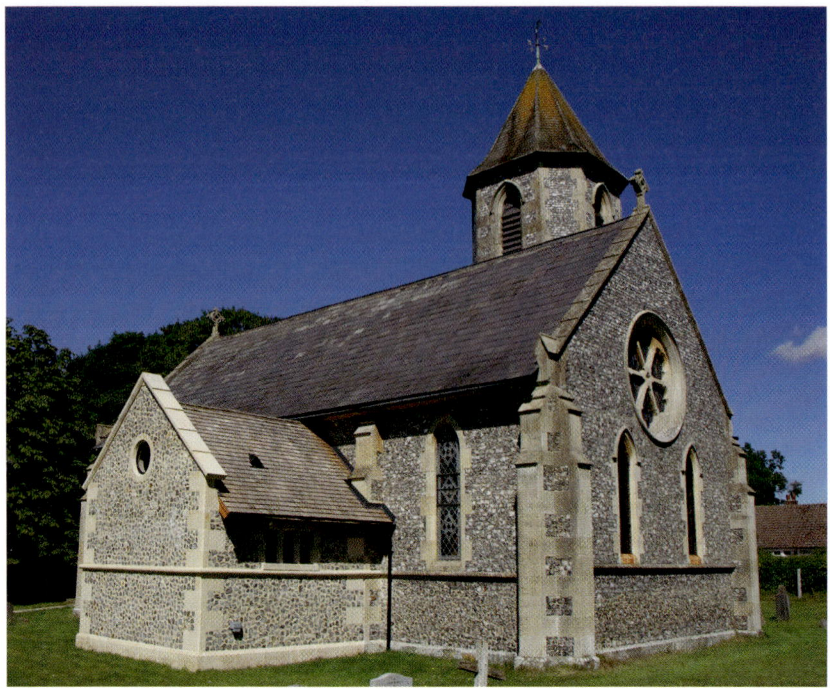

St John the Evangelist, Stoke Row, Oxfordshire

St John the Evangelist was designed by R.C. Hussey (1806–87) in 1846 and its conscientious medievalism led to his appointment to the architects' committee. He will also have been recommended by his partnership with the remarkable Thomas Rickman, whose early death predated the committee.

failed. Rickman, not on the ICBS committee, is a crucial figure in the early history of the church-building boom, a self-taught regional architect whose major achievement was to involve himself swiftly and centrally in the movement to create new churches. He moved to Liverpool in 1808 to work as an insurance clerk but began to take an interest in Gothic church architecture. He met John Cragg, the owner of an iron foundry, and with him designed three churches for Liverpool – St George's, St Michael's and St Philip's – using cast iron for their construction and decoration. In 1817 he both opened an architectural office in Liverpool and published *An Attempt to Discriminate the Styles of English Architecture from the Conquest to the Reformation*, the first systematic treatise on Gothic architecture and a milestone in the Gothic Revival. It ran through many editions and defined the basic chronological classifications of English medieval ecclesiastical architecture that we still use today: Norman, Early English, Decorated and Perpendicular. The next year, he responded smartly to the creation of the Church Building Commission and submitted a plan in open competition for St George in the Fields, Hockley, Birmingham and, having won, opened an office in that city in 1820. The Bishop of Chester asked Rickman to prepare plans for new Cheshire churches and recommended that the Commission use them as a template, calling him 'a very ingenious deserving man', but it maintained the principle of open competition.

By 1830 Rickman had become one of the most successful architects of his time, building nineteen Commissioners' churches in total, several with his first partner, Henry Hutchinson. He and Hutchinson also worked extensively on restoration and repairs including at St Mary Magdalene, Clitheroe, Lancashire in 1828–9 with an ICBS grant, rebuilding everything apart from the tower and east window. Of their many other new churches,

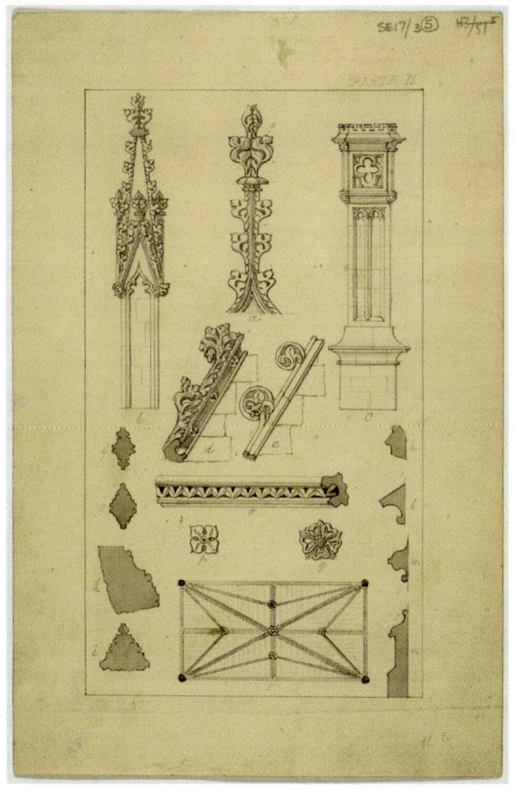

THOMAS RICKMAN
Development of English Gothic architecture: details
Ink on paper, 1808
One of the original drawings made for the first edition of Rickman's 'An Attempt to discriminate the styles of English architecture from the Conquest to the Reformation', 1817.

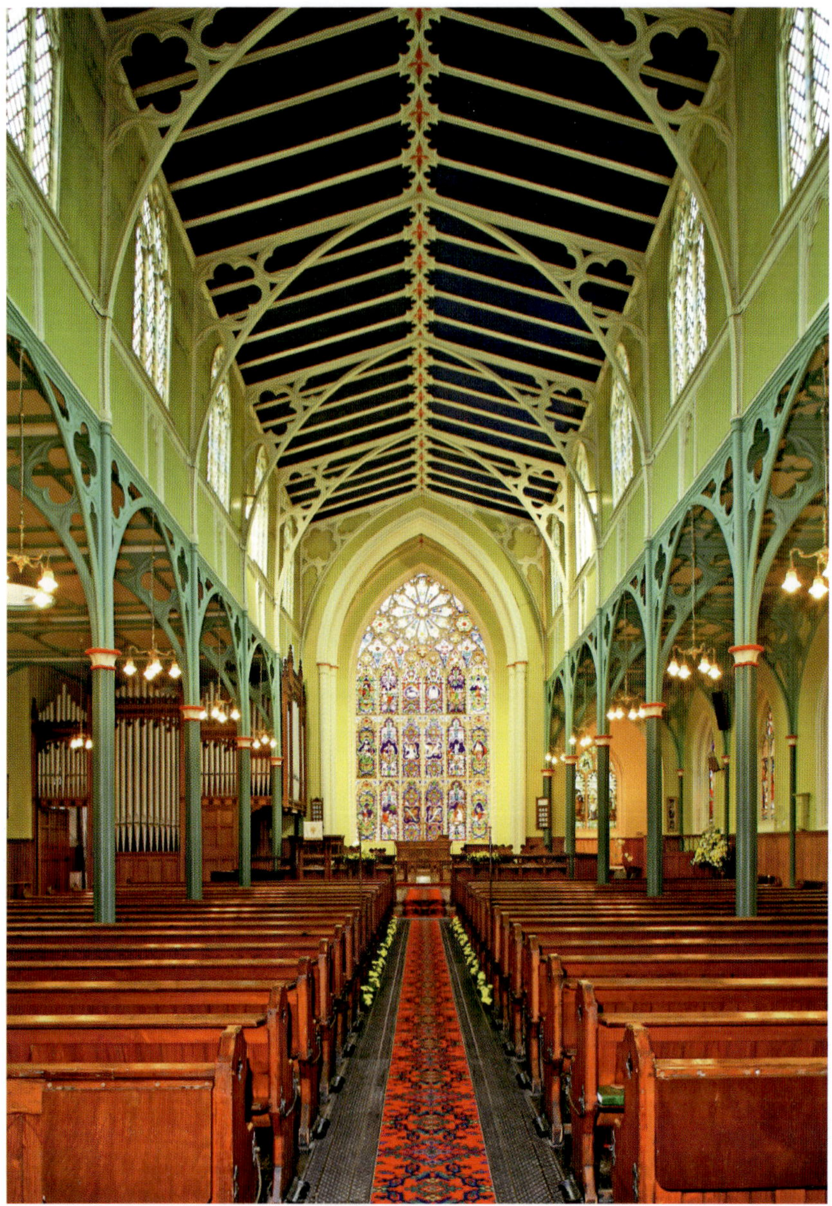

St Michael in the Hamlet, Liverpool

Thomas Rickman was always interested in new technologies including cast iron frames for churches which he designed in Liverpool with iron founder John Cragg. St Michael's was a wealthy parish and its church, built 1813–15, is Grade I listed; the citation in the National Heritage List for England states it has 'one of the earliest and most thorough uses of industrial materials in a major building'.

receiving a grant from neither the CBC nor the ICBS, St Peter ad Vincula in Hampton Lucy, Warwickshire, designed in 1826, is their masterpiece. Rickman played a vital role in the revival of taste for medievalism in church building, perhaps second only to Pugin. St George in the Fields, Hockley was demolished in 1960 but Rickman's tomb (1841), designed by Hussey, remains.

Hardly anything is known of the two remaining architects on the committee, Joseph Clarke and W. Richard. Clarke's scant biography suggests he was only twenty-eight, making him probably the youngest of the eleven, but reveals nothing more. As for W. Richard, all we have is his name.

Gothic Revival architecture was believed at first to be virtuous because economical and was later argued to be the liturgical ideal. The ICBS appointed mostly young Gothic enthusiasts to its board of architects while the CBC started out with a flurry of Neo-Classical metropolitan churches by three star architects before following the Gothic line. Having won the battle at Waterloo, England fought the war of ecclesiastical style and content for most of the rest of the century and the ICBS drew up many of the battle plans. Like Aesop's tortoise and hare, the slowest and least showy won the race, resulting in more churches but with less style or panache than those built with private funds.

SEVEN

'The style of the future':
Gothic versus Classical

The first decades of nineteenth-century church building can be seen as binary, sometimes complementary but often confrontational: the Society and the Commission, ICBS versus CBC; Hackney versus Clapham, High & Dry versus the Saints; the Oxford versus the Cambridge movement, often thought of as head against heart. While these pairings always differed in the detail they had profoundly similar aims – more churches, extended congregations, better buildings. But the real division came between early Neo-Classicism and triumphant Gothic, London versus the rest of the country in a war of styles. It is irresistible to recall W. C. Sellar and R. J. Yeatman's idiosyncratic history of Britain, *1066 and All That*, when looking at the glamour of London's first CBC churches and some of the first, worthy but ugly, regional attempts by the ICBS. The Cavaliers (in this case, the CBC) are described as 'Wrong but Wromantic' and the Roundheads (the ICBS) as 'Right but Repulsive': apposite for church building, too. Later, in the twentieth century, the two contrary positions would be taken by Pevsner and Betjeman, academic rigour versus popular feeling. Pevsner noted that Gothic architecture for churches became 'the style of the future'.

A vast amount of committee time must have been devoted to the drafting of the new 1842 'Suggestions', one of whose primary authors, one presumes, was Joseph Henry Good, both surveyor to the Commission from 1826 to 1857 and, from 1829 to 1848, examining architect to the Society. He was also clerk of works at the Tower of London, the Royal Mint, Kensington Palace and the Royal Pavilion, Brighton, largely a theorist rather than a designing architect. The only building credited to him personally is Armourers' Hall, built in 1839 for The Worshipful Company of Armourers and Brasiers in London. Curiously, the hall was one of the very few not destroyed in the Great Fire of London in 1666 and, while it was enlarged in 1795, a decision was taken in 1839 to rebuild it completely. Good's building is described by Pevsner as 'modest, late neo-classical'.

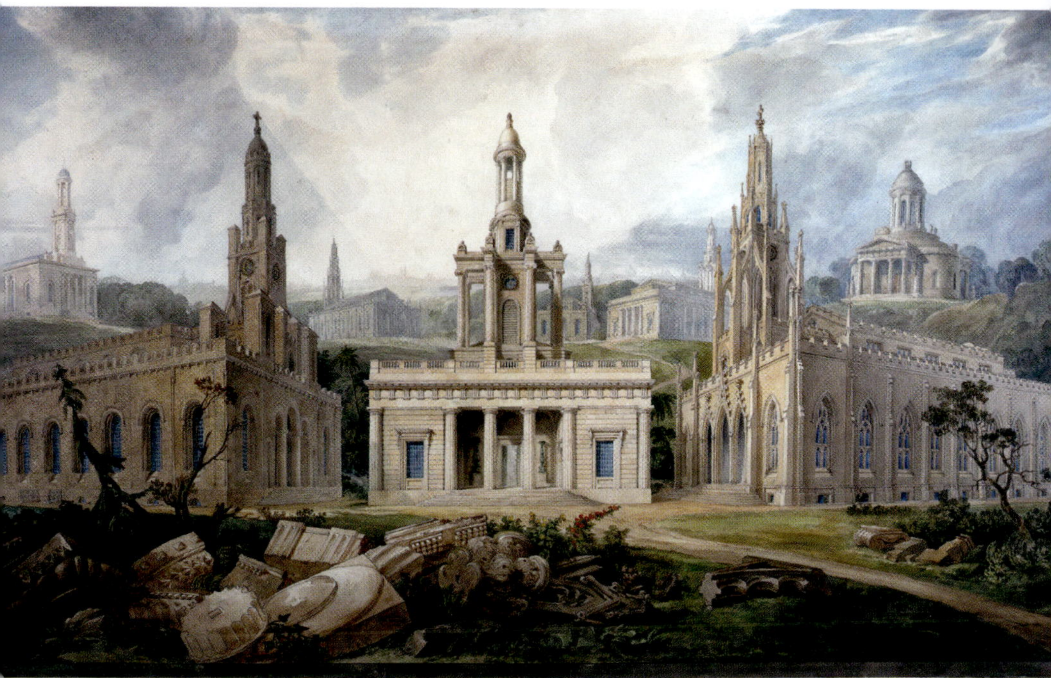

JOSEPH MICHAEL GANDY **A Group of Churches, Designed by Sir J. Soane (1825) to Illustrate Different Styles of Architecture, 1825**
Watercolour on paper

Gandy worked regularly for John Soane to present his designs in a theatrical and academic manner, akin to a history painting. This image shows three churches designed by Soane to show off the architect's range of styles and panache. The examples here are Holy Trinity, Marylebone, St Peter, Walworth and the chapel at Tyringham, Buckinghamshire. It was exhibited at the Royal Academy in 1825.

Neo-Classicism in Britain developed as a style across the arts, but most especially in architecture, from the 1750s. The study and the fashion were prompted by discoveries from Pompeii and Herculaneum and expanded through the young aristocrats on the Grand Tour to Greece and Italy: here they saw original works of art and buildings, in ruins or not, then came home with ambitions to recreate their own property in this style. In terms of public buildings a Greek Revival style was considered ideal to contain the institutions of the law, civic administration and culture, emphasising an eternal association with the values and qualities of ancient Greece, its democracy and civilisation. It also lay at the heart of all urban planning in eighteenth- and early nineteenth-century England, of which

Bath, Cheltenham, Newcastle upon Tyne and London's Regent Street are prime examples. The most obvious characteristics of the style are cool smoothness from pale, often Portland, stone; portico frontage of columns, usually plainly Doric or Ionic; and direct quotations from ancient buildings like the Tower of the Winds in Athens. Together they gave elegance, symmetry and rhetoric. The style reached its apogee in Britain just before 1830, but did not disappear.

The earliest Greek Doric building in London was Robert Smirke's first major work, the Covent Garden Theatre, built in ten months in 1808–9. Next was his largest and best-known building, the British Museum, designed in 1820. The first ever Greek Revival design in Britain was by William Wilkins in 1804 at Downing College, Cambridge, but it was still incomplete as late as 1821. His National Gallery (1832–8) was the movement's last flourish in a square started by Nash and completed by Wilkins, commemorating Nelson's victory at the Battle of Trafalgar.

Neo-Classicism was by definition associated with novelty and paganism. It also flourished in France, where the 'Louis Seize style' inevitably became linked, in some British minds, with revolution. The newly independent American nation built its first United States Capitol in Washington, DC, as an ideal of monumental Neo-Classicism. No wonder that much of the British establishment was conservative and nervous as they planned their new churches; they strove where possible to show that ancient tradition was seamlessly preserved.

By 1841 Gothic architecture was established as the national British style of public architecture as Charles Barry's Houses of Parliament began to develop. The Fine Art Commission was appointed that year with Sir Charles Lock Eastlake, director of the National Gallery and uncle of his near-namesake the architect, as secretary and Prince Albert as chairman to plan the internal decoration and, as Lucy Hartley has recently pointed out, it followed the German model of nationalism in mural paintings. This echoes the church builders' final rejection of Classicism in favour of a national, Christian style to the exclusion of foreignness.

Gothic architecture evolved in the British Isles in the late twelfth century, superseding the Romanesque or Norman French style. Thomas Rickman divided the historic styles into periods, based on the reigns of

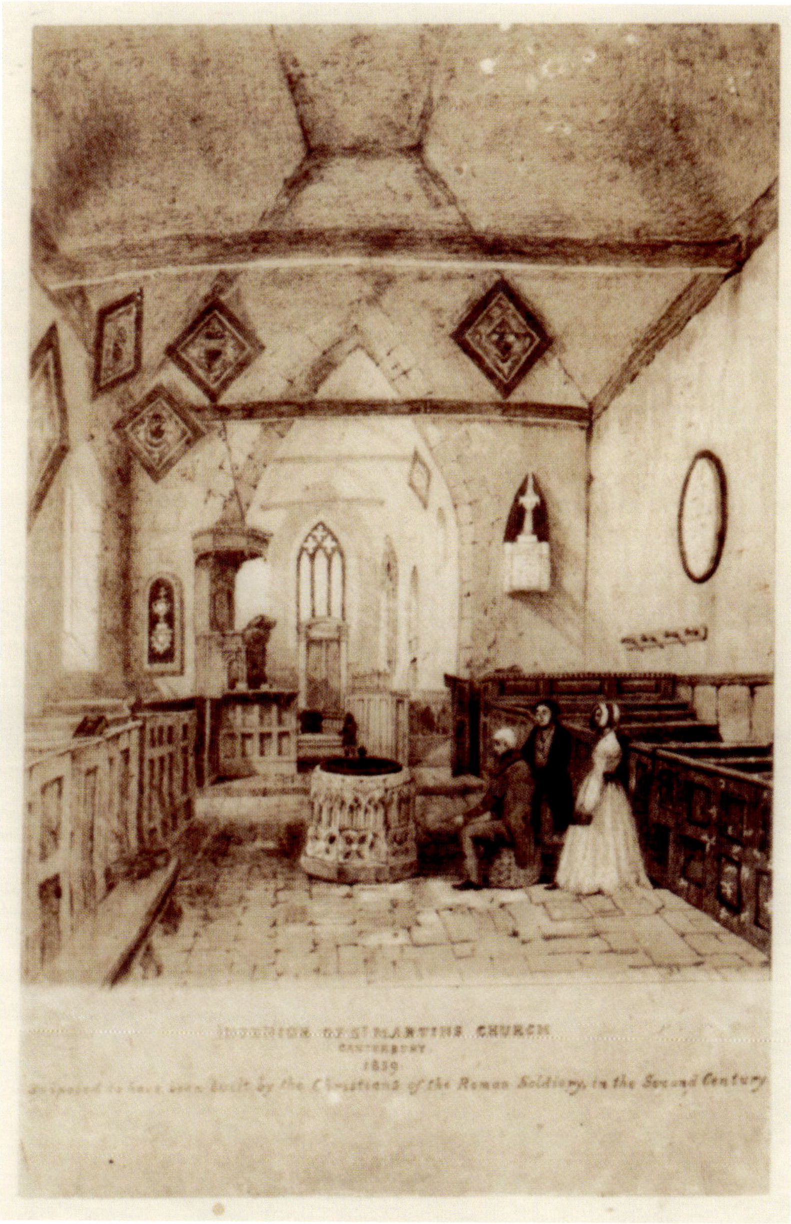

BRITISH SCHOOL **St Martin's, Canterbury, 1839**
Watercolour on paper, reproduced as a postcard
St Martin's is the earliest surviving parish church in Britain, built in AD590. It received a grant for repairs from the ICBS in 1951, nearly 1,400 years later. This interior view shows early Victorian tourists admiring the ancient font.

monarchs: Early English (c. 1180–1275), Decorated (c. 1275–1380) and Perpendicular (c. 1380–1520). While Durham Cathedral shows an overlap of the change from Norman to English, Canterbury is the first pure English Gothic cathedral and the city is also home to the earliest surviving parish church in the country, St Martin's (built about 590 AD, it received a ICBS grant for repairs 1,400 years later).

At its purest, Gothic architecture is austere, emphasising height through pointed arches and slim columns rather than heavy pillars and tall spires as if reaching to heaven. The Decorated style added flamboyant tracery, carved foliage, a play of light and shadow, while the Perpendicular introduced technological sophistication in larger windows, even slimmer clusters of columns and the further refinement of fan vaulting. The Decorated style (from the reigns of Edward I, II and III) was the version most used as inspiration for Gothic churches in the nineteenth century although the ICBS always emphasised simplicity.

New Gothic church building as supported by the Society differs from the lively and frivolous Gothic Revival of domestic buildings like Horace Walpole's Strawberry Hill or his novel *The Castle of Otranto*. Like the Neo-Classicists, the new Gothic church builders were attempting, more or less, to use antiquarian studies as their rule books rather anything more imaginative: often replicating doggedly rather than evoking atmosphere. The later Gothic Revival builders of the mid- to high Victorian period are another matter, as are those who strove to restore ancient churches, albeit sometimes with more enthusiasm than experience.

The more ancient a church the more it stands out from its neighbouring town hall, terraced cottages, pub or manor house. A Neo-Classical or Baroque church was often designed to fit a town plan and harmonise with other public and civic buildings; a Gothic church implied longevity and functional distinctiveness. So the church-building movement by its sheer scale of numbers and early preference for recreating a kind of medieval countryside church in an expanding modern town – *rus in urbe* – determined an entirely new approach to church architecture. The ICBS often simply helped an old church survive and stay standing but increasingly became part of a movement to change the total appearance and function of churches.

The architect Charles Locke Eastlake, an apologist for the Gothic Revival and the Arts & Crafts Movement, remembered from his childhood in the early 1840s some poor examples of Neo-Classical churches:

> Who does not remember the air of grim respectability which pervaded, and in some cases still pervades, the modern town church of a certain type, with its big bleak portico, its pretentious beadle, and muffin capped charity boys? Enter and notice the tall neatly grained witness-boxes and jury boxes in which the faithful are impanelled; the 'three-decker' pulpit placed in the centre of the building: the lumbering gallery which is carried round three sides of the interior on iron columns; the wizen-faced pew-opener eager for stray shillings; the earnest penitent who is inspecting the inside of his hat; the patent warming apparatus; the velvet cushions which profane the altar; the hassocks which no one kneels on; the poor-box which is always empty. Hear how the Clerk drones out the responses for a congregation which is too genteel to respond for themselves … Observe the length, the unimpeachable propriety, the overwhelming dullness of his sermon.

The origins of the church-building impetus lay in eighteenth-century philanthropy, a new social awareness, post-war shock at the impact of industrial change and a generation of influential laymen willing to commit their time and money. Their approach remained in place until the first years of Victoria's reign when a new movement informed the appearance of churches and the grants that supported them.

At 5 a.m. on 20 June 1837, William Howley, Archbishop of Canterbury, accompanied by the Lord Chamberlain, went to Kensington Palace to inform Princess Victoria that she was now queen. Howley had been archbishop during the repeal of the Test and Corporation Acts (1828), the passing of the Catholic Relief Act for the emancipation of Catholics (1829) and the passing of the Great Reform Act (1832). The bench of bishops was generally opposed to all three measures and Howley was their spokesman with an innate personal opposition to the Great Reform Act: his carriage was attacked in the streets of Canterbury. Architecture was of particular interest to him and he rebuilt his town residence in St James's Square and Fulham Palace while he was Bishop of London, and made extensive renovations to Lambeth Palace, carried out by Edward Blore from about 1828, mainly in the Gothic Revival style.

Like very many other bishops at that time, Howley was a High Churchman with Catholic beliefs but consistently anti-Roman. However, the Church as a whole had long been considered by many as passively latitudinarian or laissez-faire, taking too broad or 'low' an approach in order to encourage wider congregations. In the years after Waterloo, the High Church movement began to gather pace with laymen often setting the speed, and within the universities of Oxford and Cambridge a younger generation was flexing its muscles. In Oxford, in 1833, a movement arose for the renewal of theology, ecclesiology, sacraments and liturgical practices at the centre of the Anglican Church, which simply came to be known as the Oxford Movement, while the Cambridge Camden Society began in 1839 as a club for Cambridge undergraduates with an interest in ancient Gothic church design. Evocatively, J. Mordaunt Crook sets the scene:

> Trinity College, Cambridge, in May 1839. It is 10 o'clock at night and three undergraduates named Neale, Webb, and Boyce are trying to persuade one of their dons, Archdeacon Thorp, to become senior member of a new society. They refuse to leave until he agrees. The Cambridge Camden Society is born. J. M. Neale becomes President, Benjamin Webb Secretary, and E. J. Boyce Treasurer. Within a year they are joined by another Trinity man with influence in a much wider sphere, Beresford Hope. By 1843 the membership list includes two archbishops, sixteen bishops, thirty-one peers and M.P.s, seven deans or chancellors of dioceses, twenty-one archdeacons or rural deans, sixteen architects, and seven hundred ordinary members.

The society first collected detailed information about the architecture of parish churches across the country and in 1841 published a pamphlet, *A Few Words to Churchwardens*, summarising its ideas about the ideal modern church. In the first edition they recommended the Early English style for small buildings and Decorated or Perpendicular for larger ones but, by the third edition of 1844, the Decorated style was the overall choice. In 1841, too, Neale read his thoroughly researched *History of Pews* pamphlet to members, in which he stated: 'America has always loved pues.'

The Oxford Movement argued for the reinstatement of older Christian traditions into Anglican liturgy and theology. The principal figure in Tractarianism, the philosophy underlying the movement, was John Henry Newman, a popular Oxford priest, who was received into the Roman Catholic Church in 1845. The Tractarians introduced daily services as well as *Hymns Ancient and Modern*; the frequency of communion services was also increased. Above all ceremony and adornment were to be sought. To some extent the Tractarians were the inevitable link between the High Churchmen of the eighteenth century and the High Victorian ritualists; the ICBS drove a careful path alongside them.

The Oxford philosophy was known as Tractarianism after its publications *Tracts for the Times*, published from 1833 to 1841. In Cambridge the Camden Society, too, published relentlessly and the popularity of their first handbook led some churchwardens to seek advice on how to restore their often dilapidated buildings as restoring was not the approach taken by the ICBS. The Camden Society soon changed from enthusiastic antiquarians to architectural consultants through *The Ecclesiologist*, first published in October 1841, which reviewed over one thousand churches in its twenty-year span and doggedly attacked all buildings and architects for anything inconsistent with its view of the 'middle pointed' (i.e. Decorated). From 1845 it was largely known as the Ecclesiological Society and ICBS-funded churches did not escape its venom. *The Ecclesiologist* loathed cheaply built churches with amateurs acting as architects. Yet Thomas Rickman was heavily criticised by them in spite of his scholarship because he was a Quaker: 'he did very little … and his churches are monuments of extreme ecclesiological ignorance'. Augustus Pugin, the Gothic revivalist par excellence, was condemned because he was Roman Catholic. The preferred Cambridge Camden architect was William Butterfield, who broke many of the rules but always refused to build for Roman Catholics.

There were many points of sympathy between the Cambridge Camden Society and the ICBS, not least in the abolition of pews. The Oxford and Cambridge movements, too, had much in common in terms of doctrine but the Camden Society's bylaws forbade theological debate, leaving that to Oxford. The Camden Society was able to present

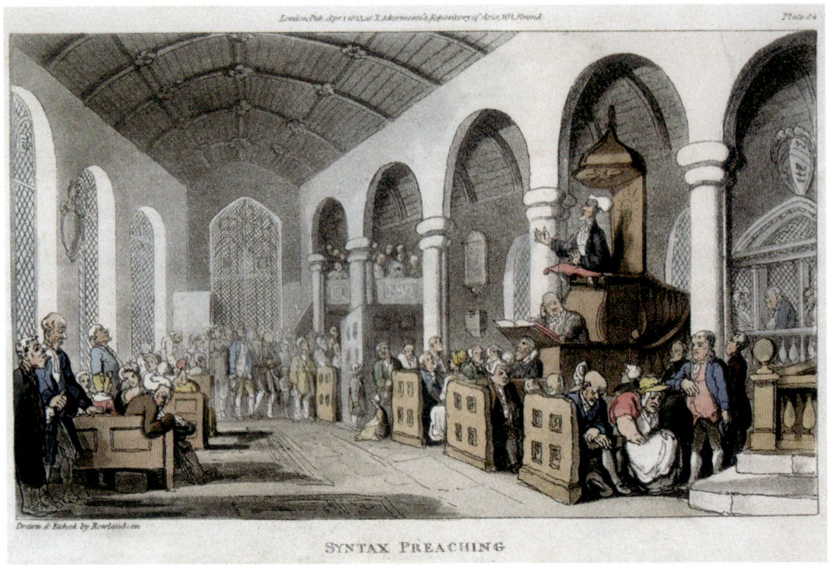

THOMAS ROWLANDSON **Syntax Preaching**, 1812
Hand-coloured etching with aquatint
Published as part of The Tour of Dr Syntax in Search of the Picturesque *(1812),*
a satire by William Combe on the fad for picturesque tourism:
'Soon a ruddy Curate came, | To whom he gravely told his name,
His rank and literary fame; | And said, as he'd been us'd to teaching,
He'd give him half an hour's preaching. | This was accepted with a smile.
And they both strutted up the aisle; | When, in due time, and with due grace,
Syntax display'd his preaching face.'

itself as solely architectural in its mission and campaigned vigorously, and successfully, for the revival of the rood screen and the chancel, which it largely achieved by the installation of choir stalls in chancels: a clever ruse to retain a traditional function.

The traditional Anglican interior had always had a pulpit for the priest to give his sermon and a reading desk for laymen to read lessons, at either side of the eastern end of the nave, and a separate chancel beyond, offering a space for the altar and reserved for the sacrament. Rood screens as a barrier between sacrament and congregation had largely been removed by the Reformation but the position of the altar had been a contentious point from the early seventeenth century when the church was thought of in terms of two spaces, keeping preaching and the sacrament separate. The eighteenth-century pulpit was often central, even in front of the altar, and formed as a 'three decker', tiered rather like a wedding and christening cake: the bottom tier was for the parish clerk, the middle for gospel readings, and the top tier was reserved for the clear delivery of the sermon by the priest alone.

The eighteenth century had seen experiment, often radical, in church layouts but by the 1820s a return to some kind of liturgical orthodoxy was attempted then overtaken by the energies of Oxford and Cambridge. They despised the type of church design that created what they saw as no more than 'preaching boxes'. Wren's carefully executed plans to deliver the sermon clearly to the multitude through soaring spaces with a high pulpit, and sounding boards to help carry the voice, were disparaged. The ICBS's support for large, plain churches was often not far removed from Wren's intention but lacked his flair.

The separation of pulpit from reading desk, each placed to either side of the chancel opening, was a vital intention of both the ICBS and the CBC. The altar was usually raised by several steps and sited in a shortened chancel, as the priest no longer conducted the sacrament privately, hidden from the congregation. One of several new, pre-Tractarian, approaches was successful at St Andrew's, Wiveliscombe, Somerset, where, in 1826, the pillars in the church were found to be out of perpendicular and the tower wobbled when the bells were rung. The county surveyor, Richard Carver, concluded that repairs would cost £3,109 whereas a new building to his Gothic design would cost £4,185. The Society gave a grant and the new St Andrew's was consecrated on 27 October 1829 with the seating capacity increased by 558 seats to 1,250. Previously, the nave, aisles and west end of the chancel had all been pewed. Carver's plan rebuilt and shortened the chancel and all seats were to face east. The pulpit and 'stranger's pew' were placed at the north side of the chancel arch and the reading desk and vicar's pew opposite them at the south. The altar stood four steps above the level of the nave. Galleries were removed except for the western one which retained its organ but an outer south aisle was added with a porch at one end and a vestry at the other.

The subject of galleries, north, south and west, was a vexed one. They were a rare feature in medieval churches but came into their own in the late seventeenth century as the site for the organ or similar instruments until Cromwell's Commonwealth banned and destroyed them. Singing

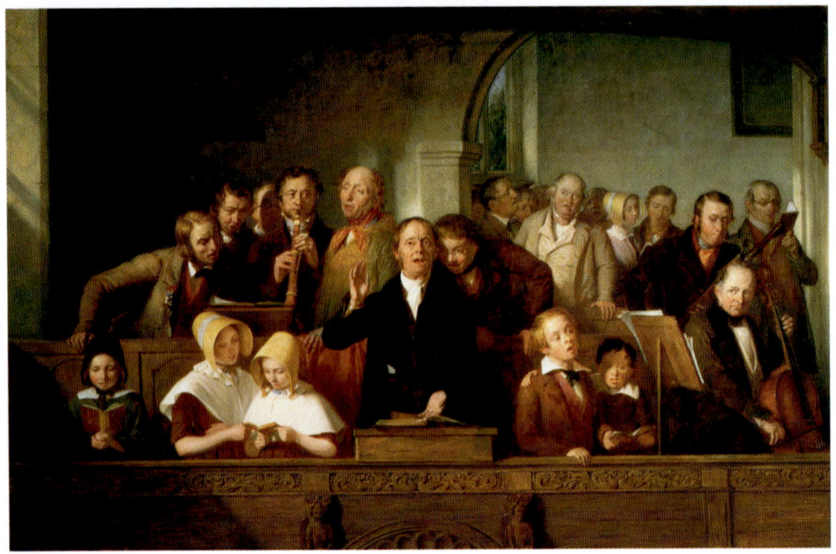

THOMAS WEBSTER, RA **A Village Choir, 1847** Oil on canvas
This work illustrates Washington Irving's 'Christmas Day', from The Sketch Book of Geoffrey Crayon *(1820), a comical and sentimental account of an old-fashioned village choir and its musicians.*

and church music were reintroduced during the Restoration period under Charles II but there was a shortage of organs, so local amateur musicians formed bands to play during services. New galleries at the west end were built for the purpose, often using wood from dismantled rood lofts and screens, and the congregation would turn to face the gallery, away from the altar, when the band played.

'West gallery' music was often recalled with nostalgia by Thomas Hardy, including a moment in *Life's Little Ironies* when the drunken choir awoke and launched into a dance tune:

> And the squire, too, came out of his pew lined wi' green baize, where lots of lords and ladies visiting at the house were worshipping along with him, and went and stood in front of the gallery, and shook his fist in the musicians' faces, saying: 'What! In this reverent edifice! What!'

Organ playing became prevalent again in the 18th century, preferred for its simplicity and solemnity, and many minstrel or music galleries were then simply used as extra seating.

The Oxford Tractarians believed that overall the Church had become too plain, architecturally and liturgically. They had less interest than the ICBS in the quantity of worshippers but were devoted to the quality of the church experience, through emotion and symbolism. While the ICBS and others influenced by Cambridge built the theatre, its stage and auditorium, the Oxford Movement provided the drama and actors. The appearance of churches was thoroughly changed and when the last issue of *The Ecclesiologist* was published in 1868 it left the Cambridge Camden Society with what it called 'the satisfaction of retiring from the field victors'.

Of course, neither the Commissioners up to 1856 nor the ICBS, before and after, were the sole builders of churches in England and Wales. Wren's churches and Queen Anne's had not stood alone either: private individuals had continued to build churches for public worship as had colleges and institutions. Acts and Letters Patent tinkered with the format of the Commission from about 1840 and, in that year, Sir Robert Inglis, the High Church, fiercely anti-Jewish and anti-Catholic MP for Oxford University, pleaded in the House for more funds for church extension:

> I have heard elsewhere, and I shall perhaps hear to-night, as an unanswerable argument against my motion, that the nation cannot afford to make the grant which I require; that the grants in 1818, and 1824, were in seasons of great financial prosperity; that I ought to wait till such return; and not select a year when the revenue is decreasing, and the public expenditure is already necessarily increased … What has been the amount of war-taxes remitted to the people in the last twenty-five years, during which, by God's providence, we have been blest with peace? My object will require a small proportion only of the wealth which has been so returned to the people … Why, the war duty on malt alone, if continued to this day, would have drawn £38,580,000 from the people; and the property-tax, which was repealed in 1816, would, if continued to 1840, have taken from the people the enormous sum of £350,827,752.

He gave the touching example of the vicar of Calverley, near Bradford, who sent a note with a petition: 'I am sorry that it is so late, and that the paper is so soiled; but it is the genuine petition of working clothiers in a small village, who left their looms to sign it.'

Radicals of all complexions had urged church reform, politically, liturgically and architecturally. Philanthropists, of whom the ICBS is the clearest example, put into action their desire to improve the lot of the impoverished clergy and expand church room for the common good and the protection of the establishment. Evangelicals, like the Clapham Sect, wanted to return to the pure gold standard of the Gospel, reaching penitents and making converts. Increasingly, and gathering momentum during Victoria's reign, there was a romantic impetus to recreate the glory of the Middle Ages or even just the seventeenth century, and a return to Catholic, but never Popish or Roman, worship. The latter medievalising group had the most lasting effect on architecture and liturgy, partly with the support of the ICBS, and to a lesser extent the CBC, which overall had the biggest impact simply through the number and spread of new or extended churches.

The ICBS was steadfast in its fundraising and grant giving even though it was not as generously supported as other church societies and, like them, depended heavily on the clergy themselves rather than the wider community for donations. As Timothy Parry says, 'Perhaps its activities lacked the romance of the great Church missionary organisations; certainly it maintained a gentlemanly modesty in the manner in which it pressed its claims for support amongst clergy and laity, together with a scrupulous integrity in the handling of any funds with which it was entrusted.'

EIGHT

'A pungent aroma of cement, fresh paint and incense': 1851–1862

Church building continued apace in early Victorian London but grants from the CBC were diminished and, in spite of a spike in income just after incorporation, the ICBS was also severely stretched and, as usual, mostly focused outside the capital. However, in 1840, a remarkable church was begun with joint ICBS and CBS support in Streatham, south London. Christ Church is a landmark on the South Circular Road and also in the history of church architecture. Described as the most original early Victorian church, it is the most important surviving work of James Wild

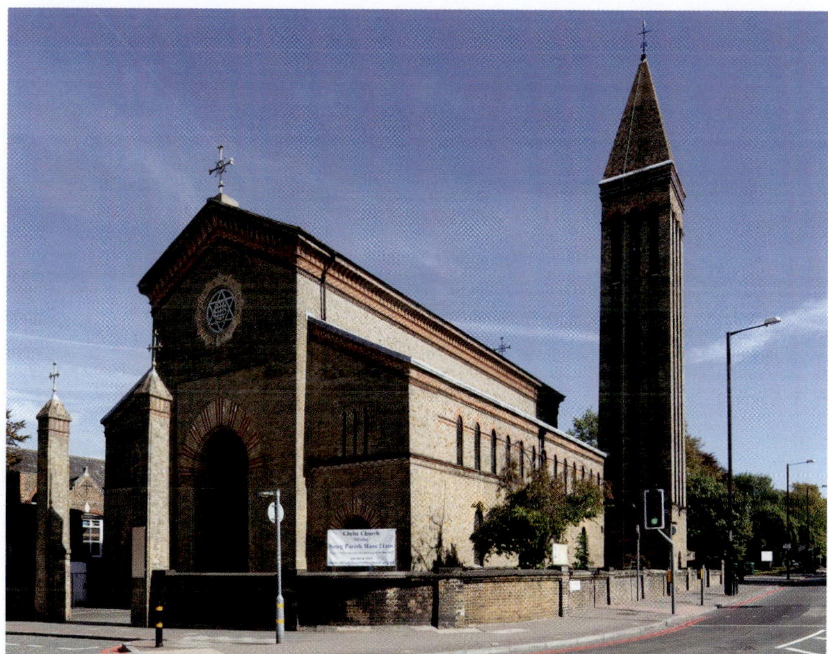

Christ Church, Streatham, London

Christ Church is a landmark on the South Circular Road and in the history of architecture. The most important surviving work of James William Wild and Owen Jones , it contains the work of later artists such as John Hayward, J.F.Bentley and Walter Crane, as well as fine Italian mosaics. It is Grade I listed and was built in 1840 with joint support from the ICBS and the CBC.

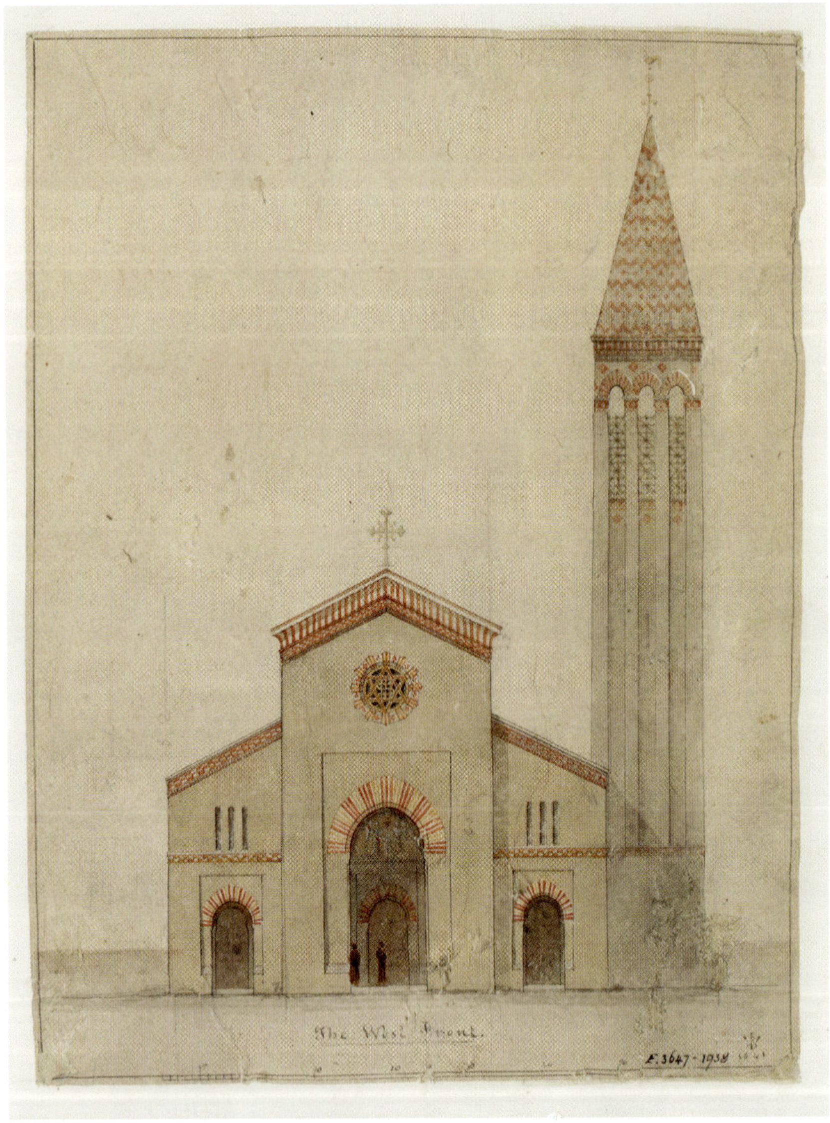

JAMES WILLIAM WILD **Christ Church, Streatham, London 1841**
Pen, ink and watercolour

Scale drawing of the west front of Christ Church by its architect J. W. Wild (1814–92).
Pevsner called it a church of impressive design and historic importance and the most
important example in England of the modern round-arched style which started in Germany.

and Owen Jones and shows influence from Ancient Egypt to the Alhambra with fine mosaics and stained glass by John Hayward, J. F. Bentley and Walter Crane. It is the first example in modern times of the use of different coloured bricks in polychrome pattern and was included in the first list of buildings of special architectural or historic interest, made in 1955; the church is now Grade I listed.

In 1843, the pragmatic Robert Peel, as Prime Minister, was looking at further ways to enhance church provision and discussed the problem with W. E. Gladstone, the leading churchman in his government, who had started his career as a High Tory and became Liberal Prime Minister for the first time in 1868. Peel finally gave £600,000 in Exchequer bills from the ever-giving Queen Anne's Bounty to the Ecclesiastical Commission for new churches in new parishes throughout the country through the New Parishes Act, sub-titled 'An Act to make better Provision for the Social Care of Populous Parishes'. Although these 'Peel districts' very soon ran out of money, anyone, layman or clergyman, could now suggest the founding of a new church, but the result was that new divisions of a district created a patchwork of smaller and smaller parishes with bigger churches and fewer endowments. There was also a new emphasis during the 1850s on the importance of open air and tent meetings, anything to spread the Word rather than having to wait for a permanent building.

In 1851, in response to a papal bull which resulted in twelve new Roman Catholic dioceses in Britain, Charles Blomfield, now Bishop of London, created the Metropolitan Churches' Fund, with the support of Joshua Watson, in 1836. Having untangled the ecclesiastical revenues within his diocese the bishop began to target London landowners for contributions in the way that rural parishes had done. It fell short of its target of fifty churches but had a successful offshoot thanks to William Cotton, now Governor of the Bank of England and an ICBS trustee in 1830, whose father Joseph had chaired the first ever committee meeting of the Society. Together Blomfield and Cotton created the Bethnal Green Fund (1839–50), building ten churches independently and without ICBS help.

Blomfield then introduced the London Diocesan Church Building Society in 1854, which supported parochial extension, ensuring decent parsonages and schools, too, declaring that men were more important than buildings. However, he also aimed to provide one church and one clergyman for every community of 3,000 people. Blomfield was buried in All Saints, Fulham in 1857, a church which an ICBS grant had helped extend in 1840. In 1880, the church was replaced by one designed by his son, Sir Arthur Blomfield. Between 1866 and 1909 the Society helped to fund nine new churches in Fulham.

The Georgian pattern of new churches completing residential schemes in middle-class areas was repeated in newly developed parts of Victoria's London, especially Kensington, which had become fashionable after William IV moved his court there. St James's, Norlands received grants from both the Commission and the Society. Designed in the Gothic style of the twelfth century by Lewis Vulliamy, in 1844–5, galleries were added five years later; the ICBS supported the enlargement of the church in 1876 and repairs again in 1972. St Matthias's, Earls Court (1868–72) was another ICBS-funded church, with a stealthy plan by a controversial vicar. Samuel Haines was passionately High Church and out of favour with his bishop and he started building his new church before he had raised the money. First he erected an temporary iron-framed building then a permanent chancel with, two years later, a wooden-ceilinged nave and aisles. The architect was J. H. Hakewill, from the ICBS advisory committee. The builders insisted on bonds guaranteeing payment from twenty private patrons of the church as fundraising was going so slowly and Haines took out life insurance as collateral with the premiums paid from the church-building funds. He insisted on side entrances to avoid 'the gathering of idle persons around the entrance'. The temporary church was dismantled and removed to another site which Haines was also promoting. His services were both extremely fashionable and fashionably extreme and, in 1873, while building work was not quite complete, W. G. Grace married Agnes Day there shortly before embarking on a cricket tour to Australia. Grace's biographer Richard Tomlinson evokes the 'pungent aroma of cement, fresh paint and incense' as the ceiling of the chancel was still being altered and notes that Grace brought his own preacher as Haines's sermons were notoriously long.

The temporary church burned down so Haines then turned his attention to what would eventually become St Cuthbert's, Philbeach Gardens, supported

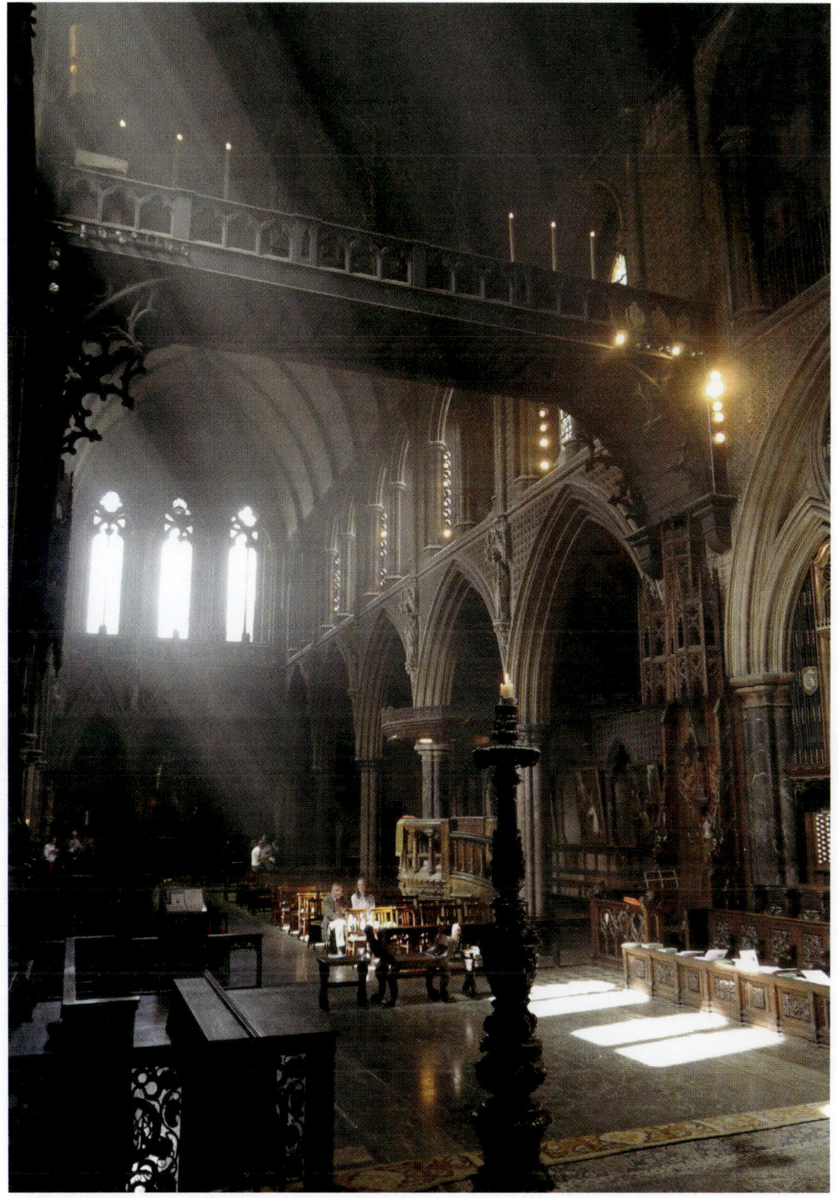

St Cuthbert's, Earl's Court

St Cuthbert's was designed by Hugh Roumieu Gough and supported as a new church by the ICBS. Plain and elegant, it became a canvas for the later elaborate interior (and events) overseen by its vicar Henry Westall. Further Arts and Crafts embellishments were made by William Bainbridge Reynolds between the 1890s and 1930s.

by the ICBS. Haines's former curate Henry Westall took over the project in spite of a battle with a local incumbent who demanded recompense for the loss of a lucrative part of his parish. Westall invoked a private patronage act and finally succeed in building what was often known by some of its congregation as 'the dustbin'. Finance was difficult and slow and a second temporary church stood alongside the building site which the Survey of London later compared to a Swiss chalet perched on a mountain beside a deep ravine. The finished church seated about 950; the cost of its construction was about £11,000, of which £8,000 had been borrowed from the London and County Bank. This version of the church was comparatively plain and elegant, a canvas for the elaborate decoration planned for the future. The church rapidly gained a fashionable and flourishing High Church congregation, known for Anglo-Catholic ritual, and in 1898 became notorious. On Good Friday a Protestant agitator called John Kensit attended the service of the Adoration of the Cross. *The Survey of London: Volume 42, Kensington Square to Earl's Court*, evokes the moment:

> Kensit with some of his followers duly attended this service, and waited until his turn came to kneel down and kiss the cross. Instead, he seized the crucifix, and, holding it aloft, said in a clear and distinct voice, 'I denounce this idolatry in the Church of England; may God help me.' A scrimmage ensued, and Kensit and his supporters were with difficulty ejected from the church, to cries variously reported in court as 'Murder. I die a martyr for the Protestant faith', 'Latimer', 'Ridley', 'My bonnet', and (according to *The Guardian*) 'Hallelujah, my wife … Hallelujah, my wife', 'Hallelujah, my hat'. Kensit was charged at Kensington Magistrates Court for behaving in a riotous and indecent manner, found guilty, but acquitted on appeal, though without costs … It became Kensit's fate to be depicted on one of the misericords in the chancel, with protruding asses' ears.

The development of Victorian city churches which attracted a fashionable congregation, now easily able to travel out of their locality to follow an idiosyncratic or glamorous preacher, began to break up parish loyalty. This was a familiar pattern for the Methodists but new to the Church of England. St Matthias's was merged with St Cuthbert's due to a diminished congregation and finally demolished in 1958.

In its last few years, the CBC mostly supervised church extensions, discussed new parish formations, looked at pew rentals and decided on sites for churches, parsonages and burial grounds; similar, in most regards, to the approach of the ICBS. Joshua Watson remained closely involved with both bodies and their administrations. By 1845, CBC funds were virtually exhausted although a few expensive churches were grant-aided including St Paul's, Wilton Place, in Belgravia, London, with 540 seats perhaps meant for the servants of the immediate vicinity. The Commission's term of office ran out in 1848; a ten-year extension was hoped for but it was only granted a further five. The 'attached architects' had been disbanded in 1832 and from 1848 it was decided to rely on reports made by local surveyors with regard to churches seeking grant aid from both the Church Building Commission and the Ecclesiastical Commission in the new Peel districts. The two commissions were drawing closer together to each other as well as to the ICBS, whose grants were now even paid through the CBC. The CBC and ICBS jointly approved plans and attached their physical seal of approval before giving grants from 1851 onwards. Gradually, this co-operation developed until neither would accept a plan if unacceptable to the other. Then they agreed that whoever received a plan first would only pass it on when satisfied. In 1851, a new Act enabled the Commission to forego pew rents if a satisfactory endowment was in place: another ICBS objective had been achieved. In 1856, an Act finally gave CBC its final extension of six months, after thirty-eight years.

The CBC's last church in London was All Saints, Haggerston, designed in 1855–6 in the Gothic style by Philip Hardwick, best known as architect of the now demolished Euston Arch and Euston's twin station, Birmingham Curzon Street, the oldest surviving railway terminal building in the world. Neatly, Hardwick had also been responsible for one of the earliest CBC churches, part of the Neo-Classical Marylebone group, Christ Church, Cosway Street (1822–4). The Church Building Commission continued to function until 1 January 1857, when it was absorbed into the Ecclesiastical Commission, which took on its task of parish division and establishing scales of pew rental.

In 1851, a census of religious practice had been taken to establish attendance at Christian religious services in England and Wales. Reports were collected from local ministers of the church, who reported attendance at their services on Sunday 30 March. It was instigated and organised by Major George Graham as registrar-general and he sought educational as well as religious statistics that year. His brother, Sir James Graham, had failed as Peel's Home Secretary to secure a Bill on factory education in 1843 and he realised the importance of information for the provision of education and religious worship.

There were three separate forms issued: one to the clergy of the Church of England, one to Nonconformists, Catholics and Jews, and one to Quaker meeting houses. The clergy were asked for the date of construction of their church or chapel of ease, if erected after 1800; the number of sittings available for worship; the number of people at morning, afternoon and evening services that Sunday; the number of Sunday school pupils at the same times; and the average attendances over a stated period for both congregations and children. There were additional questions on church endowments and other sources of income. The forms sent to Nonconformist ministers did not ask for information on income but asked if the building was used exclusively as a place of worship. Those sent to Quakers were similar but asked for the measurement of the building and the estimated number of seats. The project was organised by a 28-year-old barrister, Horace Mann, later the secretary to the Civil Service Commission, who rejected the idea of asking for individual religious affiliations,

> partly because [collecting the reports] had a less inquisitorial aspect,
> – but especially because it was considered that the outward conduct
> of persons furnishes a better guide to their religious state than can be
> gained by merely vague professions. In proportion, it was thought,
> as people truly are connected with particular sects or churches,
> will be their activity in raising buildings in which to worship and
> their diligence in afterwards frequenting them; but where there is
> an absence of such practical regard for a religious creed, but little
> weight can be attached to any purely formal acquiescence. This
> inquiry, therefore, was confined to obvious facts relating to two
> subjects. 1. The amount of ACCOMMODATION which the people
> have provided for religious worship; and 2. The number of persons, as
> ATTENDANTS, by whom this provision is made use of.

The published figures included the overall number of places of worship for England and Wales: 34,467 buildings providing some 10.2 million sittings, of which the Anglicans provided 51.9 per cent. These were enough to seat 58 per cent of the population but Mann noted the imbalance of provision, especially in the industrial towns of the north of England: '…a sadly formidable proportion of the English people are habitual neglecters of the public ordinances of religion'. Some 10,896,066 out of a population of 17.9 million attended a Christian church: among them 5,292,551 attended Church of England services, 5,169,727 other Protestant services, and 383,630 Catholic services. The tables attached to the report provide detailed information on each of thirty-two different Protestant denominations including nine different types of Methodists. Owing to the controversy this census attracted, it has not since been repeated.

The dynamism of the Nonconformist movement is apparent from its construction of over 14,000 new chapels in England and Wales during the first half of the nineteenth century. At the same time the Roman Catholics built 352 churches and the Church of England added 2,292 to its existing stock of around 10,000. The effect of the ICBS and CBC is evident in these statistics as only 152 of these are shown to have been built in the first two decades of the century.

The ICBS continued raising and allocating funds, being indispensable: a Royal Commission on the sub-division of parishes in 1853 had reported that there was still an immediate need for 600 new churches. Yet, in 1854, the royal letter prerogative was withdrawn and ICBS fundraising was badly affected: the letters had accounted for more than half its income. Between 1828 and 1851 it had received £258,009 as a direct result but the letters were seen as means of favouring High Church societies, representing too close a link between Church and Crown. In 1855, archbishops and bishops sent out their own letters of 'recommendation' and, after that, some bishops did persist but too few. There were a few exceptional donations or bequests: 'munificent' was always the ICBS word. Charles Hoare's generosity was consistent and regular, like the Society itself; he gave £100 each year for twelve years, beyond his subscription. The largest donors were Lord Farnborough, Mrs Mary Chandler and George Davenport, each giving or bequeathing £2,000 in the 1830s.

Charles Long, Baron Farnborough (1760–1838), was Beeston Long's son (see page 31) and an important patron of the arts. From 1802 he was the chairman of a 'committee of taste' to supervise plans for monuments to the heroes of the Napoleonic wars. Howard Colvin in the *Oxford Dictionary of National Biography* confirms his importance: 'Whether it was the appropriate order for the façade of the privy council offices in Whitehall (1824) or the need for a fig-leaf on the heroic statue honouring the Duke of Wellington that had been subscribed for by the ladies of Great Britain (1821), Long was sure to be consulted.' The Prince Regent relied on his judgement. His wealth was insufficient to allow him to be a major patron or collector in his own right, but as a minister and MP, he was able to use his influence to further cultural causes such as the purchase of the Elgin marbles and the establishment of the National Gallery. When an Institution of British Architects was first proposed it was in the form of an open letter to Farnborough.

Mary Chandler is a rare female presence in the story of the ICBS. She was almost certainly a cousin to William Cotton and heiress to a fortune from Jamaica, like the Long family. George Davenport of Lime Street, Lincoln's Inn was a different case. He was from a Nonconformist family and was believed by some to have lost his mind. He was convinced that Satan was taking over the British Isles – with the exception of the Isle of Man, so he rushed there to found a church and become its vicar, giving £6,000 for the purpose. During a few months in 1838 he gave away a further £15,700 for religious purposes including £2,000 to the ICBS. He promised £1,000 towards Holy Trinity, a new church for Ashby-de-la-Zouch in Leicestershire, but, as his mental state became a case for the House of Lords, some of his generosity was curtailed, including that important £1,000. An advertisement in the *Derby Mercury* on 17 June 1840 announced 'a bazaar, under the august patronage of Queen Adelaide, of useful and ornamental fancy work for September of that year to raise funds for the building of the church'. The CBC gave a grant and, quite rightly, the ICBS gave a larger one.

London-based philanthropy came from the wealthy elite, usually those with a house in the country, who visited their local church in 'Town' during the Season. Sarah Few has pointed out that London contained an

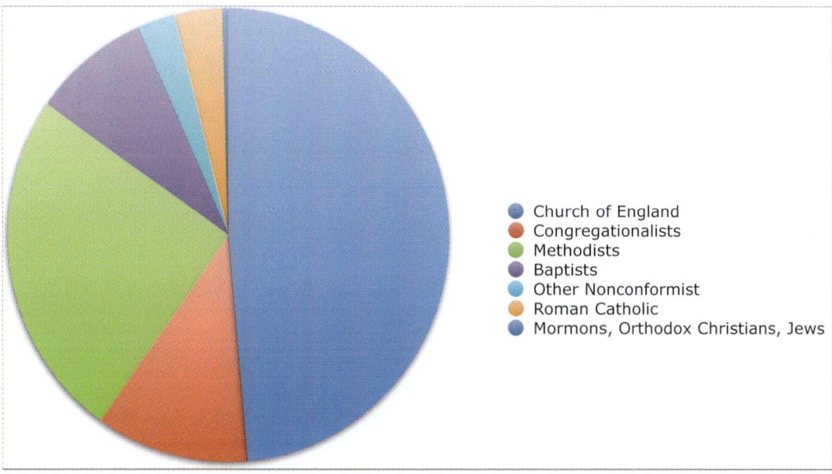

Attendants at public worship on Sunday 30 March 1851

unrivalled concentration of wealthy Anglicans employed in professions and industries such as finance and brewing, like the Hoare family and Joshua Watson. A modest reserve had been built up for the ICBS but, by 1864, it was almost finished except for a generous bequest from John Hines of Devon of £14,530 to be used partly in his own county and otherwise as the Society saw fit.

The ICBS, however, seems to have found a new resolve and outlook. In 1862, it began to publish the *Church Builder: A quarterly journal of the work of the Incorporated Church Building Society and of other works of church extension*, which listed newly built or restored churches with the date of their consecration, the name of the architect employed and a summary of the architectural work carried out. It also carried editorial on the widest range of church subjects: stained glass, mission houses, church restoration, gravestones, churches in towns, 'Handsome Churches', brickworks in the Middle Ages and 'The Church in the Collieries', together with illustrations and poems. It listed grants, sermons and meetings in aid of the ICBS. The editor remained anonymous but articles were often signed by initials.

The impetus might have been from the then secretary, the Reverend George Ainslie (1803–1871), son of Sir Robert Sharpe Ainslie, Baronet, of Park Street, Mayfair. Sir Robert Ainslie was a mysterious character, briefly an MP and diplomat, who inherited the baronetcy from an uncle. As the

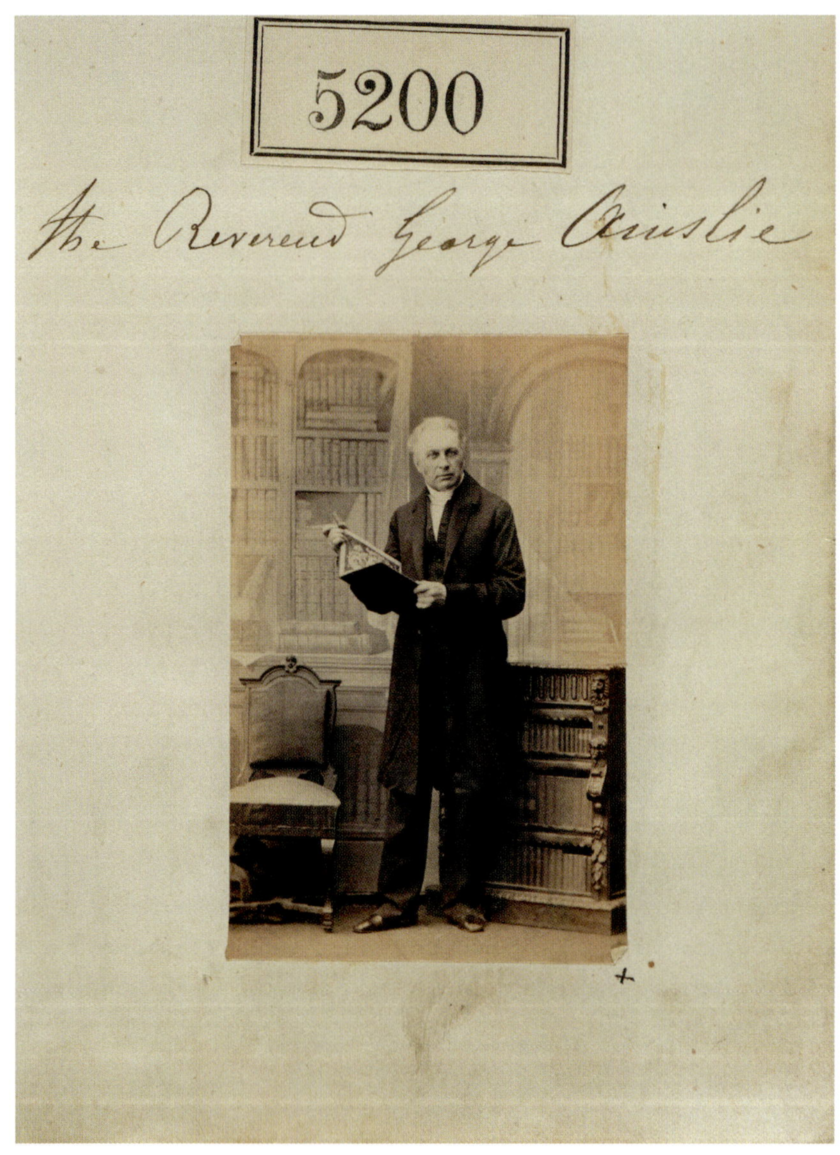

CAMILLE SILVY **Portrait of George Ainslie, 1861**
Albumen print

A photograph made for a carte de visite not long after the Reverend George Ainslie (1803–71) became secretary to the ICBS and a year before the Society began to publish its **Church Builder** *magazine, which continued until 1916.*

title died out with him, it is usually reported that he had no surviving male heirs. However, he actually left three sons and four daughters, although he and his wife did not marry until 1834 when George, the eldest child, was thirty. George became a priest in 1829, first at South Willingham in Lincolnshire then at St Peter's, Walworth, Soane's first Commissioners' church. He then, briefly, became incumbent at St Mary Magdalene, Barkway, Hertfordshire, under circumstances which seem to have caused him some distress judging by a sermon to his previous parishioners in 1837; his irregular family circumstances may have lain behind this. Finally, he moved back to London to take care of St Philip's, Granville Square, Clerkenwell, from 1850 to 1854.

Three years later, on the death of his father, Ainslie was appointed secretary of the Society, a position he kept for thirteen years until his own death. He never married and lived with his family in Mayfair until his father died, whereupon he moved to a much more modest address in Pimlico, half an hour's walk from the ICBS offices at 7 Whitehall. He was portrayed in 1861 by the fashionable French photographer Camille Silvy as a dignified scholar in a *carte de visite*. Ainslie was a distant relation of the Hoare family; his paternal grandmother was niece to Charles Hoare, the first ICBS treasurer, and the Society seems to have given him a stability that his early years lacked and the church could not provide. His brother Canon Robert Ainslie (1812–95) pursued a more orthodox clerical career, retiring as vicar of St James's, Grimsby and a minor canon of Lincoln Cathedral in 1879. A third brother, Charles, was an architect.

The voice of the ICBS through the quarterly was less prescriptive than its own previous 'Suggestions' and now altogether more genial and confident. The *Church Builder* was published by Rivington's, long associated with church literature, until 1916.

NINE

'To fulfil the ideal of the English parish church':
to 1900; the Hoare and Scott families

From 1857 onwards, the ICBS had a very different role from that of its first forty years. Many of its earliest champions had died either in the 1830s or, in the case of the tireless Charles Hoare and Joshua Watson, in 1851 and 1855 respectively. On the last day of 1856, the CBC was enfolded into the Ecclesiastical Commission so from January 1857, the ICBS stood alone. Archibald Tait also replaced Charles Blomfield as Bishop of London that year. The new secretary, George Ainslie had no connections, apart from distant cousinage to the Hoare family, with the original founders so, in its fortieth year, the ICBS achieved independence and full maturity. It also received a rather remarkable gift.

In May 1857, the Prussian consul to Britain passed on a letter from the King of Prussia's architect, Friedrich August Stüler, addressed to the Reverend Thomas Bowdler, secretary to the ICBS, who had in fact died the previous year. The letter came before the board of the Society in July 1857.

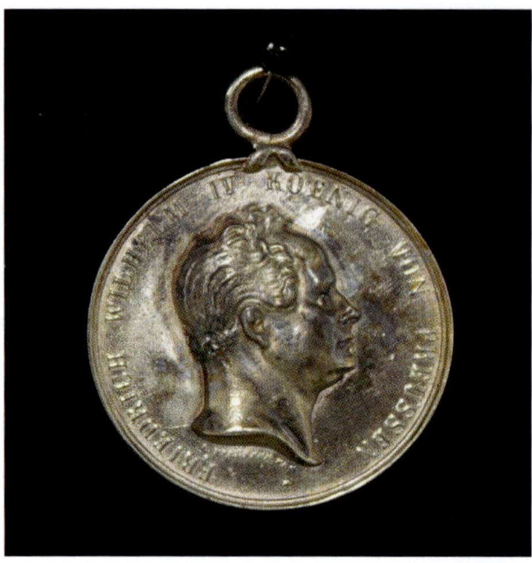

CHRISTOPH CARL PFEUFFER
Gold medal, 1850s
Now known as the King of Prussia Medal, it was first presented to the ICBS in 1857 by Friedrich Wilhelm IV, King of Prussia, a passionate and committed patron of architecture. Today, the National Churches Trust, with the Ecclesiastical Architects and Surveyors Association, presents it annually to the winner of a competition for 'innovative, high quality church conservation or repair work projects'.

Stüler was a very distinguished architect, a pupil of Schinkel, and had just completed his masterpiece, the Neues Museum in Berlin. He was commanded by King Friedrich Wilhelm IV, a passionate and committed patron of architecture, to express thanks to the ICBS for some architectural plans and drawings that he had received 'showing the very satisfactory activity of the Society'. He enclosed a gold medal 'to be presented by the Society at its own discretion in the name of his Majesty to the Architect whose exertions may have been most conducive to its success'. It was clear from the rest of the letter that Stüler had either recently visited London or had wider correspondence with someone in the ICBS. At the time of writing he was involved in the design of three churches in Prussia and the completion of the Gothic cathedral of Cologne, a particularly important project for the King.

Even though a royal gold medal was on offer to celebrate its achievements the ICBS board still looked long and deeply into the mouth of this gift horse. They discovered a 'communication' from a Mr Teulon about plans that Bowdler had suggested be sent to Prussia and the board postponed discussion yet again to find out what this all meant. Samuel Sanders Teulon was an architect, close to both George Gilbert Scott and Ewan Christian and therefore very well known to the ICBS, but the committee had no idea which plans had been sent or why. Finally, in December 1857, they carefully stated that 'the Board cannot admit that there exists any claim on the Society for the expenses of the same' and resolved to ask Bowdler's executors if the board should follow the King's wishes. Almost a year after the letter was sent it was decided to award the medal, at some point, as there appeared to be no quid pro quo or hidden financial problem.

However, in June 1857 Bernard Hubeler, the consul, wrote also to the Reverend F. F. Stooke, honorary secretary of the London Diocesan Church Building Society, in Pall Mall. Hubeler had been in correspondence with Mr Silk (another official there) the previous June and had received 'further drawings' from a Mr Gough (almost certainly the architect Alexander Dick Gough). In return, another gold medal was sent to the LDCBS to be awarded to an architect in the King's name. Sadly, Friedrich Wilhelm suffered a stroke the same year.

The medal had been designed by Christoph Carl Pfeuffer, who worked at the Royal Mint in Prussia for twenty years. It seems to have been inspired by a medal designed by Benjamin Wyon that Friedrich Wilhelm himself had received on a visit to England in 1842 for the christening of the future Edward VII, for whom the King stood as sponsor (or royal godfather). This visit was a tricky diplomatic matter but finally Prussian politicians were persuaded that the King would take the opportunity to promote, along with Christian von Bunsen, the Prussian ambassador, and the Archbishop of Canterbury, his pet idea of turning the Prussian Church Anglican. There was also a parallel plan to create an Anglican bishopric in Jerusalem with the support of the London Society for Promoting Christianity Amongst the Jews (see page 40).

Naturally, christening gifts were exchanged between the royal cousins and it is possible that the medal given to Friedrich Wilhelm was one later mounted into a small box and returned to Edward VII by Kaiser Wilhelm II in 1909. The King gave a set of vases and a magnificent Shield of Faith to the baby prince. He also presented one of his own medals for arts and science to Wyon, who had designed the Great Seals for George IV, William IV and Victoria. Stüler, too, is known to have been in England in 1842, possibly travelling with the King or sent later, specifically looking at cast-iron buildings. Presumably his research would have included the iron churches built in Liverpool by Thomas Rickman in the 1820s.

Having languished, unused, in a drawer at the ICBS for over a century, the medal is now awarded annually as the King of Prussia's Award for the best repair or conservation work. The presentation is made, fittingly, by Prince Nicolas von Preussen, a direct descendant of the donor, Kaiser Wilhelm.

In 1859, Charles Darwin published *The Origin of the Species* and rocked the traditional Christian world. More prosaically, but with a modernising eye, a sub-committee in the same year looked into ICBS finances and from then on the category of trustee was abandoned and replaced by a rule that stated that four committee members would be appointed as signatories to any cheque.

THE HOARE FAMILY

The Hoare family provided nine of the ICBS treasurers between 1818 and 2012, an astonishing continuity of service. Charles Hoare, the first treasurer of the ICBS, was one of the four ICBS trustees for thirty-three years until his death in 1851 and over the years gave one of the largest personal donations.

Hoares is the oldest bank in the United Kingdom and the world's fourth oldest bank, founded in 1672 by Sir Richard Hoare. The Hoares, as High Church Anglicans, had already participated in 1698 in the founding of the Society for the Propagation of Christian Knowledge (where six members of the family were treasurers until 1841). They were also high Tory and close to the new administration under Edward Harley. It was natural, therefore, that both Sir Richard and his son 'Good' Henry be elected Commissioners in 1711 to build Queen Anne's fifty new churches financed by a tax on coal.

Henry demonstrated his banker's prudence in reducing the price paid to the proprietor of the Three Cups Inn in Holborn for land for a new church from £2,200 to £1,900. He also succeeded in preventing Nicholas Hawksmoor from charging his habitual high fees for the new church of St Giles in the Fields, in London. In his place was employed the then unknown Henry Flitcroft, who built a competent church and went on to become the Hoare family architect, designing buildings for them at Stourhead, Barn Elms, Boreham and Clapham.

Charles Hoare was also actively involved in architectural projects. In 1799, he bought an estate at Luscombe in Devon where he employed John Nash to build a house, Thomas Chippendale the younger to provide the furniture and Humphrey Repton to design the garden. Charles was the main force in the rebuilding of the Bank's offices in Fleet Street in 1829 ('very restrained' as Pevsner says) and took an active interest in St Dunstan's in the West, the church directly opposite the bank. It had escaped the Fire of London but in a poor state and was rebuilt from 1831 by John Shaw, who designed an original octagonal church in the Gothic style, facing north–south, set back to allow road widening and with a fine tower copied from the Boston 'Stump'. Finance was provided by a private Act of Parliament that taxed all parishioners, regardless of faith, and from bank loans. No ICBS grant was sought.

Hoares were bankers to the ICBS for nearly 200 years, from the Society's inception; the full detail of the Society's account, handwritten in copperplate, can be consulted in a series of leather-bound ledgers still kept at Fleet Street. Henry Hoare was treasurer of the ICBS from 1852, son of William Henry Hoare, who had been the first treasurer of the Church Missionary Society. Henry believed strongly in the necessity for reform in all aspects of church administration. As a child he shared lessons with Samuel Wilberforce (his father, William Wilberforce, was Henry's godfather), who later became Bishop of Oxford. Known as 'Soapy Sam', Bishop Wilberforce was one of the greatest public speakers of his day but the nickname derives from a comment by Benjamin Disraeli that the bishop's manner was 'unctuous, oleaginous, saponaceous'. He is probably best remembered today for his deep opposition to Charles Darwin's theory of evolution.

Henry Hoare invested much time and money in successfully reviving Convocation, a mechanism, fallen into disuse, through which all clergy in the provinces of Canterbury and York assembled to debate and vote as a democratic counterbalance to the power of the bishops. This was finally, after 1,000 hours in meetings over four years and seven volumes of correspondence, achieved in 1861 and a few years later parodied in Arthur Featherstone Marshall's *The Comedy of Convocation of the English Church* through characters which include Deans Blunt, Pliable, Primitive, Pompous and Critical, and Archdeacons Jolly, Theory and Chasuble.

Henry's single partner at the Bank, his cousin Peter, was equally religious and built two chapels for his own use, one in the country and one at his London estate in Beckenham. He also financed the building of a new church in Beckenham. He, however, supported the bishops and disapproved strongly of any attempt to fetter their power. Despite (or perhaps because of) being married to two sisters, the cousins were unable to reconcile their differences on religious and other subjects to the extent that they agreed that the Bank would best be managed by each of them running it separately for six months of the year.

Henry's own chosen London church was St Martin in the Fields, where he left his mark in the form of a new school, a mission chapel and a revolutionary 'free' Sunday afternoon service to encourage those without the means to pay pew rents to come to church. Henry also financed other Anglican initiatives such as Cuddesdon Theological College, founded by Samuel Wilberforce in 1853 to train Oxford and Cambridge graduates. Henry's old college, St John's, Cambridge, employed Sir George Gilbert Scott, better and later known as Sir Gilbert Scott, to replace its medieval chapel and master's lodge with buildings more fitting to the nineteenth-century. Scott proposed a French thirteenth-century design but Henry found the spike on the crossing effeminate and agreed to pay for its replacement by an English-style stone tower. Henry was mortally injured in 1866 when he hit his head on a tree while leaning out of a train on his way to Cambridge to see progress.

Henry's younger brother William Henry Hoare, who was a fellow at St John's, wrote a number of theological works including *Outlines of Ecclesiastic History before the Reformation* and William Henry's son Henry William Hoare wrote *The Evolution of the English Bible – A Historical Sketch of the Successive Versions from 1382 to 1885*, still one of the best-known works in the country on the subject. His scholarship is leavened by a ready wit. He describes the Geneva Bible of 1560 as a 'Calvinist manifesto; the characteristic distaste for all forms of recreation and amusement, which comes out so curiously in the heading above St Mark's account of the murder of the Baptist, "the inconvenience of dancing"'.

A second Henry Hoare, son of the ICBS treasurer with the same name and treasurer himself until 1873, was a rather different character. He was obliged to retire from the Bank in 1874 following losses sustained in unsuccessful speculation in US railway stocks, land in New Zealand and various other ventures, not helped by the 1873 financial crisis. Despite financial support from the family he was finally declared bankrupt in 1891. Earlier, on his father's death, only part of the £5,000 cost of the St John's tower in Cambridge had been paid. Henry offered to continue payments on condition that a friend should be given the living of Staplehurst in Kent, near where he lived. The fellows declined, considering that the 'purchase of livings' was the sin of simony. Henry, therefore, ceased further funding. As a result, the college had difficulty finishing the tower, which to this day has yet to be equipped with bells.

THE SCOTT FAMILY

Like the Hoares, to whom they were later related through marriage, the Scott dynasty played a limited hand with their chosen Christian names. Thomas Scott spawned a family that produced a large number of architects and an even greater number of Anglican priests. His three sons were all priests. The eldest, John, was vicar of St Mary's, Hull, followed in the same church by his own son and grandson and resulting in the pub opposite being called the Three John Scotts. Thomas Scott was a vicar himself and a prolific biblical commentator. He became the first secretary of the Church Missionary Society. His final parish was at Aston Sandford in Buckinghamshire, where his sermons attracted such large congregations that a tent had to be erected outside the church. He died in 1821.

One of his grandsons was George Gilbert Scott (1811–78). Unlike his elder brothers, both of whom went to Cambridge and later entered the church, Gilbert Scott was not perceived as clever enough to go to university. Money was tight and his father, to supplement his own stipend, ran a small private academy for young men wishing to enter the Church of England. In his early career Gilbert designed many workhouses and also Reading gaol. His first church, designed for his uncle Samuel King at Flaunden in Buckinghamshire, was part financed by the ICBS, which would contribute to several of his later church designs. He went on to design many iconic buildings, including the Midland Grand Hotel at St Pancras Station, the Albert Memorial in Kensington Gardens, the Foreign and Commonwealth Office and Glasgow University.

Gilbert Scott ran a large professionally staffed office, the biggest in Europe and then a novelty in the architectural profession. This enabled him to handle a multitude of commissions at the same time (103 during 1867 alone) and to train a large number of young architects including G. E. Street, G. F. Bodley, John Micklethwaite and his own two sons, John Oldrid and George Junior.

As one of Britain's most prolific architects he suffered during his lifetime much criticism. Palmerston, when at last Prime Minister, was able to impose a Classical idiom on Whitehall after a decade of opposition to Gilbert's designs; other proponents of Gothic felt that he had betrayed the purity of his style. William Morris and fellow Pre-Raphaelites founded the

Society for the Protection of Ancient Buildings as a reaction against his over-restoration of Tewkesbury Abbey and John Ruskin refused the RIBA's gold medal while Gilbert was its president.

His son George Gilbert Scott Junior (1839–97) was often known as 'Middle Scott', as two of his sons, Giles and Adrian, became architects themselves. George Junior's output was small and a number of his major works were destroyed but his son Giles considered him 'a genius – a far better architect than my grandfather'. 'Middle Scott' and two other leading late Victorian church architects both trained by Gilbert Scott Senior, George Frederick Bodley and Thomas Garner, co-founded Watts & Co. in 1874 to design ecclesiastical furnishings, wallpaper and vestments. This was a sensitive year for such a company as it saw the passing of the Public Worship Regulation Act, by which clergy could be imprisoned (and five indeed were) for improper use of ritual and ornamentation such as candles. His father's substantial inheritance in 1878 enabled him to provide capital for this venture but its involvement in 'trade' forced him to resign from the RIBA.

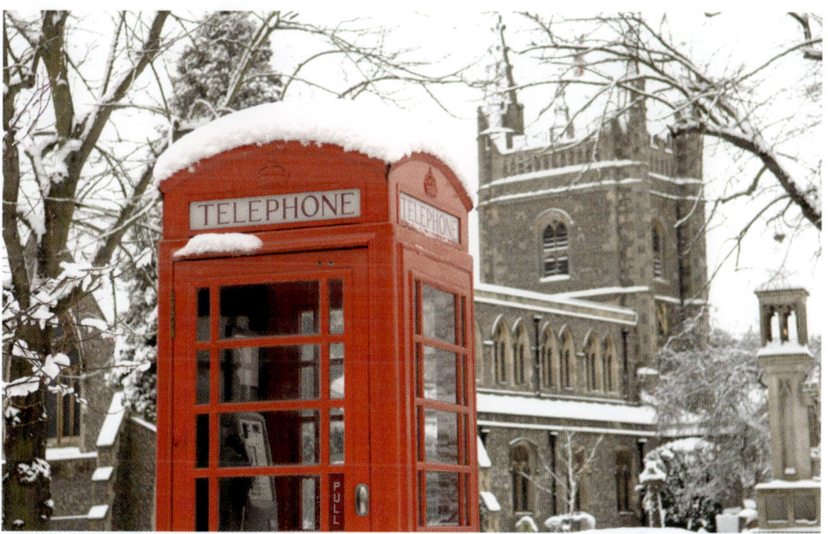

A red phone box outside St Mary's, Beaconsfield, Buckinghamshire

The church was given a grant by the ICBS for enlargement in 1868. The iconic telephone box was designed in 1924 by Sir Giles Gilbert Scott (1880–1960) while he was trustee of Sir John Soane's Museum. Scott's design was in a classical style, the curved top of which is reminiscent of the mausoleum Soane designed for himself in the churchyard at St Pancras Old Church, London.

George Junior had a strong sense of aesthetics, not only in buildings, wall coverings and furniture but also in music, apparel and even humans. At a dinner in 1871, he dressed in 'black knee breeks, black silk stockings, high-heeled shoes with large buckles, blue coat, yellow vest, white neck cloth with stiffener and frilled shirt'. In his later years he was apparently to be seen with his architect's dividers seeking to establish the measurements of the perfect female form.

In 1880 he became a Roman Catholic, a step out of keeping for a member of such an austere evangelical family, which obliged him to relinquish several of his architectural commissions. Three years later his unstable behaviour caused him to be confined to the Bethlem lunatic hospital, from which he escaped through the laundry window and made his way to Rouen. His wife and brothers had had him certified of unsound mind in Britain, but the French authorities judged otherwise, which led George to enquire, 'where in crossing the channel do I lose my wits?' Returning to Britain, he took to drink and was intermittently interned. The family went to live in Sussex, and his loyal pupil Temple Moore and younger brother Oldrid completed outstanding commissions. He died in the Midland Hotel, designed by his father, where he had taken up permanent residence.

Sir Giles Gilbert Scott (1880–1960) recalled he only met his father twice in George's troubled life. From an early age, his mother decided that Giles and his brother Adrian were to become architects and took them 'steeplechasing' on bicycles around the Sussex countryside. Giles was articled to Temple Moore and, in 1902, won a competition to build an Anglican cathedral in Liverpool. When the committee learned of the decision to employ an inexperienced 22-year-old Roman Catholic, they imposed Bodley, one of the assessors, as joint architect. This was an unhappy partnership that ended with Bodley's death in 1907, when Giles completely revised his plans. The cathedral finally built is the longest in the world and one of the splendours of twentieth-century design. It dominated Giles's life. Work was curtailed during the First World War but was sufficiently advanced by 1924 to justify consecration. The tower was finished in 1942 during another war which later brought damage from enemy bombs, and work again ceased. When Giles died, as a Roman

Catholic he was buried in what was planned to become the porch for the west door. Tightness of funds meant that when the cathedral was finally finished in 1978 it was a bay shorter than planned and Giles found himself under a black cobble cross in the middle of the road. In 2012 he was moved to a more suitable spot opposite under a fine memorial stone designed by his son.

Giles's secular works include Cambridge University's library, Battersea and Bankside power stations (the latter now Tate Modern), the Guinness brewery at Park Royal (demolished 2006) and the red telephone box, the last of these inspired by his time as trustee of the Soane Museum. He was also the architect of the new Waterloo Bridge, finally completed in 1945 and replacing the version, built in the wake of the battle of Waterloo, by John Rennie. By bizarre coincidence, in 1841 an American daredevil was killed while hung by a rope from a scaffold on the bridge; his name was Samuel Gilbert Scott but, for once, was no relation.

Giles's brother Adrian was commissioned, after the Second World War, to design a new, more modest, Catholic cathedral in Liverpool, on the foundations laid by Sir Edwin Lutyens, but his design, a reduced version of Lutyens's, was rejected. A few years earlier Elisabeth Scott (1898–1972), granddaughter of George Senior's brother John, designed the Shakespeare Memorial Theatre at Stratford-upon-Avon, the first important building in Britain to be designed by a female architect. She features, with her second cousin Giles, on the new British passport.

The Scott and Hoare families were united by Elizabeth (Betty) Scott (1915–2001), granddaughter of George Junior, who was married to Graham Hoare in September 1939. She started her career as an actress but later, together with her husband, took over the management of the family company, Watts & Co., then still at 30 Baker Street. Business for textiles and wallpapers was not easy in post-war austerity; the secular market was non-existent and the church provided but a modest living. In 1950, the company moved to 11 Dacre Street in Westminster but in 1965 the building was sold, Betty purchased the other family shares, and thanks to the hospitality of the MP Ivor Bulmer-Thomas, who was secretary of the Society of the Faith at the time, Watts & Co. moved into the Society's fine Lutyens building nearby at 7 Tufton Street, where it still has its showroom today.

Betty Hoare abhorred 1970s modernism and built up a collection of historic church embroidery that would otherwise have been destroyed. It is now displayed at the Elizabeth Hoare Gallery – with great appropriateness – in Liverpool Cathedral.

Dizzying as this dynastic tapestry may be, it becomes even more tightly woven. Opposite Watts & Co., which is still a family firm today, lies Church House, partly built to a design of Sir Arthur Blomfield in 1888; most of it dates from the 1930s and is by Sir Herbert Baker, who also designed the Partners' Room at Hoares Bank in Fleet Street. A room in Church House is named in honour of Henry Hoare to recognise his work on the modernisation of Convocation.

Finally, the threads are firmly tied to the present day. Betty Hoare's son Michael followed eight other family members as treasurer of the ICBS and oversaw the Society's transfer into the care of the National Churches Trust (NCT), whose chairman he was from 2007 to 2013. The NCT headquarters are now also, fittingly, at 7 Tufton Street.

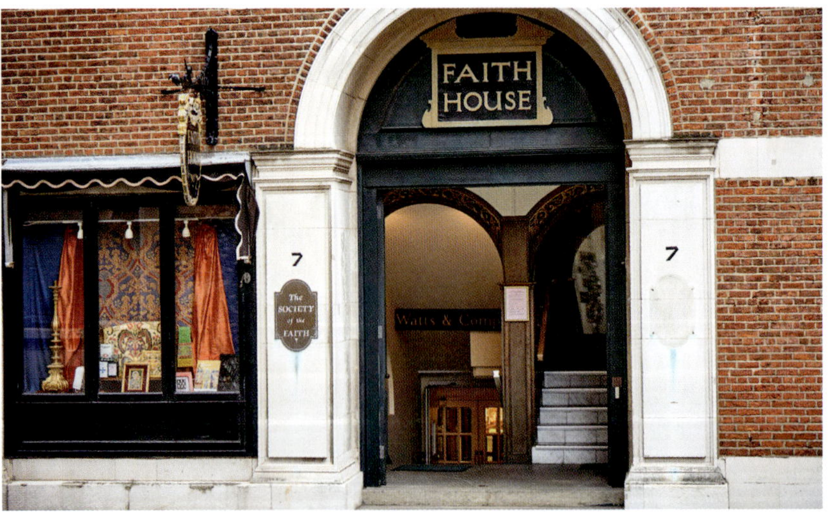

7, Tufton Street, Westminster, London

7 Tufton Street, designed by Edwin Lutyens, is home today to Watts & Co., specialist in ecclesiastical vestments, and also the National Churches Trust, which took over the responsibility for the ICBS. This was overseen by Michael Hoare, whose mother, Betty Hoare, ran Watts & Co., which had been co-founded by her grandfather George Gilbert Scott, Junior. She gave her private collection of ecclesiastical embroidery to Liverpool Cathedral. The cathedral was designed by her uncle Sir Giles Gilbert Scott.

The ICBS had moved between premises a number of times over the years from 1818 (Lincoln's Inn, Parliament Street, St Martin's Place) but, in 1850, a former treasurer, Newell Connop, who had been in post from 1829 to 1846, gave it stability. He bequeathed the lease of his house at 7 Whitehall, at the Trafalgar Square end of the street, which remained the Society's address until the house was demolished in 1886. The Additional Curates Association was a tenant. To give an impression of the Society's costs, by 1863, *The Church Builder* was costing £248.66 to publish each year; the salaries amounted to £778.10 and office expenses were £262.

The 1848 committee of architects inevitably changed although appointing younger men allowed for a long association. The young Turks were gradually joined then replaced by John Loughborough Pearson, George Edmund Street, Richard Norman Shaw, Aston Webb and others, above all Ewan Christian. Most of these architects were closely associated with George Gilbert Scott as his pupil or indeed relation and many also served the Ecclesiastical Commission. In 1952, the ICBS annual report commended the work that they had all undertaken 'quietly and without ostentation'.

Naturally, churches took several years to complete and claim grants but, at a rough count, between 1857 and the end of the First World War, an astonishing 2,240 new churches were built with some form of ICBS grant. All told, from 1818 to its absorption into the Historic Churches Preservation Trust in 1983 – from the first in Ripley in Derbyshire to the last at Bayston Hill, Shropshire, both solid industrial regions – 3,222 new churches were enabled with the help of the ICBS. This is an average of eighteen churches every year, including smaller mission churches and school chapels. It does not include the thousands of extensions, reseatings and repairs that were always the mainstay of ICBS work.

Nearly half of the new ICBS-aided churches were built in the High Victorian period, when a vast number of other churches, often very elaborate indeed, were created by private patrons, landowners, institutions and factions, the largest burst of religious building since the Middle Ages. While the ICBS was therefore swept up in a swell, it is equally clear that the Society itself stood, quietly and modestly, behind the original impetus. The ICBS was not the only reason that churches were built in such great numbers in the long nineteenth century but it played a crucial role and lasted the course longer than any other institution. The ICBS inspired and irritated many other regional church-building societies into existence as both a model and a spur.

In the 1860s, few distinguished churches were started and not many survive today out of the 400 that received ICBS grant aid but, in Droitwich, St Nicholas's still serves the west end of the town. It was designed by local architect John Smith in 1866 as the salt trade was beginning to decline and a spa was being developed. The church stands opposite the train station, which had been built fourteen years before. The first church of St Nicholas in Droitwich was destroyed in the town fire of 1293; a second church from the early fourteenth century survived until the mid-seventeenth century. It is a typical example of an ICBS church of the time, following a familiar pattern of urban development and ICBS grant. It exemplifies Anthony Trollope's satiric view in Clergymen of the Church of England of the many occasions when a clergyman found a modest living in a suburb or country town, far removed from the port-drinking, hunting and shooting parson of a previous era. Now he was simply 'the professional gentleman who has taken his family in to the last built new house in Albert Terrace'.

Elsewhere, more glamorously, G. E. Bodley, Sir George Gilbert Scott's first pupil, had an early success with All Saints, Selsley, Gloucestershire (1860–8). Its spectacular stained glass is due to his association with William Morris and his company, and the church is one of the very few built with an ICBS grant listed in Simon Jenkins's *England's Thousand Best Churches*.

The 1870s proved a richer decade. In 1870, a missionary curate in Kennington, south London, sought a permanent church and a site was acquired off Camberwell New Road, with an architect appointed. However, this plan was changed in 1871 when the assistant curate, Charles Edward Brooke, put forward a design by George Edmund Street for what became St John the Divine. A public appeal began in 1871 and the ICBS made a grant but the greatest support was from an anonymous donor who gave no less than £10,000, later discovered to be Charles Brooke himself. Street was duly appointed as architect and Samuel Wilberforce, by then Bishop of Winchester, became chairman of the Building Committee.

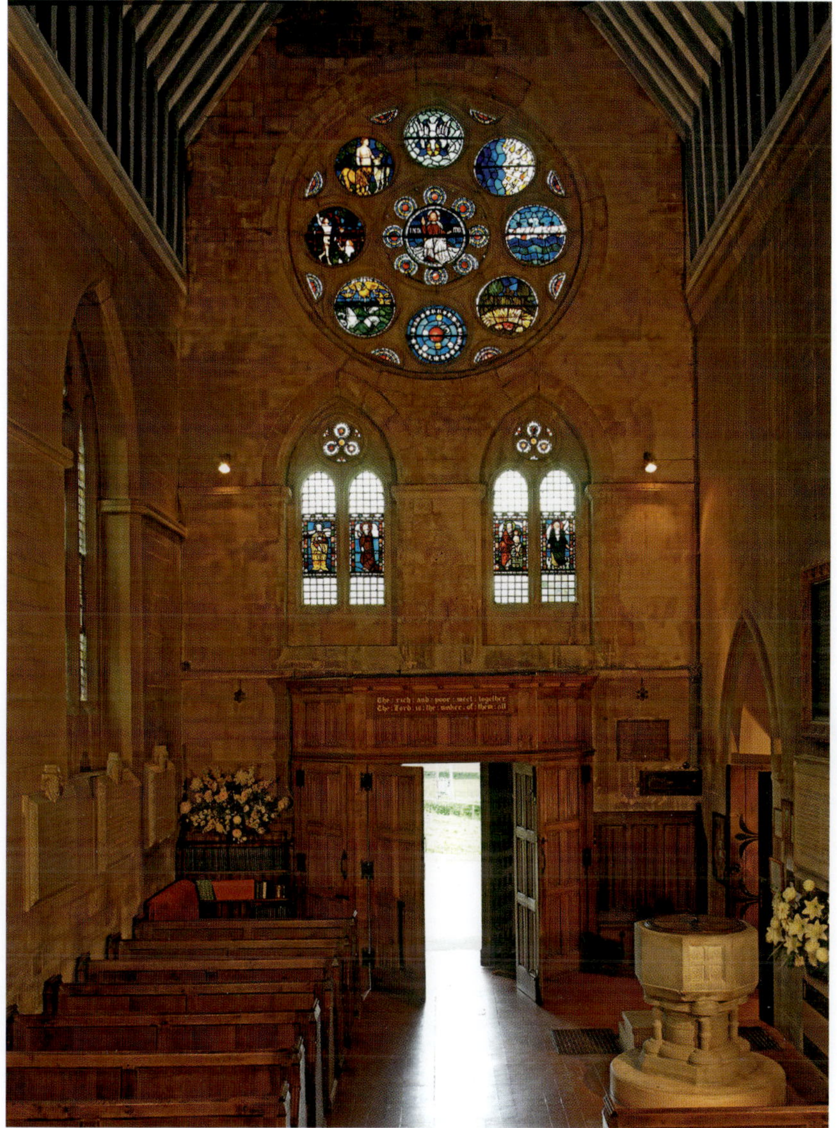

All Saints, Selsley, Gloucestershire

All Saints was an early success in 1862 for George Frederick Bodley (1827–1907). He was the first pupil of Sir George Gilbert Scott, to whom he was related by marriage. Bodley was a friend of William Morris and at Selsley he gave Morris & Co. their first commission for ecclesiastical stained glass. Because of this, it is one of the very few built with an ICBS grant listed in Simon Jenkins's England's Thousand Best Churches.

Another anonymous donation enabled the capitals of the columns to be carved and some of the pillars themselves to be in marble not stone. This turned out to be from Brooke again, enabling Street and G. E. Bodley to create the interior that they wanted. The spire was added at a later date by Street's son, A. E. Street. John Betjeman called it 'the most magnificent church in South London'.

Street was an active member of the Ecclesiological Society and in 1855 he published *The Brick and Marble Architecture of Northern Italy*, and in 1865 a book on the Gothic architecture of Spain. These works inspired the wider use of polychromatic brick and stone work, mocked as the 'Streaky Bacon style'. His majestic Royal Courts of Justice on the Strand, London, opened in 1882. He worked extensively throughout Britain and especially Oxfordshire where one of his best churches is SS Philip and

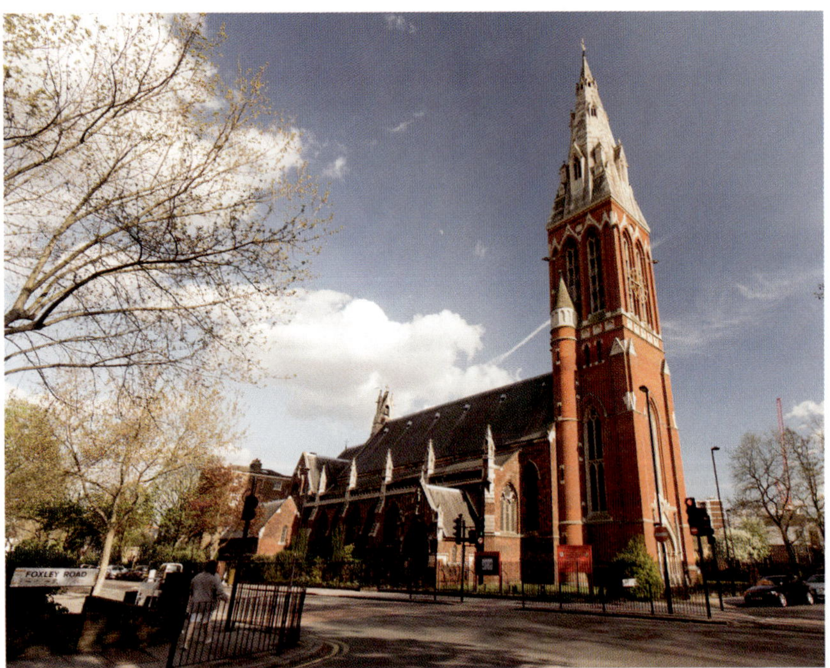

St John the Divine, Kennington, London

St John the Divine has another Bodley interior with an overall design by George Edmund Street. Charles Edward Brooke, the assistant curate, launched a public appeal in 1871 and the ICBS made a grant but the greatest support was from an anonymous donor who gave no less than £10,000, later discovered to be Brooke himself. John Betjeman called it 'the most magnificent church in South London'.

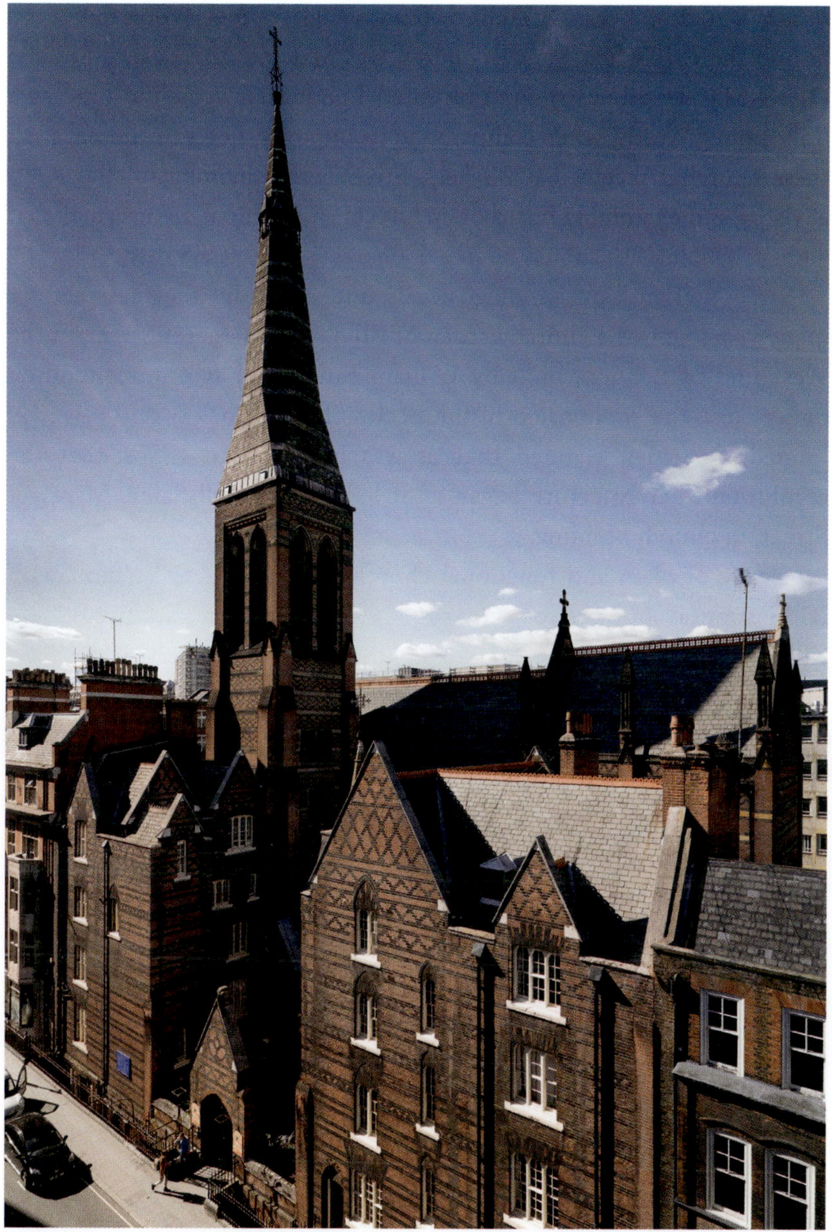

All Saints, Margaret Street, London

Simon Jenkins has described All Saints as 'architecturally England's most celebrated Victorian church'. It was commissioned by Alexander Beresford-Hope MP from William Butterfield to conform to the rules for a model church laid down by the Ecclesiological Society. It cost £70,000 in 1850.

James, Woodstock Road, Oxford, built while Samuel Wilberforce was bishop there. His first London church was St James the Less in Pimlico (1858–61), described by the Illustrated London News at the time as a 'Lily among Weeds' when compared to its impoverished surroundings. All these churches received ICBS help. Street was a member of the ICBS advisory and examining board of architects and particularly insistent that all seats in churches should be free of charge: a loyal ICBS man.

Street's High Church allegiance is underlined by the fact that for many years he was a churchwarden of All Saints, Margaret Street, in the West End of London, built by William Butterfield as a model church under close the supervision of the Ecclesiological Society and privately funded. Betjeman claimed that 'it was here, in the 1850s, that the revolution in architecture began … It led the way, All Saints Margaret Street, in church building.'

Plenty of plain and functional churches continued to be built with ICBS support but so, too, did some real splendours. St Augustine's, Kilburn, the 'Cathedral of North London', was built in 1871 by John Loughborough Pearson and replaced an iron church with one of rich red brick, vaulted ceilings and a wealth of internal stone sculpture. While it was being built it was already referred to as 'one of the finest examples of ecclesiastical structures in London'. Betjeman called Pearson a 'vista-man, vistas and vaulting'.

Perhaps the most surprising of all ICBS grants is for another Pearson building: Truro Cathedral (1880). There had been a church on the site since at least 1259 and, while no other cathedral received an ICBS grant before or since, it fulfilled many of the ICBS's criteria. The Diocese of Truro was only created in 1879; the ICBS had helped build twenty new churches or mission churches in Cornwall while it came under the care of Exeter and many more were to follow. Truro's industrial importance increased late in the nineteenth century and it had its own iron-smelting works, potteries and tanneries. The Great Western Railway arrived in Truro in the 1860s with a direct line from Paddington; the Bishopric of Truro Act 1876 gave the town its bishop, then the possibility of a cathedral. The next year Queen Victoria granted Truro city status and plans for a cathedral began. The elements that secured ICBS support were both the local needs of a

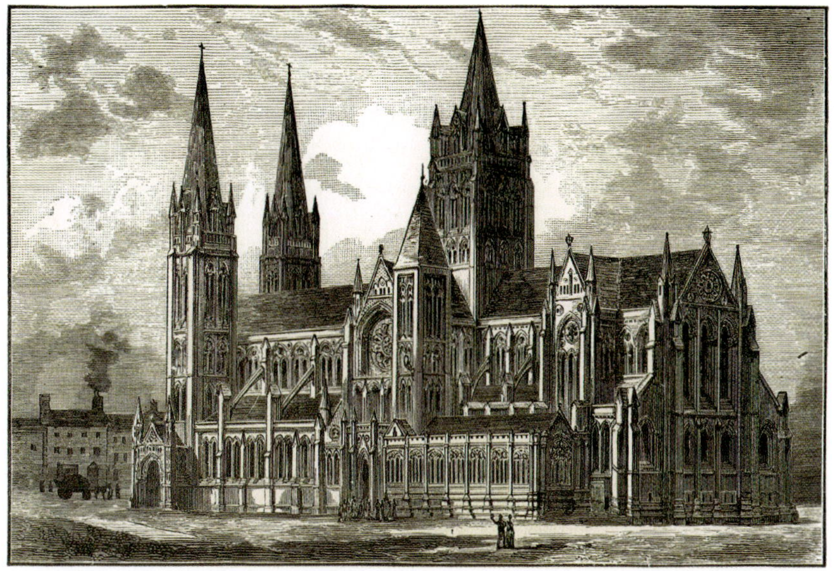

BRITISH SCHOOL **Truro Cathedral**, Late 19th century, Engraving

This image of the south elevation of Truro Cathedral was published as the frontispiece of
The Cornish See and Cathedral. *John Loughborough Pearson's 1880 building was unique
in ICBS history: no other cathedral received an ICBS grant before or after. The influence
behind the project was Edward White Benson, the first Bishop of Truro (1877–83), and later
Archbishop of Canterbury. Bishop Benson created at Truro not only the first brand new
cathedral built for the Church of England but also the Service of Nine Lessons and Carols.*

growing town and Pearson's success in arguing, surprisingly, to retain part
of the ancient parish church. Another guarantee of the project's success
was Edward White Benson, the first Bishop of Truro (1877–83), previously
chancellor of Lincoln Cathedral and, from 1883 until his death in 1896,
Archbishop of Canterbury. In 1880 Bishop Benson created at Truro not
only the first brand new cathedral built for the Church of England but also
the much-loved Christmas Service of Nine Lessons and Carols.

The new argument of the High Victorian period between two
passionately committed groups was about 'restoration', back to an
assumed ancient pattern which allowed a decaying church to function
and flourish, against a new approach to 'preservation' of original stone,
timber and layout for historic and aesthetic reasons. Today, the argument
for conservation not restoration is firmly supported by the National
Churches Trust, the successor to the ICBS. William Morris founded the

Society for the Protection of Ancient Buildings (SPAB) in the 1870s to protest against and counterbalance the 'restoration' of medieval buildings, especially churches:

> No doubt within the last fifty years a new interest, almost like another sense, has arisen in these ancient monuments of art; and they have become the subject of one of the most interesting of studies, and of an enthusiasm, religious, historical, artistic, which is one of the undoubted gains of our time; yet we think that if the present treatment of them be continued, our descendants will find them useless for study and chilling to enthusiasm. We think that those last fifty years of knowledge and attention have done more for their destruction than all the foregoing centuries of revolution, violence and contempt.

Morris believed that something vital and irreplaceable was being lost; Gilbert Scott, Ewan Christian and others believed, in theory at least, that they, too, were following a moral code but acted with less nuance. In 1850 Scott stated in 'A Plea for the Faithful Restoration of our Ancient Churches' that 'as a general rule it is highly desirable to preserve those vestiges of the growth and history of buildings which are indicated by the various styles and irregularities of its parts'. However, he generally did away with all later changes so as to reconstruct a church in a uniform early style often on the evidence of just one remaining original element. This is why Morris thought of such 'restoration', most notably Scott's approach to Tewkesbury Abbey, as a kind of forgery and why SPAB was also known as the Anti-Scrape Society. It has been estimated that 80 per cent of all Church of England churches were affected in some way by the restoration movement, led by the Oxford and Cambridge ecclesiologists, from minor alterations to complete demolition and rebuilding. John Dobson, funded widely by the ICBS in the north east, often carved a completely fictitious early date into the stone of his restoration projects. As Betjeman complained later:

> *The Church's Restoration*
> *In eighteen eighty-three*
> *Has left for contemplation*
> *Not what there used to be.*

But not all crimes against church fabric were committed in the latter part of the nineteenth century. St Peter's, Great Berkhamsted, Hertfordshire was originally built at the beginning of the thirteenth century, possibly on the site of an even earlier church. It was then extended with an ICBS grant in 1819–21 at the same time as restoration by Jeffrey Wyatville, who moved or destroyed many original features and covered the exterior in stucco. The church was restored again (with no ICBS grant even requested) by William Butterfield in the 1870s. He no longer had an entirely ancient building upon which to work and his alteration, although drastic in some cases, is more appreciated than Wyatville's. Refurbishing and reordering was again undertaken in the twentieth century.

During the late nineteenth century Ewan Christian (see page 151) was a dominant and influential voice. Christian was elected vice-president of the RIBA in 1880 and reached the height of his career as president from 1884 to 1886. Much of his church work, particularly his 880 chancel restorations, was in his capacity as architect to the Ecclesiastical Commission and, on his appointment, Christian moved his practice into the commission's office premises in Whitehall Place, a stroll from those of the ICBS, for whom he was also consulting architect for nearly fifty years from 1847. In addition to his building and restoration work he produced thousands of reports on designs for Church of England buildings that were submitted to the commission and completed surveys on the fabric of ancient churches including fourteen cathedrals. He was responsible for a substantial reorganising of Hawksmoor's Christ Church, Spitalfields, in the East End of London, when he removed the side galleries, blocked in the windows at the corners and combined the upper and lower aisle windows in 1850. The ICBS helped fund some repairs there in 1910 but refused more in the 1960s.

At the turn of the twentieth century, the ICBS helped to create a magnificent church in Marylebone which sits well alongside the glamorous group of Commissioners' churches of the 1820s. At that point in its early history, the ICBS had been concentrating more modestly on enlargements and occasional new buildings all over the country but, back in Marylebone nearly a century later, it helped make a splash.

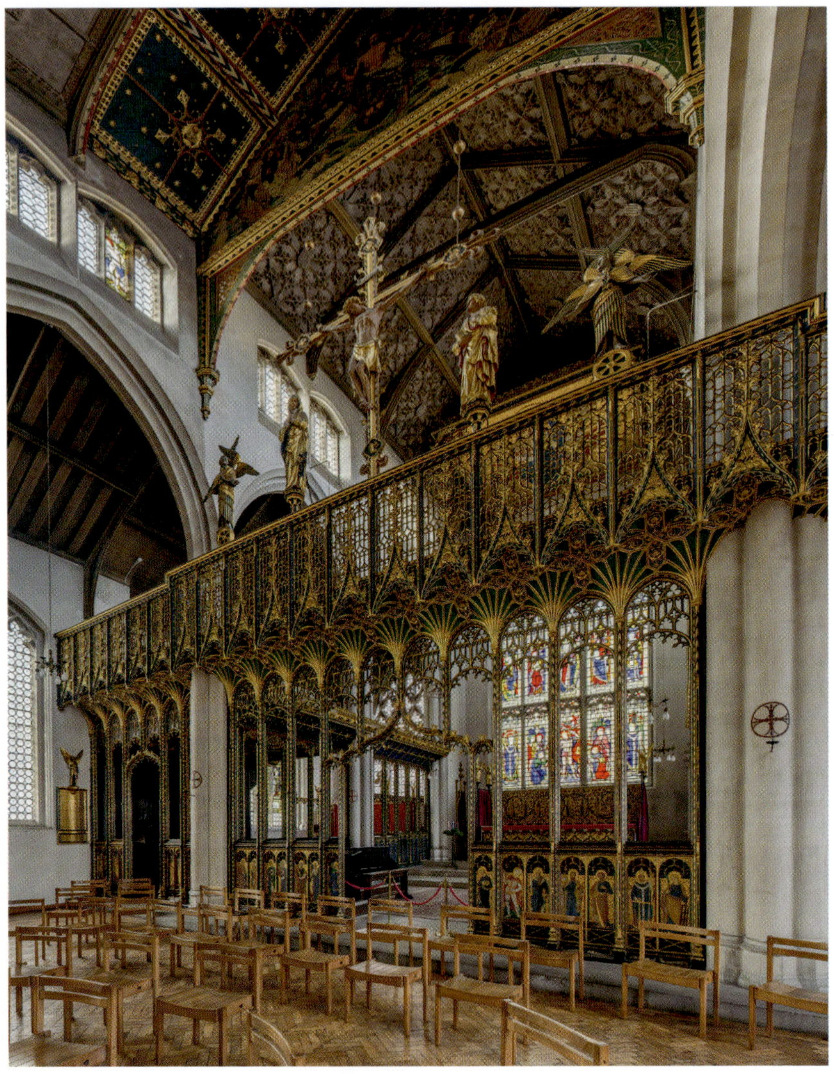

St Cyprian's, Clarence Gate, London

The image shows the white and gold interior of St Cyprian's and its rood screen. The church was designed in 1866 by Ninian Comper 'to fulfil the ideal of the English Parish Church ... in the last manner of English Architecture'. It received a grant from the ICBS.

As early as 1866, Father Charles Gutch, who was previously curate at nearby All Saints, Margaret Street, was seeking a church of his own. He was a mathematician and fellow of Sidney Sussex College, Cambridge, and later a close friend to the poet Christina Rossetti. His title reveals that he was very High Church indeed and consequently was disapproved of by the local church authorities and also Lord Portman, the local landowner. Nevertheless Gutch argued successfully for a mission church in an impoverished north-eastern corner of Marylebone, yet near the palatial Nash terraces of Regent's Park. It could only hold 180 people and Father Gutch died before a new building was permitted but his successor, the Reverend George Forbes, argued successfully for a spacious new church. Lord Portman sold a plot of land under market value on the condition that all monies were in place and that the church was completed speedily. The ICBS contributed and a church was designed, in the words of its architect, Ninian Comper, 'to fulfil the ideal of the English Parish Church … in the last manner of English Architecture'. The exterior was complete by 1903 and Comper then slowly completed his glorious interior, following his principles of the Classical style informing the Gothic through 'unity by inclusion'. Ian Nairn describes St Cyprian's as 'a sunburst of white and gold and all-embracing love … the moment you go in through the door you know that everything is absolutely right'.

TEN

'A dignified distinct building dedicated to the service of the Church': ICBS support throughout England and Wales

The ICBS gave grants all over the country: from north, as far as the border with Scotland, to south; from east to west, across Wales and to the tip of Cornwall; on the Isle of Man, the Channel Islands and the Isle of Wight. Not many idyllic picture postcard villages received new churches but many icons of English church beauty were propped up and made useful and safe with ICBS help. Every city benefited; even, as we have seen, a new cathedral was built with the support of the ICBS. But its real heartland lay in villages that had turned into towns or suburbs, places that had become urban rather than peripheral. An early argument was made in Parliament that if an increase in churches always means an improvement in morals then Norwich must be the most saintly town in England as it had the greatest concentration of churches from the Middle Ages. Instead, the ICBS and other bodies doggedly built in hope, responding to changing needs, which often changed yet again. Some of their churches have disappeared altogether and others that were new in the 1800s did not even outlast the century. It is impossible, of course, to pick out every interesting church here or cover the whole country fairly but looking closely at certain places tells a tale with richness and detail. The story of the church-building boom and the people behind it can be seen in many different ways in Wales, the north east, Cumberland and Westmorland, Nottingham, Essex and Brighton.

WALES

Between 1819 and 1826, during the ICBS's crucial early years, the Bishop of Llandaff was William Van Mildert, a close friend to Joshua Watson and his circle. Van Mildert broke with the practice of his predecessors by actually residing in his diocese, which was more remarkable than it seems as no palace was built until 1850. His indirect predecessor Richard Watson was a reformer who played a key role in the drive towards the CBC and the ICBS. Watson died in 1816, after twenty-four years as bishop there, at which time Henry Handley Norris, both curate and brother-in-law to John Watson in Hackney, was prebendary at Llandaff Cathedral.

The Welsh dioceses were part of the Anglican Province of Canterbury from the reign of Elizabeth I until the passing of the Welsh Church Act 1914; the independent Church in Wales was created on 31 March 1920. More than any other part of the British Isles, Wales was the home of Dissenters and, at the 1851 church census, they claimed 85 per cent of the population. Between 1800 and 1851 500 chapels were built in the Llandaff diocese. The annual revenues of Llandaff in 1835 were only £924, the smallest in England and Wales: bishops of Llandaff and also St David's held other offices, at St Paul's or Durham. In 1850 the Llandaff Church Extension Society was created for a 'Holy Enterprise'.

The Society responded swiftly to a request for a new church in Pontypool, Monmouthshire to a design by the engineer Watkin George. George had been a partner at Cyfartha Ironworks, the largest in the world when he left it behind with nearly £40,000 in his pocket. St James's was built as a simple Georgian hall in 1819, fifty years later extended without ICBS help, in the Gothic revival style. It is now redundant and its future is under consideration.

The CBC also responded with some alacrity to the chance to make changes in Wales but built only St Matthew's Church, Buckley, Flintshire with the first parliamentary grant in 1822, which awarded £52 more than the final cost of £4,000. Thirty-three churches in Wales were built in the second phase. In 1879 the Dean of Bangor complained that one million people spoke Welsh and 800,000 were Nonconformist; new churches were 'doomed to be kept empty by ordained illiterates and mouthers of marvellous Welsh'.

The ICBS next supported St Paul's in Newport in 1829 but the church was not begun until the CBC gave a grant in 1835 to create the first Gothick church, as opposed to the more scholarly Gothic Revival, in Wales. It was built by Thomas H. Wyatt while he was also district surveyor for Hackney and shortly before he became a member of the ICBS's panel of architects. He also built St Catherine's, Govilon, Monmouthshire with Society funds, in 1850. Wyatt had distinguished patrons in the Herbert

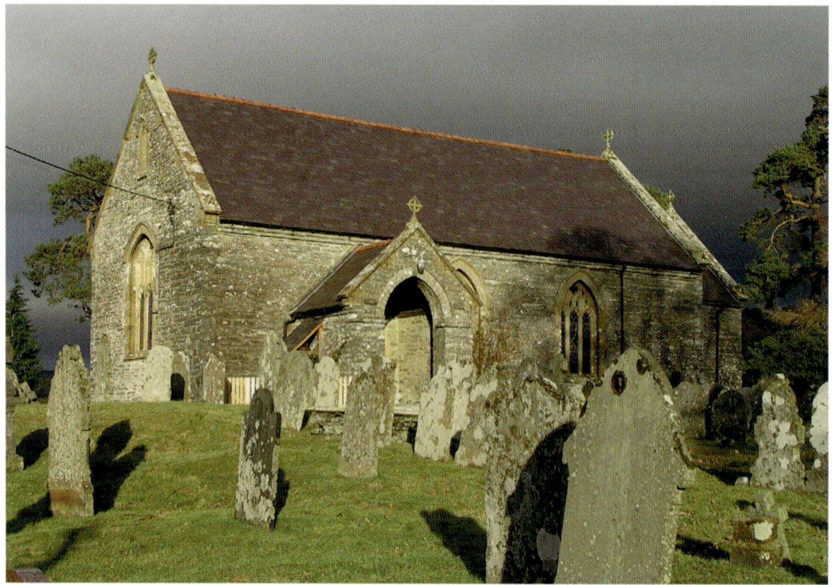

St Harmon, Radnorshire
St Harmon was the church of diarist and priest Francis Kilvert from 1876 to 1878. The church had been built without a grant from the Society in 1821. Kilvert wrote: 'The church was built in the Dark Ages of fifty years ago and was simply hideous.' In 1906, the ICBS gave it a grant for restoration.

family of Wiltshire and the dukes of Beaufort, for whom he substantially restored St Cadoc's, Raglan, Monmouthshire in 1867 with an ICBS grant.

The diarist and priest Francis Kilvert was vicar of St Harmon in Radnorshire from 1876 to 1878. The church had been built without a grant from the Society in 1821, in Van Mildert's time, which also refused to help extend it a couple of years later. Kilvert wrote:

The church was built in the Dark Ages of fifty years ago and was simply hideous. But ugly as it appeared externally the interior was worse and my heart sank within me like a stone as I entered the door. A bare cold squalid interior and high square ugly boxes for seats, a three-decker pulpit and desk, no stove, a flimsy altar rail, a ragged faded altar cloth, a singing gallery with a broken organ, a dark little box for a vestry, and a roof in bad repair, admitting the rain.

Eventually the ICBS did help it in 1906 and also grant-aided the ancient St Peter's, Painscastle, in the same county, church of the Reverend John Price,

Kilvert's eccentric 'Solitary of Llanbedr', who lived in personal poverty in a cabin. The ICBS gave a grant in 1866 towards 'rebuilding of west wall and window, porch and nave north wall, with new roofs, restoration and reseating' at Price's church. The Society helped build seven mission or church schools in Brecknockshire during the nineteenth century and that modest scale of support is most typical of its grants within Wales. Kilvert reported a tale in which a widower, entering a little-used church to marry his second wife, found a handkerchief belonging to his first wife still hanging on the altar rail.

NORTHUMBERLAND AND DURHAM

After Llandaff, William Van Mildert became Bishop of Durham for ten years from 1826 and the end of his tenure coincided with the passing of the Established Church Act. He also helped to found the University of Durham in 1832 and was the last Bishop of Durham to hold the ancient title Prince Bishop in the County Palatine, acknowledging spiritual as well as temporal power. His see contained the most northerly church in England and, in Berwick, the only one left standing that was built during the Commonwealth. Just down the coast at Lindisfarne or Holy Island, the ICBS also helped the church next to the abbey founded by St Aidan when he first brought Christianity from Iona to the island in AD635. Van Mildert had in his care innumerable churches built in the earliest coalfields and, later, in the growing suburbs within Durham and Northumberland.

When Van Mildert arrived in Durham, the only other city in the region was Newcastle upon Tyne. The coal industry had been long established and the Tyne had been the principal route to export coal and, before that, leather to London since the thirteenth century. By 1800, Newcastle was also the centre for making window glass.

In 1826, the centre of Newcastle was being transformed into a fine late Georgian city by the developer Richard Grainger and his architect, John Dobson, who was also responsible for many churches in the area. Grainger was said to have found Newcastle of bricks and timber and left it of stone. As well as medieval churches, Newcastle also had new churches including the elegant All Saints, an elliptical, Neo-Classical building designed by David Stephenson (to whom Dobson was apprenticed), which opened in

1796, at a cost of £27,000. Forty-three pews, containing 283 seats, were sold for £2061 19s. to freeholders in the parish to be annexed to their property for ever. It received an ICBS grant for repairs in 1854–5.

Between 1812 and 1820, Sir Charles Monck was MP for Northumberland and a moderate Whig. He suggested in Parliament that, to solve the church room problem, endowments should be used and that there should simply be more services conducted rather than more churches built, perhaps not fully aware of the working day of the average working man. He further believed that local commissioners for each city should apply to Parliament for grants but it was not in the vested interest of the bishops or the landowners in the Lords to support this moderate and reasonable proposal which would have destroyed the *status quo*.

Monck was also an innovative architectural patron and avid Neo-Classicist. After his return from a two-year Grand Tour honeymoon during the Napoleonic Wars, he built an austere Doric Northumbrian mansion to his own design with Dobson's help between 1810 and 1817. During the same period, the Moot Hall, or courts, had been built in Newcastle by William Stokoe, a remarkably pure and ambitious example of Doric building outside London. It was opened in 1811 by Earl Percy, who, as 3rd Duke of Northumberland seven years later, proposed the motion that set the Church Building Act on its way. The ICBS funded no Neo-Classical churches in the north east, nor were any Commissioners' churches built to complement the fashionable local style.

The first ICBS grant for a new church to be built in the city was for St James's in the (then) largely rural area of Benwell. Designed by Dobson, in a Gothic Revival style, it opened in 1833 and followed a standard pattern of extension and improvement. In 1864 a chancel and south aisle were added to a design by Dobson; in 1879 it gained an organ chamber and vestry; in 1884–5 a new baptistry, choir vestry and tower with spire and clock were added, then in 1903 a north aisle and a chapel to the aisle in 1910. St James's received a further grant for repairs in 1977–8. Richard Grainger, creator of Georgian Newcastle, is buried in the churchyard, at the heart of his grander but failed plan for the area, which included quays, railway junctions, workhouse, factories, housing and even a zoo. The project bankrupted him. The land on which St James's was built was given by John Buddle, a very successful mining engineer and colliery owner, who is also buried in the churchyard within a coal seam.

In 1856, Richard Clayton, a very popular evangelical preacher in Newcastle upon Tyne, died and was replaced against the wishes of his parishioners by a High Church incumbent, in keeping with all other city centre churches at the time. Clayton's congregation voted instead to build their own church in Jesmond, then fields and farms on the edge of the city, in 1861, with the unusual dedication 'in memory of the late Rev. Richard Clayton' and with no saint's name attached, as outlined in the parish committee minutes:

1   To testify the veneration and affection of a bereaved congregation for their departed minister…
2.   To provide additional church accommodation and spiritual superintendence for a town in which such provision, in connection with the Church of England, is at present so fearfully inadequate;
3.   To erect a church, which by having the patronage in perpetuity vested in trustees nominated by the promoters, will form a central point for the maintenance and promulgation of sound scriptural and Evangelical truth in a large and prosperous town…

It is a very late example of a traditional west gallery church and did not approach the ICBS for funds.

Church building was also continuing under private patronage, most notably by the largest landowners of all, the dukes of Northumberland. In the 1880s the 6th Duke of Northumberland began the planning for a church in the fishing village of Cullercoats in memory of his late father, the 5th Duke, and chose a site on the sea, near the family's previous summer home. The foundation stone was laid in 1882 and the church was finally dedicated in 1884, built by J. L. Pearson in a French Gothic style. Its soaring spire was used as a navigational aid by the fishermen of Cullercoats as well as by major shipping approaching Tynemouth, some of which had possibly sailed past the other Pearson spire in Truro.

The new twentieth century saw the Society funding a remarkable church in Roker, near Sunderland. The Roker and Fulwell New Church Committee had been set up in 1903 to raise funds for the church and

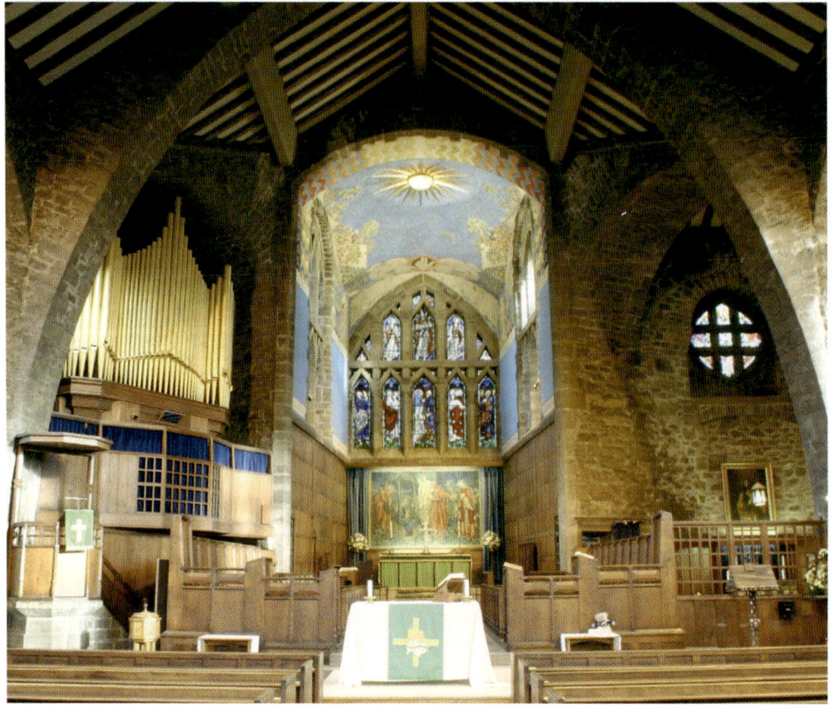

St Andrew's, Roker, Sunderland

One of the first churches to which the ICBS gave a grant in the 20th century, the local patron was a labourer turned shipbuilder millionaire. E.S. Prior's masterpiece shares the title 'Cathedral of the Arts and Crafts Movement' with J.D. Seddings's Holy Trinity in Sloane Street, Chelsea, commissioned by Earl Cadogan, a long way away both geographically and socially.

a local shipbuilder, John Priestman, offered £6,000 in memory of his mother. His conditions stipulated that the church had to be completed by 31 December 1905 and he retained the right to approve its design. He 'wished the church to seat 700, and most importantly for the entire congregation to have an uninterrupted view of the altar and pulpit, with no chancel screen and good acoustics'. The architect chosen was Edward Schroeder Prior, RA, because of his local connections and his own belief that he would create 'a dignified distinct building dedicated to the service of the Church. Church architecture, least of all, has been able to go beyond the trivial efforts of traditional picturesqueness'.

Prior had grown up in the Clapham Sect and then became a pupil to Richard Norman Shaw. He took over Shaw's work at St Margaret's, Ilkley,

Yorkshire, which probably brought him to the attention of the ICBS when it helped fund this new church. Here Prior learned 'that the idea of wonderful construction was all an imposture: there was no science of construction, but there was an experience of construction to be gained by the man who worked with his hands and not the man who made the drawing'.

Experience, practical application, dignity and avoiding the merely picturesque are proper ICBS principles and St Andrew's, Roker is a masterpiece.

CUMBERLAND AND WESTMORLAND

Over on the other coast, Cumberland and Westmorland produced a curiously high proportion of the protagonists in the early years of the new church-building movement. Bishop Watson and Joshua Watson were both Cumbrians and, synonymous with the region, so was the Wordsworth family.

William Wordsworth, the poet, was the older brother of the Reverend Christopher Wordsworth, employed by Charles Manners-Sutton, Archbishop of Canterbury between 1805 and 1828, as a tutor for his son. Christopher Wordsworth then became master of Trinity College, Cambridge, and one of the founding committee members of the ICBS. His son, also Christopher, became a bishop. Christopher senior and Joshua Watson met at William Van Mildert's London house while he was the rector of St Mary-le-Bow and the two men became close and lifelong friends. William Wordsworth was also part of this circle of friends and published his curious *Ecclesiastical Sonnets* in 1822, a history of the Church in England, inspired by looking at the land upon which his patron, Sir George Beaumont, planned to build a new church. The philosophy that lay behind the new churches inspired this long suite of verses, not his finest writing but deeply felt and in harmony with the church-building impulse of his brother and friends in the years after Waterloo: 'in rival haste the wished-for Temples rise'. The year that Wordsworth published his *Sonnets* found Joshua Watson leaving Hackney for Park Street (today Queen Anne's Gate) in Westminster, nearer to the commissions and societies that so absorbed his time. He lived there for sixteen years and, in 1835, there is mention of Wordsworth's visiting card bearing Watson's Park Street address. The poet admired Watson very much indeed and suggested

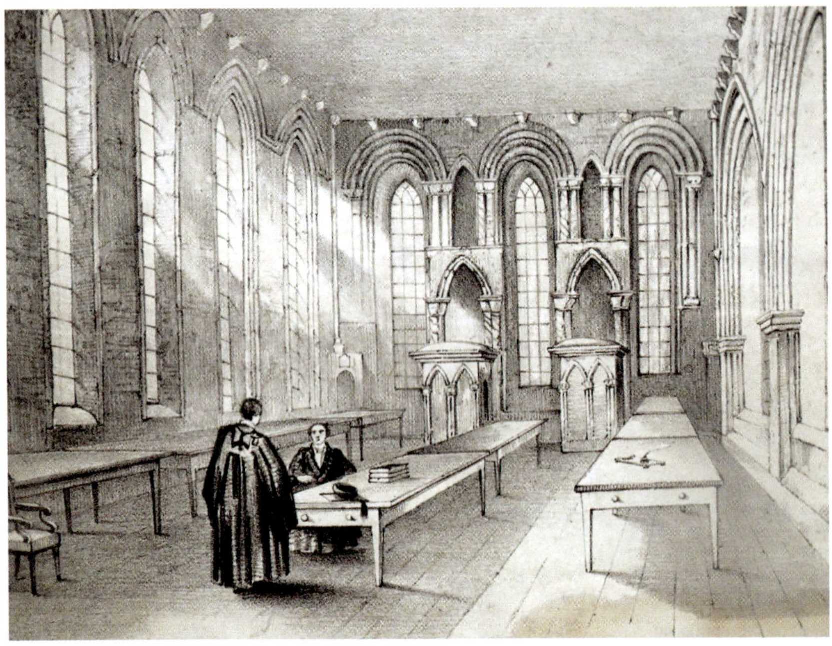

BRITISH SCHOOL **St Bees Theological College**, Cumbria 1843
Watercolour on paper
*The main lecture room of the college, now known as the Old College Hall. St Bees was the first
independent college for the training of Church of England clergy, breaking a monopoly controlled
by Oxford and Cambridge. It was founded in 1816 by George Henry Law, Bishop of Chester.
Joshua Watson's friend William Wordsworth wrote: 'Prosper the new-born College of St Bees!'*

that the words 'and also Joshua Watson' should be added to the petition
of the Litany which includes thanks for 'all Bishops, Priests and Deacons'.

All Saints, Cockermouth, where the poet was christened, received a
very early enlargement grant from the ICBS although this simple church
burned down in 1850 and was replaced. Many of the ICBS grants went to
churches in the coastal and mining towns – including Millom, Whitehaven
and Cleator Moor – which were expanding throughout the century with
migrant workers who were often Irish Catholic. A few miles along the coast
from Whitehaven was St Bees Theological College, the first independent
college for the training of Church of England clergy, breaking a monopoly
controlled by the universities of Oxford and Cambridge. It was founded in
1816 by George Henry Law, Bishop of Chester, and Wordsworth wrote in
his *Sonnets:* 'Prosper the new-born College of St Bees!'

NOTTINGHAM

In the east Midlands, during the first two decades of the nineteenth century, Nottingham's vast hosiery industry slipped into a deep depression. There was then an industrial revival due to 'twist net fever' between 1822 and 1825 when the industrial lace trade developed and workers again flooded into the town. Houses were built on every available piece of land until Nottingham became so overcrowded that, by the 1840s, it had some claims to have the worst slums in the country. In 1831, residents of these slums rioted in protest against the Duke of Newcastle-under-Lyne's opposition to the Reform Act of 1832 and burned down his mansion, known as Nottingham Castle. Between 1822 and 1903, twelve new parishes and churches were created from the mother church of St Mary the Virgin, the most ancient church in the city, four of these funded by the ICBS.

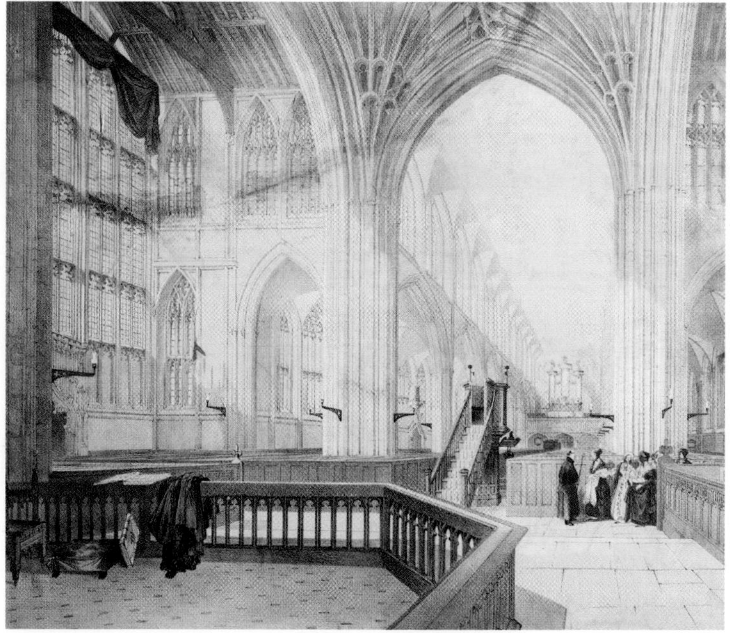

BRITISH BCHOOL **St Mary's, Nottingham**, circa 1848, Engraving
The medieval church of St Mary, Lace Market, Nottingham, received grants from the ICBS in the 1830s and again in the 1840s, having been rebuilt many times; a Classical temple front had been added in the 1720s. This mid-19th-century print is entitled 'Interior of St Mary's Shewing High Pews' and may have been published to celebrate its reopening after four years for major repairs.

Between 1821 and 1825, St Mary's had itself requested ICBS grants for enlargement and been refused; in 1838 it successfully petitioned for funds to repair and reseat. Between 1844 and 1848 the church was closed so that more major repairs, again funded by ICBS, could be undertaken. A five-year restoration programme enabled the roofs and west front (where a Classical version had been added in the 1720s) to be returned to the Gothic style by George Gilbert Scott. It is now Grade I listed, one of only five such buildings in Nottingham.

Just outside the church, under the windows of the Lace Market Hotel, a public hanging took place in 1844 as the church closed for repairs. The crowds were so huge that a stampede followed which resulted in at least twelve more deaths. The trial had taken place opposite the church in the courthouse, an eighteenth-century building remodelled and panelled in the nineteenth century, by which time the use of a bar across the front of the court to hold defendants had been replaced by a dock, a term which comes from criminal slang meaning a cage or rabbit hutch. This was often a small box with panelling similar in height to the rest of the court seating, all bearing a distinct resemblance to church pews and galleries and probably often constructed by exactly the same joiners.

ESSEX

Leytonstone in Essex saw the building of two churches whose histories are full of the associations and ups and downs which punctuate the story of the ICBS. An attempt to build a chapel in Leytonstone faltered in the 1740s when the vicar reported to his patron that 'there could be no occasion for such a chapel where the gentry all kept coaches, and where the tradesmen, farmers and servants were none of them more than a mile-and-a-half from the Church'. Nonetheless a chapel was built and worship took place without the benefit of the vicar until official permission was granted in 1754 followed by agreement, in the auspicious year of 1818, that a larger chapel should be built. The ICBS supported the new building of St John the Baptist in 1830 on land purchased by William Cotton (see page 129), who was buried there in 1866.

Leytonstone grew steadily throughout the nineteenth century, helped by the arrival of the Great Eastern Railway in 1856. The ICBS gave grants for the construction of twelve new churches in the immediate area from 1876 to 1904 as well as extensions to St John's in 1893 and 1908. One of the new churches was St Andrew's, whose parish stands within the estate of Wallwood, which Cotton had purchased in 1817. It was sold off for development on his death but his family reserved a site for a church to be built in their father's memory. His eldest son, William Charles Cotton, was chaplain to the Bishop of New Zealand in the 1840s and introduced beekeeping to the North Island. Cotton senior gave the ICBS an elegant cupboard whose original owner had been John Howard, the famous prison reformer, who died in 1790. The cupboard is still in use today in the offices of the National Churches Trust.

St Andrew's became known as the Cotton Memorial Church. Initially a corrugated iron structure was provided and a building fund instigated. The foundation stone was laid on 18 June 1886 by the Duke of Connaught, and in recognition of Cotton's importance to the area and church building as a whole, the Lord Mayor of London and five bishops were present. The architect was Sir Arthur Blomfield and he built in stages; the chancel and first bays of the nave were completed in 1887. The chancel was paid for by Cotton's children as their memorial to him but its elaborate design that meant the congregation was unable to pay for continued work and building stopped. Further fundraising followed, and in 1893 the building was complete. Its website history explains:

> The Church was immensely fashionable – weekly total congregations in 1903 exceeded 1,500 people. Unusually, St Andrew's charged no pew rents and there was no endowment. Until the 1920s the clergy were paid entirely by the congregation. Neither was a Vicarage provided (despite local myths to the contrary): the parish rented a house in Chadwick Road for the Vicar until well after the Second World War … In its Edwardian heyday St Andrew's also offered day and evening classes for both children and adults, an amateur orchestra, gym, tennis and cricket club.

St Andrew's thrived until the early 1930s, when in spite of large congregations, the finances became a serious problem, so much so that a formal decision to close the church was taken in 1967; the ICBS turned down a grant request in 1960 as work had already begun before the application was made. But, almost at the last hour, St Andrew's was reprieved and today is Grade II listed.

BRIGHTON

Brighton provides another link with the founders of the ICBS through Joshua Watson's son-in-law and indeed with the Duke of Wellington. Henry Michell Wagner was vicar of Brighton between 1824 and 1870. He was a descendant of Melchior Wagner, a hat maker to the royal family, and first married into a wealthy Sussex family with a longstanding ecclesiastical connection with Brighton. He had three sons from his first marriage. On the death of his first wife in 1838 Wagner married Mary Sikes Watson, the 38-year-old daughter of Joshua Watson, described on Wagner's Wikipedia page as 'a lady of too great Victorian piety for comfort ... letters between her and Wagner during their courtship discussed administrative matters and philosophical principles'.

In 1824 there were only three Anglican churches in Brighton; four proprietary chapels followed. The CBC gave an interest-free loan for a chapel of ease and built three more churches between 1826 and 1847, the first of which was the ambitious St Peter's by Charles Barry, which cost more than £20,000 instead of Barry's estimated £14,700. Wagner had disputes with the vestry about pew rental, to which he was much opposed. The vestry demanded a lower proportion of free pews to reduce the debt more quickly; Wagner, who had authorised 1,100 free pews in the 1,800-capacity church, disagreed. The Commissioners eventually agreed to alter the balance to 900 free and 900 rented pews. By 1866, there were twenty-seven churches in the town, six of which Wagner himself had founded. Of these six, only St Paul's Church remains in Anglican use. Of the rest, one is now used by the Greek Orthodox community and the others have been demolished. The ICBS helped build seven churches in Brighton between 1833 and 1883.

Wagner died in 1870, his wealth and church-building enthusiasms inherited by his eldest son, Arthur Douglas Wagner, named in honour of the Duke of Wellington, to whose sons Henry Wagner had been tutor. Wagner built one church, St Paul's, especially for Arthur, who was even

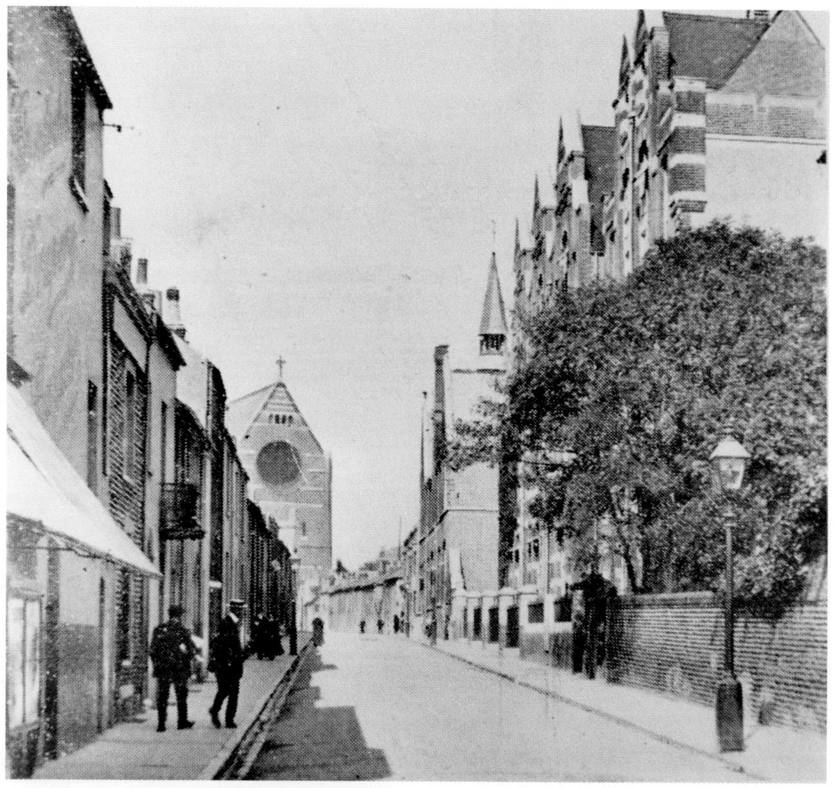

Exterior of St Bartholomew's, Brighton,1912

St Bartholomew's Church was the one Brighton church that Arthur Wagner planned entirely himself, working with local architect Edmund Scott between 1872 and 1874. It was the first church in Brighton to offer universal free seating from its opening. Without a tower or spire it claims to be the tallest church in Britain and its proportions are often compared to Noah's Ark.

more aggressive in his views about ridding the Church of pews. He wanted his church to have free seating for all but his father insisted that 460 of the 1,200 seats should be reserved for rental. It opened on 23 October 1849, grant-aided by CBC and ICBS with substantial funding from the Wagner family. Arthur Wagner assumed responsibility for the church in 1850 when his father presented the curacy to him in perpetuity. He held the curacy until his death in 1902. Pugin, Morris and Burne-Jones contributed to an overall redesign by George Bodley in 1861 and a new tower was later added after the death of Henry Wagner. In 1873 the parishes were reorganised and pew rentals abolished at St Paul's.

In the 1860s, Arthur Wagner was strongly associated with the second phase of the Oxford Movement and St Paul's displayed many of aspects of its controversial approach to ritual and Catholic liturgy: the Eucharist and 'the Real Presence' as opposed to the Ministry of the Word, the offices of Morning and Evening Prayer and an emphasis on beauty and decoration within the church. St Paul's found itself a subject of national controversy because of its emphasis on confessionals, which became public knowledge during the 1865 murder trial of Constance Kent (who had confessed her crime to Arthur Wagner). There were debates in the House of Commons and an assault on Reverend Wagner; even Henry Wagner was critical of his son's ritualism. Invited by his son to preach, he included in his sermon Matthew 17:15: 'Lord, have mercy on my son: for he is lunatick, and sore vexed…'

ELEVEN

'The burden of church buildings weighs heavily':
1900 to the present day

In 1913, the Archbishop of Canterbury wrote in the Society's annual report that the ICBS had three main principles: to give financial aid; to be a source of information; and 'upholding a high standard of what church building ought to be'. He also made reference to 'younger rivals which are attracting public attention', an accurate forecast that, throughout the rest of the twentieth century, the ICBS would have to compete for attention with myriad other national bodies with a special interest in church buildings. The Church of England's own Central Council for the Care of Churches was formed in 1917, arising from the Central Committee for the Protection of English Churches.

The year 1927 seems to have been one of particular focus for the ICBS and in the annual report the secretary, (Albert) Clifton Kelway, put his skills as a journalist to good use. He underlined the significance of the ICBS's role as an incorporated body, allowing it to act as trustee to any building or repair fund without deeds being submitted: in 1927 500 such funds were being held in trust. He set the ICBS in a national context, informing readers that one million houses had been built since the end of the war and that 'it is probably true to say that, first and last, the Society has assisted to preserve nearly all the ancient parish churches of England & Wales'. New churches and care for old churches were still seen as vital but enlarging existing buildings was no longer the main concern. Communities were still poor, badly housed and often without health provision; church room was no longer seen as the dominant crisis.

The population of England and Wales had stood at 17.9 million in 1851, of whom 5.2 million were members of the Church of England. By 1911 the population had doubled to about 36 million but there were probably less than half the number of Anglican communicants compared to 1851: at the end of the First World War the figure was estimated at 2.3 million.

The ICBS centenary took place during the last months of the war, which was no time for celebration. Instead, the 1927 annual report, under the chairmanship of the Hon. Hugh Wyndham, an historian, and with Arthur. H. Hoare as treasurer, included every single grant made in the Society's nearly 110 years: a cumulative (and not adjusted) £1,157,285 had been spent on 10,281 churches and a further £31,470 on 1,039 mission churches.

More tetchily, it also included a statement after a resolution passed on 2 February 1923, by the National Church Assembly (established in 1919):

> The National Church Assembly desires to place on record its appreciation of the services which have been rendered, and continue to be rendered, at the present stage of development of Central Church organisations by the Central Societies of the Church of England and commends their work to the earnest attention and hearty support of all Church people … The Committee of the ICBS ask their many supporters to make this resolution known as widely as possible. It answers a question which perhaps perplexes the mind of some Church people.

In 1919, parochial church councils and diocesan advisory committees (DACs) had finally been given legal status; the DACs set up their own architectural committees. By 1927, the ICBS appears to have been feeling threatened by these so-called 'Central Societies' and naturally became defensive and entrenched.

The relatively new diocese of Southwark even set up its own church-building fund, rather than relying on the Society, managed most successfully by the bishop. In 1925 he launched an appeal for funds to build twenty-five new churches to serve the extensive building in his diocese since the First World War. When the appeal closed ten years later it had raised some £133,000, enough to build twenty new churches, to enlarge five others, to acquire three sites for future building and to build ten church halls.

One of the more original projects was St Philip and All Saints in Kew, Surrey. This was built by several members of the Hoare family, inspired by Uvedale Lambert, a local historian, who provided, with his wife Cecily, née Hoare, the basic structure in the form of a disused seventeenth-

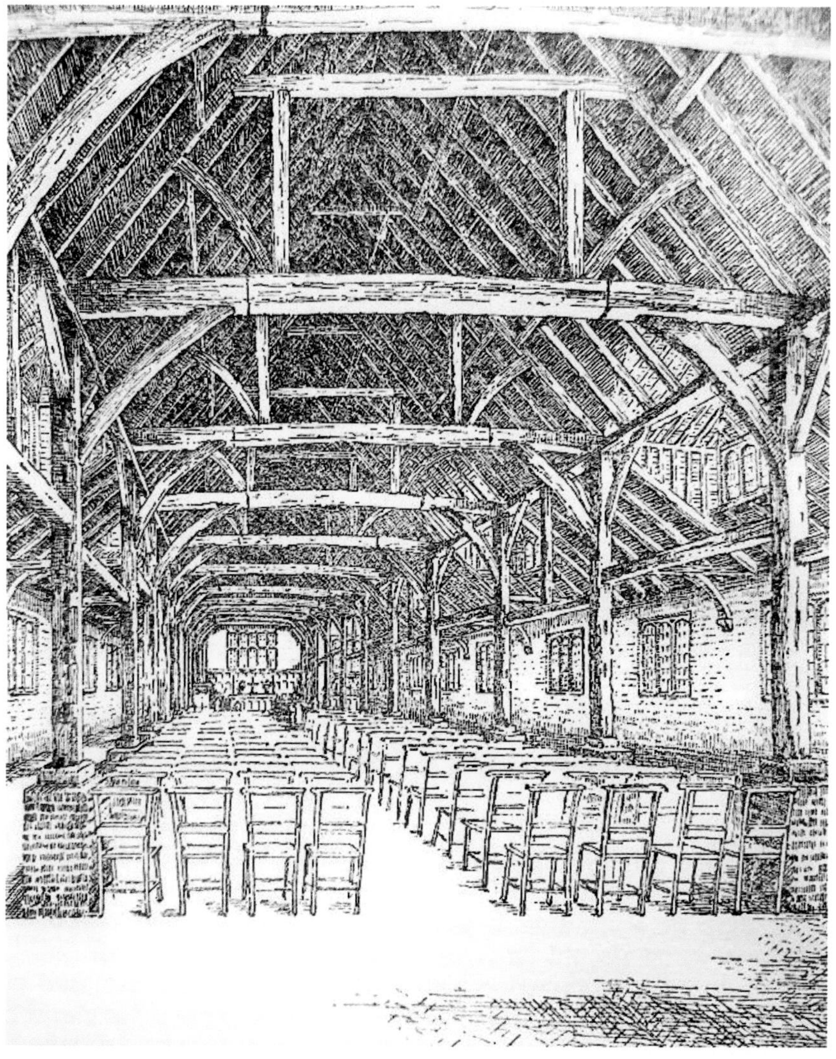

M. SWAN **The Barn Church, Kew**
Line drawing published in *The Barn Church...A brief account of the building and its conversion into a Parish Church*, Arden Press, 1936

The Barn Church was built in 1929 by several members of the Hoare family; a 17th-century barn from a family farm was carefully dismounted, transported and reassembled at Kew.

century barn from their farm. The wood frame was carefully dismounted, transported and reassembled at Kew. Some 116,000 bricks to the correct pre-Dutch shape were baked by Walter Hoare in the works that he had set up with the help of Edwin Lutyens at his house near Basingstoke. The tower frame was made of green oak from the Lambert estate, which also provided the 'Surrey marble' from which the font is carved and the heavy blue slate paving that had previously been used as a threshing floor at the farm. Geoffrey Hoare carved, from his own home-grown oak, a pulpit, copying a medieval original at Hereford Cathedral from which one of his wife's ancestors, Bishop Croft, had denounced the behaviour of Puritan soldiers during the Civil War. Uvedale purchased panelling, much of Tudor and Jacobean origin, from various local houses, and the sanctuary chairs were made of cedarwood from a large tree in the Godstone churchyard blown down in a 1927 storm and given by the Reverend Gerard Hoare, its vicar. The poppy-head stall ends, recovered from St Dunstan's in Fleet Street when it was reordered in the 1860s, had been stored for the intervening sixty-eight years by Hoares Bank, which also gave two oak lecterns. The bank's clerks donated a bible.

The result, with its well-lit forest of cattle-worn ancient timbering, is a spectacular building, 140 feet long and seating 435. It is dedicated to several other family members and in particular Henry Gerard Hoare and Gerard Croft Hoare, both killed during the First World War. It cost only £6,770, of which £2,500 was supplied by the Bishop of Southwark's fund. It can, therefore, claim to be the cheapest church of its size ever built. This did not prevent lengthy negotiations with the Ecclesiastical Commissioners, who were patently unhappy with some aspects of the design proposals, particularly the unusual proportions of the nave and the arrangement of the windows.

New research by Clare Price has shown in detail that between the two world wars, the stance taken by the ICBS's architects was deeply anti-modernist. Between 1900 and 1940 the membership of the Society's Consulting Architects' Committee varied very little. Members did not retire but served until death to be replaced by elderly colleagues, in marked contrast to the days of 1848, when the committee was first formed with architects in their prime. In 1937, Sir Charles Nicholson, who had been born in 1867, reviewed the recently published ICBS book *New Churches Illustrated*, which showcased churches funded by the Society between 1926 and 1936. As a member of the Consulting Architects' Committee his criticisms seem curious but the book does include churches not grant-aided by ICBS. He complained that many of these modern churches were 'merely eccentric' and the architects were simply 'showing off their own cleverness'. He deplored the use of western galleries for choirs and predicted that the legacy of these designs would merely be their clumsiness and oddity. He concluded with the obvious: 'Perhaps it is difficult for old eyes to appreciate the adventurous tendencies of a new generation.' It could be argued that the Society should be applauded for even-handedness, publishing details for churches of which many of its distinguished architects disapproved. Clifton Kelway, although in his seventies by 1937, and an historian of the Catholic Revival (and author of 'Church and People as seen by Mr Punch' for the satirical magazine *Punch* as far back as 1909), perhaps provided journalistic objectivity as secretary.

William Douglas Caröe, another committee member and an Arts & Crafts architect who had been articled to J. L. Pearson, was ten years Nicholson's senior. He was also consulting architect for the Ecclesiastical Commission and wrote to the ICBS secretary in 1935: 'I do not think any "modernist" style has yet been developed and I rather hope it may not be.' In 1934 a competition was held to build the church of John Keble, Mill Hill, London. The winning design was passionately criticised by the ICBS architects with Charles Spooner, another Arts & Crafts man, declaring it 'unworthy'. Yet when the first post-war architects' committee meeting was held in 1949 among the seven new members was Donald Martin-Smith, the John Keble architect.

The committee decided not to hold monthly meetings and there are no minutes recorded after 30 May 1951 although an attendance book exists up to 1994. It published a new 'Policy' in 1951, which Clare Price believes is revolutionary in a quiet way as in it the committee admits for the first time that 'some difference of opinion is bound to exist between members regarding the merits – or demerits – of the designs submitted to the Society for the erection of new churches'.

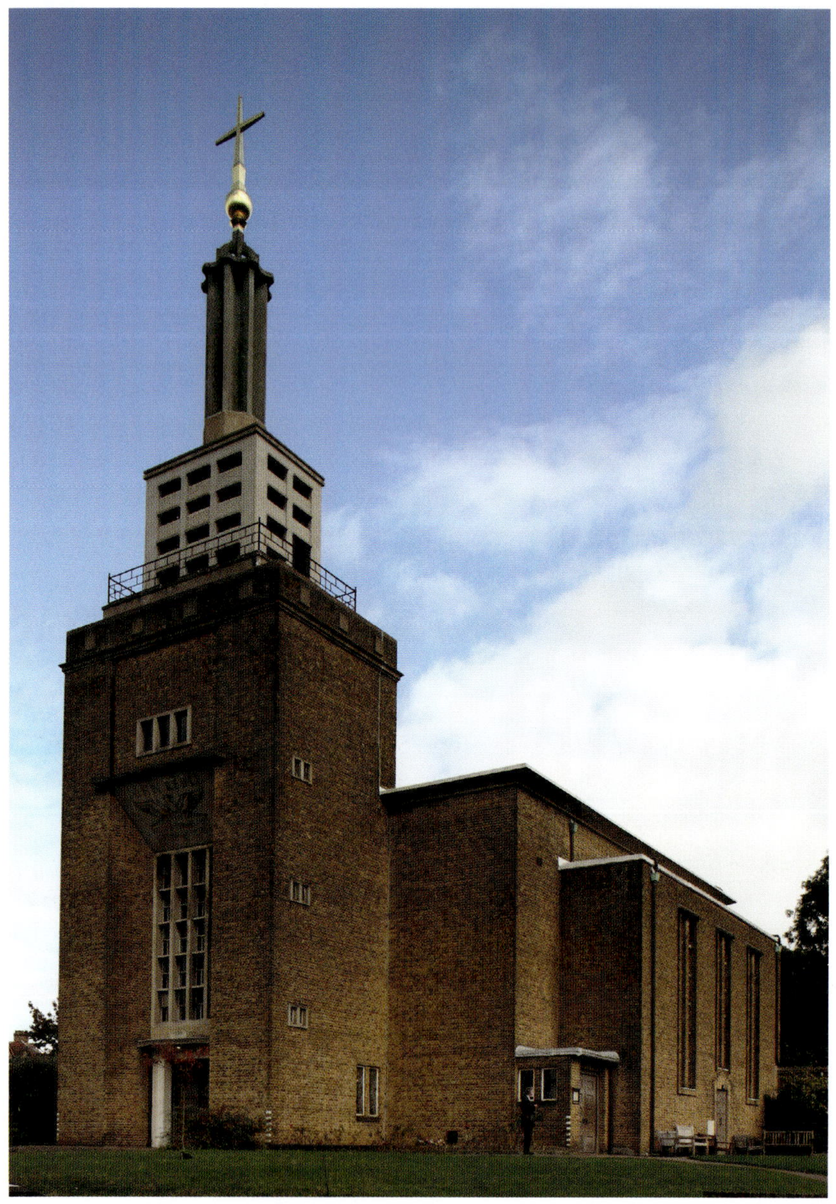

John Keble, Mill Hill, London

In 1934, a competition was held to choose an architect for a new church in Mill Hill. It was won by Donald Martin-Smith (1900–84) and the church was much criticised by the ICBS as too modern and 'unworthy' but, nonetheless, Martin-Smith was elected to their first post-war architects' committee in 1949.

Concurrently, the golden egg of Queen Anne's Bounty was focused on poor rural areas with the attention of the Ecclesiastical Commission being on urban areas. In 1948, after decades of planning, the two were merged and the Church Commissioners were formed, two thirds of whose revenues are now used to pay clergy pensions, with the remainder split between support for bishops and cathedrals and parish missions. Yet in the 1950 ICBS annual report a lament was printed that there was still 'no official central organisation' and that 'reliance on ICBS … continues to be indicated with almost distressing clarity'. The Society was well aware of parallel developments and that parish churches throughout Britain were in a very poor state of repair; while this was by no means a new problem, circumstances had been exacerbated to crisis point by the almost total cessation of maintenance and repair to churches during the Second World War.

In 1951, the Pilgrim Trust and the Society of Antiquaries urged the Church Assembly (now called the General Synod) to set up a commission. This was chaired by Ivor Bulmer-Thomas, a dynamic if contentious MP and journalist. The commission found that £4 million over ten years was needed to bring churches into a state of good repair on top of annual maintenance costs of £750,000 (somewhere in the region of £100 million and £20 million respectively in today's money) to put the ecclesiastical built heritage of the country in order. It was the new commission's recommendation that a charitable trust should be set up to raise and distribute funds to churches of architectural and historic significance. It further recommended that incumbents should be trained in the management of church buildings, churches should benefit from architects' surveys every five years and grants only be made to churches that employed a qualified architect.

After discussions in 1952, a trust deed for the Historic Churches Preservation Trust (HCPT) was drawn up in 1953 and Bulmer-Thomas was first its secretary. For over fifty years the HCPT was primarily a grant-giving trust, providing vital funds for repairs to historic churches and, from the outset, it supported churches of all the major Christian denominations, as well as chapels and meeting houses. The Hoare family were represented by Sir Frederick Hoare and Michael Hoare, who were trustees from the 1960s until 2011. In the first ten years of its life, the HCPT raised around

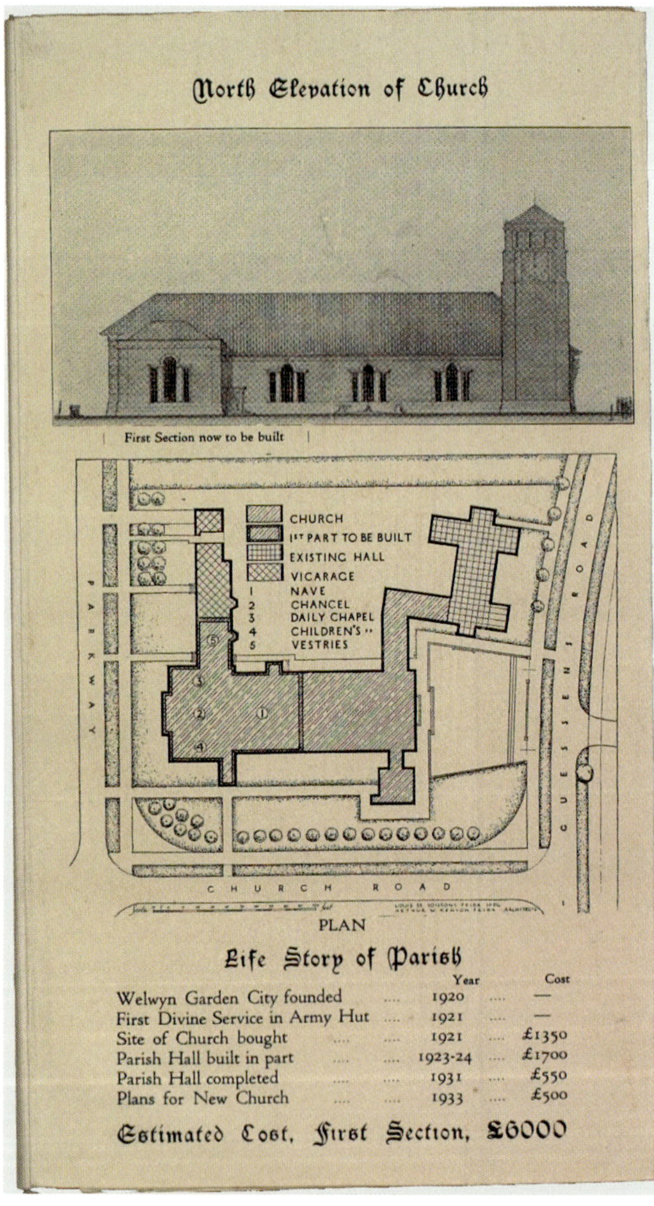

		Year		Cost
Welwyn Garden City founded	....	1920	....	—
First Divine Service in Army Hut	....	1921	....	—
Site of Church bought	....	1921	....	£1350
Parish Hall built in part	....	1923-24	....	£1700
Parish Hall completed	....	1931	....	£550
Plans for New Church	....	1933	....	£500

LOUIS DE SOISSONS, **St Francis, Welwyn Garden City**, 1929, North Elevation and Plan
Ink on paper

Louis de Soissons (1890–1962), a Canadian, was responsible for the 'master plan' (a very early use of the term) for Welwyn Garden City, a planned town created by Ebenezer Howard in Hertfordshire. The ICBS helped to fund Soissons's church of St Francis but otherwise did not get involved with the new garden city movement.

£725,000 (equivalent to £25 million in 2017 terms), helped to set up sixteen county trusts, which themselves raised a further £300,000, made some 2,000 grants and 100 loans, mostly to Anglican churches but also to around forty Nonconformist and three Roman Catholic chapels, and obtained tax relief for covenanted subscriptions. Quinquennial architect's surveys became mandatory in 1955.

Why did the Synod form a new trust when the ICBS was still in place after 145 years? Or was that very longevity the reason in a nutshell? Yet the ICBS had at least made some efforts to modernise with the 1951 policy and the inviting of new architects on to the advisory committee. In 1949, they had published *Preservation of our Churches: A Plea for Immediate Action*, followed in 1950 by a brochure by A. B. Knapp-Fisher, 'The Future of Church Building', deliberately printed in a modern, clean sans-serif font unlike the rest of the report in which it was inserted. In 1948, the ICBS annual report commented on the centenary of its board of architects that they had worked 'quietly and without ostentation', which indeed might have been seen elsewhere as an epitaph rather than praise. In 1924, in a volume of the Forsyte Saga, John Galsworthy wrote of this kind of modesty and 'dread of swank':

> And removing their hats, they passed the Cenotaph.
> 'Curiously symptomatic – that thing,' said Sir Lawrence; 'monument to the dread of swank – most characteristic … The fine, the large, the florid – all off! No far-sighted views, no big schemes, no great principles, no great religion, or great art – aestheticism in cliques and backwaters, small men in small hats.'

It should be borne in mind that the Act of Incorporation of the ICBS had never been amended: the Society had been run in much the same way since 1828. The presidency (the Archbishop of Canterbury, fifty vice presidents, exactly half laity and half senior clergy, who were *ex officio* the Archbishop of York and diocesan bishops), a treasurer and thirty-six elected committee members made a governing body of eighty-eight men. Luckily a quorum was set at a sensible five. All the same, the new HCPT was set up with a body of trustees as great and good as the ICBS presidency, including each Prime Minister from Winston Churchill to Edward

Heath. There were also 10 women trustees out of 130 (over the whole history of the HCPT) and familiar names from the world of architecture and conservation including John Betjeman and Alec Clifton-Taylor. Clearly, the HCPT was seen as a new Elizabethan organisation and ICBS was pre-Victorian.

Yet the ICBS had continued to help parishes build new churches throughout the two world wars wherever possible; another role might have been to have influence the development of churches in the post-1946 New Towns. Some of the towns, including Hemel Hempstead and Harlow, had early nineteenth-century churches funded by the Society already in place and kept to lend patina, and the towns were at first very well funded. One of the few churches helped by the Society that was part of a garden city masterplan is St Francis's in Welwyn Garden City. When the first families began to move in to Welwyn Garden City, the congregation was part of the Hatfield parish and a curate would cycle over to take services in a temporary building. In November 1921 the Bishop of St Albans conducted a service in the Cherry Tree pub (now Waitrose) as the congregation was too big to be accommodated elsewhere. In the early 1920s a site for a permanent church was found with a local wish for the dedication to be to St Francis of Assisi. Work started in 1934 but the outbreak of the Second World War prevented any building that was not absolutely necessary and the church was only half the length originally envisioned by Louis de Soissons. He had been appointed architect for much of the town's layout and buildings from 1920, building on Ebenezer Howard's original plan for an ideal garden city.

From the 1930s onwards, with increased mobility through ownership of more private cars, there was a change of attitude towards the countryside and its buildings. Urban tourists became aware of charming and ancient rural churches. John Betjeman was behind the Shell Guides from 1934 onwards, improving on the previous sort of publication that 'catches the church-crawling public and the growing numbers of amateur archaeologists'. Aiming for a slightly more discerning readership he wanted his new guides to be 'at once to be critical and selective. They had to illustrate places other than the well-known beauty spots and to mention the disregarded and fast disappearing Georgian landscape of England; churches with box pews...' Covering a similar field, Professor Nikolaus Pevsner's architectural

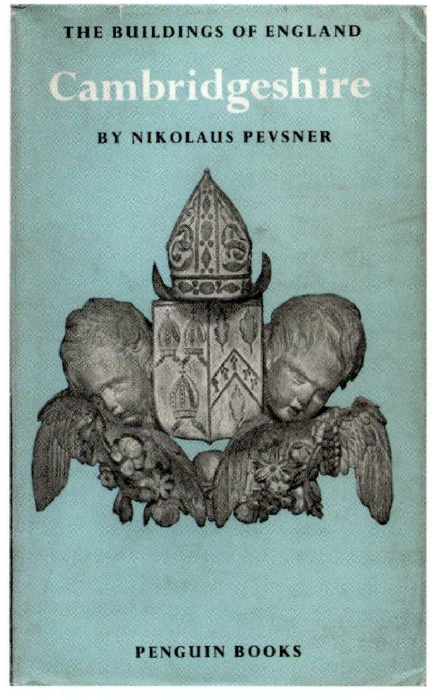

The Buildings of England:
Cambridgeshire,
Penguin Books, 1954

This 46-volume series of county-by-county guides was created by Professor Sir Nikolaus Pevsner. Begun in 1945 and published between 1951 and 1974, it is often simply referred to by his surname.

guides to each county began to be published in 1951; scholarly, acerbic and exhaustive, they concentrate particularly on public buildings and churches.

Further voluntary organisations began to appear to stand alongside SPAB (the oldest 'national amenity society' in the world, founded in 1877): the Ancient Monuments Society in 1924; the Georgian Group (which grew out of SPAB) in 1937, to campaign for the preservation of the best architecture from 1700 to 1840 in England and Wales; the Victorian Society in 1957, to protect buildings created between 1837 and 1914; and finally the Thirties Society, now the Twentieth Century Society, which focuses on buildings post-1914 and was formed in 1979.

The ICBS maintained its role in 'upholding a high standard of what church building ought to be' through its own publishing. The *Church Builder* had ceased in 1916 but by 1936 single-survey volumes with photographs began to emerge. The large-scale *New Churches Illustrated* was on sale for 3*s*. 6*d*. in November 1936, looking at fifty-two churches erected between 1926 and 1936. Its preface states that 100 churches were built with ICBS assistance between those dates and decries 'cheapness' in budgets and cramming of sittings to achieve the lowest per capita costs.

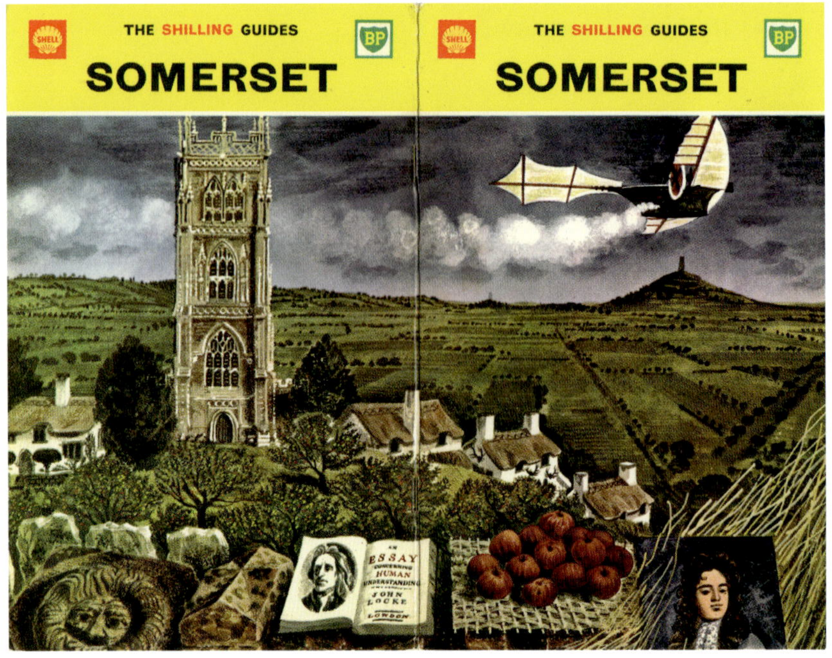

DAVID GENTLEMAN **Cover for the Shell Guide to Somerset** 1960s

John Betjeman edited the elegant Shell Guides from 1934 to appeal to a new generation of car-driving tourists who wanted something not too serious but nonetheless informative about the countryside and historic buildings of Britain. In the 1960s, a cheaper, priced at one shilling, series of 48 guides was published by Shell-Mex and BP which also published posters for schools.

Publication costs were reduced with advertisements for craftsmen and tradesmen. *Fifty Modern Churches* followed in 1947 for 10s. 6d., hardback, and contains a list of all consecrated Anglican churches built since 1930. One of these was Findon Valley Mission Church and Hall in Sussex, which was built as a temporary structure in 1935, without an ICBS grant. Why was it included? Its designer, Macdonald Gill, brother of Eric Gill, had been an assistant to Sir Charles Nicholson, had added to the splendours of Roker church in the 1920s and was the designer of the upper-case lettering used on headstones and war memorials by the Imperial War Graves Commission. His mission church is a modest addition to a survey of fifty churches but the inclusion of such buildings which would be 'used reverently for worship, but which be nevertheless will also be successful for social functions' is typical ICBS pragmatism. Finally, a pocket-sized *Sixty Post-War Churches*, also priced at 10*s*. 6*d*., illustrated 'Churches, Church Centres and Dual Purpose Churches' in 1956, noting that building costs had quadrupled since the last volume and that the ICBS 'takes no part in the controversial question of architectural form'.

WATERLOO IN HAMPSHIRE

In 1815, a pub opened north of Portsmouth on the London road. The timing was perfect: soldiers who had just disembarked at Portsmouth on their return from the Battle of Waterloo decided to stop there and celebrate their victory in English ale. Not surprisingly, the pub was then named the Heroes of Waterloo and the surrounding area became known as Waterloo although it was simply a hamlet of four cottages and outside any parish until 1858. Gradually it developed into a small village and in 1829, at a meeting in the pub, it was decided to build a church. The ICBS gave a grant so Jacob Owen designed a small chapel-like building with a large

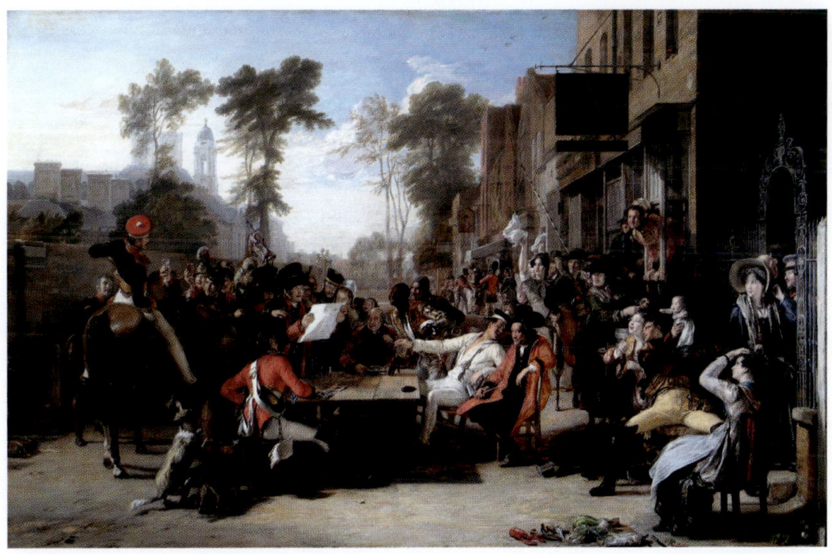

SIR DAVID WILKIE **Chelsea Pensioners Reading the Gazette after the Battle of Waterloo**, 1822, Oil on canvas
The painting shows the news from Waterloo reaching London and was commissioned by the Duke of Wellington.

west gallery and a tower in 1831. By that time, some villas had appeared as well as a butcher and baker and eventually the village was aggrandised with the name Waterlooville. A Baptist chapel followed, then a large Baptist church, an industrial school and, next, a convent. The tiny hamlet grew into a suburb of Portsmouth. By 1969, the church of St George the Martyr proved too small and, 140 years after the first church, the ICBS helped fund a new building. The tower and chapel were retained but extended and strengthened with granite and concrete under the direction of Kenneth Makins, the diocesan surveyor, and reopened in 1970.

The Diocese of Portsmouth was created in 1927 and from that date until 1982 the ICBS answered five enquiries, helped build one new church and turned down two requests from within the diocese. It refused nineteen applications in total for grant aid. It helped enlarge one church, the rebuilding of two (including Waterlooville) and the repair of twenty-five more. Starting back in 1829 with Waterlooville and finishing in 1977 with a shared church in Basingstoke, the Society helped the county of Hampshire and the Isle of Wight build precisely one hundred churches and mission churches. The bulk of these were built in the late nineteenth century and almost every one of them followed the Society's principle of helping towns and growing suburbs rather than rural parishes. Pevsner describes Hampshire as a 'bumper county' for Victorian churches and the ICBS's role was a vital one. He goes on to describe the 'individualists and the rogues' among church architects of the period and these people are, regrettably perhaps, not always part of the ICBS story.

The overall ICBS story is one of new and enlarged churches with an ambition for large congregations, following rather than leading architectural innovation; churches that were reorganised or rebuilt to accommodate changes of taste and of worship; later on, churches that were restored, repaired, conserved, preserved. The Society started its life by making a major and very public stand. Then it reacted and adapted, practically and conscientiously, raised, gave out and withheld funds as well as actively guiding and publishing. Between 1925 and 1935, 85 per cent of its grants (by number, rather than value) went towards the repair and enlargement of churches. Only 10 per cent was given to new buildings and 5 per cent to new mission buildings. The amount of time devoted to the analysis of necessary repair will have overlapped with the work done by the diocesan committees on the same subject and the sums of money voted were always small. It was fast becoming an impractical approach.

Meanwhile, at the HCPT, a difference broke out in 1956 between Ivor Bulmer-Thomas, who wanted the Trust to save *every* church threatened with closure, and Archbishop Fisher of Canterbury. Bulmer-Thomas was a remarkable but notoriously difficult man: a member of Clement Attlee's Labour government, he crossed the floor to the Conservatives in 1949 and subsequently joined the SDP and then the Liberal Party. He lost the argument with Fisher, retired from active involvement with the HCPT and went on to found the Friends of Friendless Churches, a privately funded association that now owns around fifty former places of worship, half in England and half in Wales. Its name (derived from the French term 'club for those without a club') seems faintly to echo that of the dining club 'Nobody's Friends'. Bulmer-Thomas died in 1993, only minutes after completing a letter, characteristically rude about the Church of England, to the *Daily Telegraph*: it was published with his wife's agreement on the same day as his obituary. A flurry of concerns and financial needs is revealed by the creation of these several groups: churches with dwindling congregations; churches with none at all; churches in poor repair; churches with sensible plans for their own conservation; parishes with ambitions for good new church buildings.

During the 1970s, there was real concern about the future of the ICBS. The minutes of 17 September 1980 mention the possibility of co-operating with the Friends of Friendless Churches and/or the HCPT, but conclude that they have different aims: ICBS was still being seen as existing to 'build and maintain living churches as places of worship'. The archbishops had acknowledged in their report to Synod in January 1976 that 'the burden of church buildings weighs heavily'. In 1977 an exhibition, *Change and Decay; The Future of our Churches,* was held at the Victoria & Albert Museum, following on from the hugely influential *Destruction of the Country House* exhibition in 1974. A similar focus on gardens followed in 1979; the church exhibition was by far the least attended of the three heritage spectacles but within three weeks of its opening the government ring-fenced grants to restore historic churches, administered first by the Historic Buildings Council, then by English Heritage, and since 2012 through the Heritage Lottery Fund. In 2017 it was announced that the ring-fencing of specific funds for historic churches would end.

Before 1977, churches in use, even if considered 'outstanding' (that is, given Grade I and II* status) were ineligible for government grants. Redundant churches, however, like secular listed buildings, could receive them. In that year the situation came to a head over Christ Church, Lancaster Gate, opposite Kensington Gardens in London. Built by F. & H. Francis in 1854–5 (without ICBS help), it was known in its heyday as 'the thousand pound church' because of the large sums collected from the wealthy Bayswater congregation every Sunday. During redecoration, severe dry rot was found in the roof when a painter put his brush straight through a beam. The Diocese of London proceeded to have the church demolished (even though it had a thriving congregation) and a block of flats was subsequently built on the site. The spire remains in place in a surreal fashion. If the church had been declared redundant by the Church of England, which would have taken a minimum of two years, it could have had its repairs grant-aided, but because it was in use it was not eligible and the condition of the building was considered to be dangerous. SAVE (Save Britain's Heritage) had been created in 1975 – European Architectural Heritage Year – by a group of journalists, historians, architects and planners to campaign publicly for endangered historic buildings. Dame Jennifer Jenkins (an architectural campaigner who was at that time a member of the Historic Buildings Council for England and later chair of the National Trust) and SAVE separately championed the cause of grants for churches still in use and finally a dedicated grant scheme for churches was brought in so that, in a variety of forms, money has since been forthcoming to help pay for church repairs either direct from central government, English Heritage or the Heritage Lottery Fund.

In 2007, Roy Strong, director of the Victoria & Albert Museum when the *Change and Decay* exhibition was staged there, gave a lecture at Gresham College entitled 'The Beauty of Holiness and its Perils (or, What Is to Happen to 10,000 Parish Churches?)'. He argued that many people of a certain age had had their view of church buildings set hard by Pevsner and Betjeman, often to the detriment of the churches themselves:

> The perception of the village church for most of the population is rooted in the picture postcard picturesque. For the educated the dominant forces which have taught us how to view these churches are two late twentieth-century icons, Sir Nikolaus Pevsner and Sir John Betjeman. I think that the time has come to query their contribution instead of adding to the incense on those particular altars. Was how they taught the educated to view churches a help to our present plight or not? ... What is completely missing is virtually anything about the church's social or cultural history in terms of who built it, the nature and extent of the parish, its incumbents, its place in the religious history of the area ... Pevsner I suppose can be said to speak to the intellect, whereas Betjeman appeals to the imagination and the heart ... Betjeman was to condition two generations, including my own, to look with heady nostalgia and romance at the country church.

The question of where the ICBS belonged, in an increasingly competitive charity and conservation landscape, recurred during 1981 and 1982. A steadily reducing number of members, churches and diocesan societies now provided the ICBS with an annual income of a mere £10,000, much of which was absorbed by administrative costs. By the second half of 1982, the ICBS seems to have been quite advanced in negotiations with the Central Council for the Care of Churches, which was thought to have identical aims. These negotiations came to an abrupt halt in November 1982, apparently because the ICBS would not be sufficiently represented on the joint committees. Other minutes mention the repair funds as a problem.

The HCPT suddenly emerged again as the most likely marriage partner although concern was still expressed that it, unlike the ICBS, was interested in architectural quality and historical associations. By 21 January 1983, a draft agreement with the HCPT is annexed to the ICBS's minutes. This is similar to a draft in the HCPT's papers, but there are some differences; there are also manuscript amendments to the ICBS version and it is not clear what was finally agreed, at least in detail. The substance of the arrangements is, however, clear and is expressed in a formal minute, that 'the Society should enter into an arrangement with the Historic Churches Preservation Trust whereby the ordinary business of the Society is managed by the Trust on payment of a management fee of 15% of the Total Annual Income of the Society, including the income of all the Trust Funds'. The draft agreement also states that the ICBS would remain an independent, registered, national charity.

The ICBS formal yearly meeting, known as the Annual Court, had become a low-key affair. In 1983 it followed immediately after a General Committee meeting and no other people were present. The archbishops and diocesan bishops are not mentioned in the minutes, even by way of apologies. From 1984 onwards, however, the Annual Court was much more formal. The minutes of that year record having received apologies from the two archbishops; Canterbury also sent a message referring, with approval, to the HCPT arrangement. In 1985, apologies were received from forty-six vice presidents and sixteen other members; the Archbishop of Canterbury and the Bishop of Carlisle were present.

Yet the HCPT was by no means a wealthy suitor itself and in 1980 was £15,000 in deficit. The ICBS's own administrative costs were about 50 per cent of income and their grants were still numerous (600–700 a year) but individually tiny. It adopted a policy of giving only loans, in order to save the reserves, and not engaging in competitive fundraising, operating instead through a joint grants committee with the HCPT. This echoes the situation in the last years of the Church Building Commission, when it elided more closely with the ICBS.

The HCPT, at the time, was housed in Dickensian conditions in offices at Fulham Palace, a building that the Bishops of London had vacated some 200 years previously. Into this rabbit warren of tiny rooms, with inadequate heating and outside sanitation, the ICBS added its own voluminous files to those of the HCPT. The floorboards of one narrow corridor gave way under the strain of floor-to-ceiling filing cabinets. Happily most of the ICBS's extensive archive, built up painstakingly over the previous 165 years, was transferred to Lambeth Palace from the disused mortuary chapel in Great Peter Street, Westminster, that had since 1974 served, perhaps fittingly, as the Society's last independent office. Details of the papers and images of the remarkable visual records which form the archive are available online.

Another, more trying, issue, concerned repair funds, which the ICBS held on behalf of a number of individual churches, in a scheme that had been established in the nineteenth century before a revised system of diocesan finances had been set up. The purpose of these funds was to allow churches to build up sums that would assist when repairs became essential. Most of these funds were small with only a handful above a few thousand pounds and, under the terms of the trusts, the income, but not the capital, was available to the churches concerned. The lack of any fee paid for the administration of these funds was the subject of regular contention over the years at the ICBS. In 2001, there were about 600 separate funds totalling just over £780,000, simply accumulating with no real likelihood that the majority would ever be used. A process was thus begun to return the bulk of the money either to the original church or to its successor. As the church was sometimes no longer in existence either as place of worship or even a building, there was potential for interminable negotiations, but in the end the process was completed.

In 2007, finally, a new charity, the National Churches Trust (NCT), was established that drew together the HCPT and the ICBS. The NCT eventually also took responsibility for the Open Churches Trust, which had been founded ten years previously by Andrew Lloyd Webber to encourage and help congregations open up their churches: 'to be able to help the congregations of the finest of these buildings to open them so the public can enjoy not only their beauty and structure but also the often unique history each can extol'. The NCT is therefore a 'national, independent, charity dedicated to promoting and supporting church buildings of historic, architectural and community value which receives no income from government or church authorities, and relies on voluntary contributions to undertake its work'. Today it works with any Christian denomination and throughout the United Kingdom, absorbing the principles of all its earlier constituent parts.

The NCT was formed both to simplify administration and against a concern that the charitable objects of the HCPT and the ICBS were both too narrow. They were each limited to supporting the repair or the building of churches (confined to Anglican ones in the case of the ICBS) and it was now seen as essential to raise public awareness of the issue of churches at risk and to stimulate both national and local action. The charitable objects of neither the HCPT nor the ICBS covered a campaigning role so legal advice was sought. The sticking point was that the Charity Commission would not permit a change or extension to the objects of a charity while it was still possible to fulfil the original ones. While deeply frustrating, this was a tribute to the longevity and significance of the ICBS which deserves to be celebrated.

It took eleven long years for the HCPT then the NCT to disentangle the independence of the ICBS, which was still a statutory body under the 1828 Act of Incorporation. An approach to the Law Commission complained:

> The principal concern resulting from this process is the unjustifiable length of time that it took. The change being sought was merely one of basic governance arrangements to enable the charity to operate effectively and efficiently in line with modern practice. No change in the purposes to which ICBS funds could be put was even being sought. The existence of the governance arrangements was largely one of historical accident rooted in the way society was organised at the time and predating modern charity law.

There was a poignant moment when the dissolution of the ICBS seemed to depend on a paper statement to that effect simply being pinned on the notice board of the House of Lords Library. Nothing so ignominious – or indeed straightforward – was permitted. Against the backdrop of an entirely new Charities Act in 2011, the process ground on until a vote was secured in favour of the ICBS being absorbed into the NCT, which now took control over both the ICBS and the HCPT, subject to their own specific objects. The only irony was in the Commons, where a member asked why it had been necessary to bring this case to their attention and wished to know if it was part of a tax avoidance scheme.

At the time of writing the senior vice-president of the NCT in is Michael Hoare, the tenth generation of his family to be involved with the Incorporated Church Building Society, who delivered its principles safely into the twenty-first century.

POSTSCRIPT
The future

With their magnificent architecture, artefacts, paintings, decoration, music, vestments and silver, England's churches, filled with memories of the country's past, both national, regional, local and individual, represent, and by far, the country's biggest single portfolio of cultural heritage.

Over the centuries, churches have proved their remarkable capacity to adapt to change. We are now witnessing the passing of the church as a building reserved uniquely for worship and a return to the medieval concept of one that also belongs to the local community, is open to all, is used for local events and is a store of local history.

In the 1970s the V&A held a series of exhibitions lamenting the imminent demise of the English garden, the English country house and the English church. For the first two categories, this pessimism proved totally misplaced and both have metamorphosed into rude health. Is it now the turn of the glories, the interest and the solace of our churches to be rediscovered?

The ICBS raised huge sums, but these were almost exactly matched by government money granted to the CBC at a time that the country was effectively bankrupt. Gibbon points out that the Romans actively promoted religion of all faiths to provide a structure to society and its social glue. Is it too much to expect our own rulers to encourage the use of churches and to provide funding for them through the same private/public funding partnership that existed at the time of the ICBS and the CBC?

Michael Hoare

ACKNOWLEDGEMENTS

This book marks the two hundredth anniversary of the Incorporated Church Building Society.

The ICBS archive, containing records and images from 1818 up to 1982, was deposited at Lambeth Palace Library. It was painstakingly catalogued and the catalogue information is available via the online catalogue: http://archives.lambethpalacelibrary.org.uk/calmview. In addition, 12,000 digitised plans and images (originally created by the Church Plans Online project) are available at http://images.lambethpalacelibrary.org.uk.

Researchers can now find details of ICBS grants and reproductions of ground plans, elevations and other magnificent architectural drawings of churches that the ICBS has helped. The extent of the archive means that the vast majority of material (including extensive correspondence and other papers about applications for church building) is not available online but can be consulted in the Reading Room. The Lambeth Palace Library itself holds copies of nearly all the Society's publications including annual reports and Council meetings. I am very grateful to all staff at Lambeth Palace Library for their help, especially Sarah Etheridge.

My greatest gratitude is to Michael Hoare, whose interest in and knowledge of his family's histories as well as his own rôle within the ICBS and then the National Churches Trust prompted the book. I hope that it begins to show the remarkable part that the Hoare, and Scott, families played in church building over the last two hundred years and more. Many of the ideas, some of the words, but none of the errors, are due to Michael and I want to thank him for his good humour and unfailing support. We both wish to acknowledge the many contributions made by Antony Wedgwood, who was treasurer of the HCPT (later NCT) at the same time that Michael become treasurer of the ICBS.

Michael has introduced me and the idea of the book to several people who have helped in many ways, not least of whom is Victoria Hutchings, the historian of Hoares Bank. She has been wise and kind and a welcome distaff presence in a project that inevitably focuses on men.

ACKNOWLEDGEMENTS

The book owes its elegance to Umbria Press: its publisher, Alan Gordon Walker; editor, Jonathan Wadman; designer, Louise Millar; picture editor, Sarah Stewart-Richardson; and index compiler, Colin Hynson. Both content and author have benefited from their professional and generous care.

I have learned much from conversations with and advice from:
The Reverend Dominic Coad, St James, Benwell;
Anthony Coleman, photographer;
Clare Price, Twentieth Century Society;
Charles Saumarez-Smith, Royal Academy of Arts;
Matthew Saunders, Friends of Friendless Churches;
The Reverend Henry Stapleton;
Father Steve Trickback, Christ Church, Streatham;
and Eddie Tulasiewicz, Clare Walker and staff at
the National Churches Trust.

Most of all, I want to thank my husband, Andrew Hughes, for IT support, patience and for the many visits we have always made together to churches, starting with St Peter's in Cambridge, next to Kettle's Yard, which is now in the care of the Churches Conservation Trust.

BIBLIOGRAPHY

I owe a debt to two authors above all, Michael Port and Timothy Parry. Their diligence and exemplary research has provided the basis for my own text but all mistakes are my own. Their bibliographies are also rigorous and, up to their publication dates, complete. Below, after the Port and Parry books, is a selection of the books and articles which have been especially useful to me:

M.H. Port, *Six Hundred New Churches: The Church Building Commission 1818-1856*, Spire Books Ltd., new edition, 2006

Timothy Parry, *The Incorporated Church Building Society 1818-1851*, unpublished Dphil dissertation, Oxford, 1984

Richard Yates, *The Church in Danger: a Statement of the Cause, and the Probable Means of Averting that Danger Attempted, London, 1815;* reviewed in The British Critic, vol. x, July 1818

John Mason Neale, *A few words to churchwardens on churches and church ornaments*, Cambridge Camden Society, 1841

Alan Brunskill Webster, *Joshua Watson: The Story of a Layman, 1771–1855*, S.P.C.K., 1954

Charles Locke Eastlake, *A History of the Gothic Revival: an Attempt to Show How the Taste for Mediæval Architecture, which Lingered in England during the Two Last Centuries Has since Been Encouraged and Developed*, Longmans, Green & Co., 1872

Irby C. Nicholls, Jr., *The Historian*, vol. 20, No.3, May 1958 (The Austrian War Debt)

John Summerson, *Georgian London*, Pelican Books, 1962

R.A. Soloway, *Prelates and People: Ecclesiastical Social Thought in England, 1783-1852*, Routledge & Regan Paul, 1969

J Mordaunt Crook, *The Greek Revival: neo-classical attitudes in British architecture, 1760-1870*, John Murray, 1972

Kenneth Clark, *The Gothic Revival: an Essay in the History of Taste*, Penguin edition, 1974

Victoria Hutchings, *Messrs Hoare, Bankers: A History of the Hoare Banking Dynasty*, Constable, 2005

Geoffrey Best, *Temporal Pillars: Queen Anne's Bounty, the Ecclesiastical Commissioners, and the Church of England*, Cambridge University Press, 2010

Dominic Janes, The Role of Visual Appearance in Punch's Early Victorian Satires on Religion, *Victorian Periodicals Review*, Volume 47, Number 1, The Johns Hopkins University Press, 2014

Alan Powers, British architecture after the Great War, *Architectural Review*, 30 December 2014

Lucy Hartley, *Democratising Beauty in Nineteenth-Century Britain*, Cambridge University Press, 2017

Clare Price, *The Old Boys' Club: The Inter-War Church as an Architecture of Constraint and Restraint*, paper read at The Society of Architectural Historians of Great Britain Annual Workshop, 2017

ILLUSTRATION CREDITS

Front cover: Reproduced by kind permission from Erewash Borough Council;
Back cover: All images were provided by Friends and supporters of the National Churches Trust
p.2 © The Fitzwilliam Museum, Cambridge; After extensive investigation, copyright is not known; **p.8** By kind permission of St John's Finsbury Park; **p.16** © The Collection:Art & Archaeology in Lincolnshire (Usher Gallery, Lincoln)/ © The Estate of L.S. Lowry. All Rights Reserved, DACS 2018; **p.20** Heritage Image Partnership Ltd/Alamy; **p.22** Universal History Archive/Getty Images; **p.24** Heritage Images/Getty Images; **p.27** © National Trust Images; **p.28** By William Overend Geller; after Sir William Charles Ross/ © National Portrait Gallery, London; **p.34** Collage/London Metropolitan Archives on behalf of the City of London Corporation; **p.37** National Churches Trust; **p.39** Courtesy of the Church Commissioners/The Auckland Project; **p.41** Design Pics Inc/Alamy; **p.42** © Sarah Stewart-Richardson; **p.45** Reproduced with the Permission of Lambeth Palace Library; **p.46** www.ralf-tenbrink.com; **p.48** Stephen Dorey/Alamy; **p.50** World History Archive/Alamy; **p.55** The Bodleian Library, University of Oxford. Trades & Professions 3(63c); **p.60** © Vincent Lowe; **p.67** Look and Learn/Peter Jackson Collection; **p.68** Calthrop, Claude Andrew/The Cheltenham Trust and Cheltenham Borough Council/Bridgeman Images; **p.69** Reproduced with the Permission of Lambeth Palace Library; **p.74** © Victoria & Albert Museum; **p.76** Supplied by The National Churches Trust; **p.79** *top left* John Jackson/ © National Portrait Gallery, London; **p.79** *top right* Jesus College, Oxford; **p.79** *bottom* Chronicle/Alamy; **p.81** George Cruikshank/ © National Portrait Gallery, London; **p.83** Paul Fearn/Alamy; **p.84** Look and Learn/Peter Jackson Collection; **p.85** Peter Scholey/Alamy; **p.86** CAMimage/Alamy; **p.87** lowefoto/Alamy **p.89** Cashin, Edward/Bristol Museum and Art Gallery, UK/ Bridgeman Images; **p.91** The Print Collector/Getty Images; **p.92** Guildhall & Art Gallery/Heritage Images/Getty Images; **p.93** Look and Learn/Peter Jackson Collection'; **p.94** G. Yates/© London Borough of Lambeth; **p.95** Antiqua Print Gallery/Alamy; **p.96** Nikreates/Alamy; **p.97** © Humphrey Bolton/www.geograph.org.uk; **p.98** Reproduced with the Permission of Lambeth Palace Library; **p.101** © Royal Academy of Arts, London; Photographer: Prudence Cunning Associates; **p.102** © Royal Academy of Arts, London; Photographer: John Hammond; **p.103** Reproduced with the Permission of Lambeth Palace Library; **p.105** ART Collection/Alamy; **p.106** George Landseer/ © National Portrait Gallery, London; **p.107** Michael Charles/Alamy; **p.108** *top* Hassocks5489/ Wikimedia Commons; **p.108** *bottom* James Gray Archive www.regencysociety-jamesgray.com; **p.109** © Victoria & Albert Museum; **p.110** © Tony Clarke; **p.111** RIBA Collections; **p.112** © Ian Hamilton; **p.115** © Sir John Soane's Museum, London; **p.117** www.historiccanterbury.com; **p.122** World History Archive/Alamy; **p.124** Art Collection 2/Alamy; **p.127** B.O'Kane/Alamy; **p.128** © Victoria & Albert Museum; **p.131** St. Cuthbert's Church, Earl's Court www.saintcuthberts.org; **p.138** Camille Silvy/ © National Portrait Gallery, London; **p.140** Supplied by The National Churches Trust; **p.147** Jeremy Trew/Trewimage/Alamy; **p.150** Cliff Hide Stock/Alamy; **p.153** © William Douglas; **p.154** Joe Dunckley/Alamy; **p.155** © Chris Redgrave/Historic England Archive; **p.157** Historical Images Archive/Alamy; **p.160** © David Iliff; **p.164** © Derek Savage; **p.168** © John F Pattinson; **p.170** Old College Hall/St. Bees Historical Group; **p.171** Kevin Marston www.kevinmarston.com; **p.175** James Gray Archive www.regencysociety-jamesgray.com; **p.179** M.Swan; **p.182** stevecadman on Flickr; **p.184** Reproduced with the Permission of Lambeth Palace Library and Louis de Soissons; **p.187** *The Buildings of England – Cambridgeshire* by Nikolaus Pevsner (Penguin Books, 1954). Cover copyright © Penguin Books Ltd, 1954; **p.188** Courtesy of the Shell Heritage Art Collection and the BP Archive; **p.189** Wilkie, David/ Apsley House, The Wellington Museum, London/© Historic England/Bridgeman Images.

INDEX

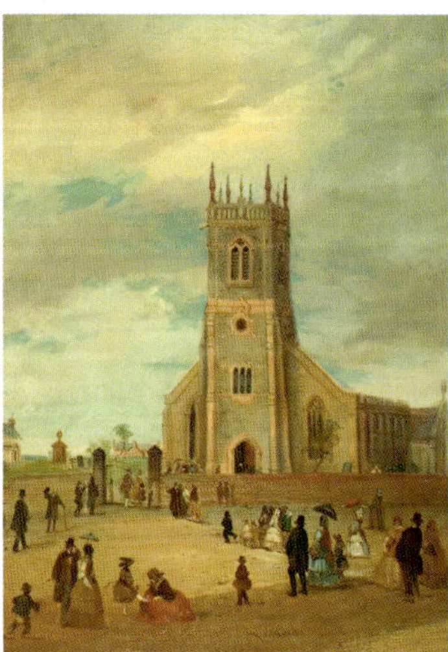

Front cover image

BRITISH SCHOOL **St. Mary's, Market Place, Ilkeston, Derbyshire, 1855,** Oil on canvas

The 13th and 14th century parish church was rebuilt between 1853 and 1855 by Thomas Larkins Walker with a grant from ICBS. The chantry chapel was rebuilt to accommodate nearly 300 children while new seating, flooring, heating and lighting were installed. It is listed Grade II by National Heritage for England.*